FESTIVALS, FAMILY AND FOOD
by
Diana Carey and Judy Large

ILLUSTRATIONS
by
Cornelie Morris and Sylvia Mehta
with
Music
by
Rob Mehta

DEDICATION
For our children and others, who reminded us of what the seasons can mean.

Hawthorn Press

PUBLICATION DETAILS

Published by Hawthorn Press, Bankfield House, 13 Wallbridge, Stroud, Gloucestershire. GL5 3JA
Copyright© 1982 D. Carey and J. Large. All rights reserved.
ISBN 0 950 7062 3X
Cover design by Charmaine Williamson.
Typesetting by B. P. Hawkins Ltd., 4 London Road, Stroud, Gloucestershire.
Illustrations by Cornelie Morris and Sylvia Mehta.
Musical illustrations by Rob Mehta.

ACKNOWLEDGEMENTS
Acknowledgement of the authors' gratitude are due to the many people who freely gave their assistance in producing, editing and in suggesting material for 'Festivals Family and Food'.
 These people include Cornelie Morris, Sylvia Mehta and Rob Mehta for the illustrations and music; teachers and parents at Wynstones school, Christine Clover and Greta Rushbroke, Mrs.F. Spencer, Alice Fuller, Rosie Franklin, Michael Carey, Elsa Lampkin, Dot Galvin and Pat Jones. Special thanks are due to Diana Clayton for her library work in tracking down copyrights. Also thanks to husbands Michael and Martin, for cups of tea and help with the manuscript.
Two groups have been helpful- the T.V. Action Group which suggested the need for this book, and the support of Faith Hall, Audrey McAllen, Honor Mackenzie and Frances Woolls. The Ariadne Women's Group has also given support and assistance.

Foreword

Medieval calendar woodcuts often illustrated the months of the year according to seasonal tasks. The following text is a typical portrayal of the year, which could also be chanted by children of the past while they acted out the stated activities in rhythmical fashion.

January
By this fire I warm my hands;
February
And with my spade I delve my lands.
March
Here I set my seeds to spring;
April
And here I hear the birds sing.
May
I am light as bird in the tree top;
June
And I take pains to weed my crop.
July
With my scythe my mead I mow;
August
And here I shear my corn full low.
September
With my flail I earn my bread;
October
And here I sow my wheat so red.
November
At Martinmas I kill my swine;
December
And at Christmas I drink red wine

In stark contrast, a friend spoke with us recently about feeling lost in today's 'instant' society. Few of us today follow the full cycle from spade and seed to bread. If we so wish, we may have strawberries for tea in January, courtesy of frozen foods. Meals needn't take any actual process of preparation; with a tin or a packet something to eat can be ready in minutes. Cakes and biscuits are available ready-baked or in convenient mixes. Indeed, 'convenience' is a commercial catchword. Some feel that major holidays are also in a commercial domain, with Christmas decorations in the shops so rapidly followed by Easter ones that the themes become superficial and any meaning, lost.

We are a mobile society; we move away from immediate family, perhaps changing home or work-place every few years, and have new or changing standards and expectations in relationships. Ideally all of these changes mean that we are no longer tied to our environment as past generations were. We can better fulfill individuality and make free choices. This is the ideal. But being tied to the environment and natural seasonal cycle of life is not the same as being in touch with it. It may be that we still need the latter.

The theme of this book is a simple but bold suggestion; that if rituals and festivals have traditionally contributed to the integration and stability of communities and societies, then in the modern context they may do the same for our personal integration and for a healthy social ethos. 'Family' today may be in new forms, with single parents or single individuals joining together or with couples and their children. It has always meant people of all ages belonging together, and for many the extended family is still important. Even if we manage only once a year to gather with friends or relatives in celebration of one festival or occasion, this is time well spent.

This book is for men, women and children who wish to relate to the seasons and at the same time to each other. It is written with children very much in mind, for children can remind us of nature and the wonder we might otherwise forget. We hope it will be used as a reference book according to the reader's own needs, situation, and resources. And we hope it will be enjoyed. Don't feel intimidated by the sheer volume; try a few ideas each year and gather some of your own, which can be added at the end of the book.

CONTENTS

INTRODUCTION: The Four Seasons   vi

I   SPRING DAYS   **1**
   1. Candlemas   7
   2. St. Valentine's Day   9
   3. Shrove Tuesday and Shrovetide   11
   4. Mothering Sunday   13
   5. Good Friday   15
   6. Eastertide   16
   7. May Day   25

II   HERBS   **33**

III SUMMER DAYS   **42**
   1. Whitsun   48
   2. Midsummer   51
   3. Picnics   54
   4. Other Summer Food and Drink   59
   5. Harvest   66
   6. The Preserving Year   70

IV   AUTUMN DAYS   **78**
   1. Michaelmas   80
   2. Hallowe'en   83
   3. All Souls Day   91
   4. Guy Fawkes Night   93
   5. Bonfire Songs   100
   6. Martinmas   106
   7. What to do with all the apples!   108
   8. Things to make with Autumn Nuts, Berries, Grasses and Leaves   112

V   WINTER DAYS   **118**
   1. Advent   121
   2. St. Nicholas   126
   3. Christmastide Decorations   131
   4. Christmas Eve   137
   5. Christmas Day   141

6. New Year   151
7. Twelfth Night – Epiphany   154

VI   BIRTHDAYS   159

VII   SWEETMAKING   167

VIII   HUNGRY TEATIMES   171

IX   RAINY DAYS & CONVALESCENCE   179

X   EXTRA TOUCHES   193

XI   BIRTHDAY CALENDAR   201

XII   YOUR OWN IDEAS   207

XIII   INDEX   209

XIV   REFERENCES AND   215
        ACKNOWLEDGEMENTS

v

INTRODUCTION

The Four Seasons

Spring brought the leggy lambs running up to their mothers for short and urgent sucking sessions. We saw the afterbirths, we knew that hens laid eggs and that baby pigs came out of the mother sow, but we never doubted that we were young, God-like creatures, mysteriously deposited under the gooseberry bush to be brought to our mothers in the midwife's bag ...

Autumn brought the fluttering leaves, piled by the winds into the banks of confetti to jump and roll in, and scatter back to the winds.

Winter seeped through our boots, aggravating our itching chilblains, but they were soon forgotten in the snowball pelting ... but Summer mornings were the best of all ...

Winifred Foley
No Pipe Dreams for Father

The Months

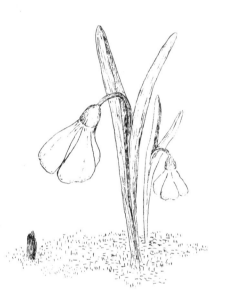

January cold desolate;
February all dripping wet;
March wind ranges;
April changes;
Birds sing in tune
   To flowers of May,
And sunny June
   Brings longest day;
In scorched July
   The storm-clouds fly;
Lightning-torn
   August bears corn;
September fruit;
In rough October
   Earth must disrobe her;
Stars fall and shoot
   In keen November;
And night is long
   And cold is strong
   In bleak December.

Christina Rossetti

The Calendar.

I knew when Spring was come –
Not by the murmurous hum
Of bees in the willow-trees,
　　　Or frills
　　　Of daffodils,
Or the scent of the breeze;
But because there were whips and tops
By the jars of lollipops
In the two little village shops.

I knew when Summer breathed –
Not by the flowers that wreathed
The sedge by the water's edge,
　　　Or gold
　　　Of the wold,
Or white and rose of the hedge;
But because, in a wooden box
In the window at Mrs. Mock's,
There were white-winged shuttlecocks.

I knew when Autumn came –
Not by the crimson flame
Of leaves that lapped the eaves
　　　Or mist
　　　In amethyst
And opal-tinted weaves;
But because there were alley-taws*
(Punctual as hips and haws)
On the counter at Mrs. Shaw's.

I knew when Winter swirled –
Not by the whitened world
Or silver skeins in the lanes,
　　　Or frost
　　　That embossed
Its patterns on window-panes:
But because there were transfer-sheets
By the bottles of spice and sweets
In the shops in two little streets.

　　　　　　　Barbara Euphan Todd

*'alley-taws' are marbles.

Recipe Notes

Ingredients.

Styles of eating are very much a question of individual choice. We would like to make a few points though:-

1. Very few meat recipes have been given but if possible it is desirable to use a good butcher, whose meat is fresh, not frozen, and where you can, hopefully, get good free-range chickens and buy sausagemeat or other minced meat which he has minced and without additives.
2. Most of the recipes given can be made with a 100% wholemeal flour or 81%. It is very much up to personal taste what flour is used but Health Food Shops have a good range.
3. When we have mentioned flavourings, it is worth investigating the possibility of using essential oils – often available from Health Food Stores, rather than the totally synthetic vanilla or other essences generally available. Sometimes we can also use vegetable colourings rather than the synthetic ones, e.g. *turmeric* produces a good yellow, *beetroot juice* gives red/purple and *onion skins* give a brown colour.

Where possible, perhaps the ideal is to buy really fresh meat, fruit and vegetables and to spend a bit of time, if you can, shopping around for good quality produce.

Recipe Conversion
(for American Usage)

4 oz flour	1 cup
8 oz butter or marg.	1 cup
8 fl oz milk	1 cup
7 oz sugar	1 cup
4 oz icing sugar	1 cup
	confectioner's sugar
2 oz rolled oats	1 cup
4 oz raisins	1 cup
4 oz nuts, chopped	approx. 1 cup
6 oz rice or lentils	1 cup

Treacle	:	molasses
Biscuits	:	cookies
Sweets	:	candies
Teatime	:	not dinner, not lunch, probably anything from a sit-down snack to a light supper!

Oven Temperatures

Mark		
1	275 F	140 C
2	300 F	150 C
3	325 F	170 C
4	350 F	180 C
5	375 F	190 C
6	400 F	200 C
7	425 F	220 C
8	450 F	230 C

Weights

½ oz.	10 gms.
1 oz.	25 gms.
1½ oz.	40 gms.
2 oz.	50 gms.
2½ oz.	60 gms.
3 oz.	75 gms.
4 oz.	110 gms.
4½ oz.	125 gms.
5 oz.	150 gms.
6 oz.	175 gms.
7 oz.	200 gms.
8 oz.	225 gms.
9 oz.	250 gms.
10 oz.	275 gms.
12 oz.	350 gms.
1 lb.	450 gms.
1½ lbs.	700 gms.
2 lbs.	900 gms.
3 lbs.	1 kg. 350 gms.

Volume

2 fl. oz.	55 ml.
3 fl. oz.	75 ml.
5 fl. oz. (¼ pt)	150 ml.
½ pt.	275 ml.
¾ pt.	425 ml.
1 pt.	570 ml.
1¾ pt.	1 litre.

Persephone

There is a story from ancient Greece which comes to mind each times Spring returns. It is the tale of Persephone, goddess of Springtime and plant-life, daughter of the goddess of agriculture, grain, and corn, Ceres or Demeter. When Ceres walked through the fields, the corn grew tall and straight and ripened to the harvest. Persephone often ran lightly and playfully before her, helping the first young shoots to grow, playing with young lambs, and singing to the wildflowers.

One day Persephone called her young friends to go with her to gather flowers for garlands on the beautiful plain of Etna. They would climb the green slopes of Mount Etna there, and seek blue speedwell, yellow narcissus, snap dragons and sweet-peas – all the spring flowers which we look for and enjoy today. The little girls sang as they wove garlands for their hair.

It happened that Pluto was passing by, riding in his dark chariot drawn by four coal-black horses. Pluto was King of caves and caverns, King or God of the underworld. He heard the song, and then he saw Persephone, sitting among the many-coloured blossoms. Long had Pluto searched for a maid to share his throne underground. So many had refused him, that he didn't ask this time. Straight through the bushes he rode, right to the spot where she was seated, with a loud noise of cracking branches and the shrieks of frightened girls, he swept Persephone up off her feet and into the chariot, and in a twinkling she had gone. The blossoms lay crumpled and fading on the trampled earth. The bushes drooped heavily, the other girls ran sobbing home, and only the wind carried the cry of Persephone back to the ears of Ceres.

Ceres was walking through the cornfields, as she did daily, when the faint cry reached her. She dropped her basket of grain, and began running towards the mountain. Faster and faster she ran, calling out for her daughter. But the hillside was transformed. All the flowers, even the red anemones, had closed their buds and bent their heads. As the sun went down, the stars came out one by one and the wind grew colder, Ceres found a broken, faded garland of flowers. Only much later did the sun travel down to tell Ceres what happened, and the grieving Cornmother went away to a far country.

Persephone was unhappy in the underground, missing the bright sunbeams and fresh grass and flowers she had once so loved. Pluto gave her a shining black dress, and jewels to wear, but these did not cheer her. He put food on a golden plate, but she would not eat.

You can imagine how much things changed up on the earth. The green grass became brown, flowers died, the leaves and fruit in the orchards fell and did not ripen. The corn drooped, dried and could not be harvested. People could no longer grind flour for bread and they began to go hungry. When the great King of all the gods Zeus heard of this, and saw the earth's sadness, he commanded Pluto to return Persephone to Ceres. If she had not eaten in the underworld, then she had no connection to it, and should therefore be free to leave. A joyful Ceres returned to meet her.

But Pluto was cunning., He offered the fair Persephone a pomegranate fruit, red, wrinkled and round like an apple, imploring that she eat just a bit before leaving. Very slowly, Persephone ate six of the yellow seeds from inside the pomegranate.

So it was, that when Zeus heard of her eating the seeds, he decreed that for each seed she ate, she must spend one month in the underground, even if this meant that things did not grow on the earth. We are quite used to this now, and call most of this time, with the early evening darkness, Winter. The other six months Persephone would resume her place among the plants and flowers. And we celebrate her return, when the snowdrops, crocus blossoms, daffodils and later the violets and other flowers appear to welcome her, as Spring.

Slumber in Spring

Grey pussy-willows
For fairy pillows
So soft for fairy's head;
Cherry-petals sweet
For a cool, clean sheet,
Green moss for a fairy bed.
Fragrant violet for a coverlet.
And hush! down the hill's green sweep,
Comes the wind's soft sigh
For a lullaby;
Sound, sound will a fairy sleep.

Elizabeth Gould

Spring is Coming Song

Spring is coming, Spring is coming,
Birdies, build your nests;
Weave together straw and feather,
Doing each your best, doing each your best.

Spring is coming, Spring is coming,
Flowers are coming too,
Pansies, lilies, daffodilies
Spring is nearly through, Spring is nearly through.

Spring is coming, Spring is coming,
All around is fair,
Shiver, quiver on the river
Spring is really here, Spring is really here.

The month it was April
The day it was sunny,
I plucked him a primrose
And the moon came up like honey.

3

The Old Cricketer

All winter long, in the slush and the mud and the
     darkness,
Treading the lonely round of the yards and the
     pastures,
Working the ploughland and tending the cattle,
He would remember the sun and the summer,
And long for the flowering of blackthorn,
The ripple and sheen of young barley.

Then when April was come he would go to his
     kitchen
And take down a bat that was slung by the fireplace,
Caressing the willow of strange antique pattern,
Tortuous of grain and darkened by wood-smoke,
More precious to him than elm, oak or beechwood,
Dearer than cedars of Lebanon.

And would call up his friends in the villages,
In the hamlets, the farms and the homesteads,
For the April annointing of cider and linseed,
Linseed oil for the bat and the cider for friendship.

And the old men would come to stand by the barrel,
Mighty men of the past, red-faced with weather
And many a glass of the plum and the parsnip;
Recalling the glory they knew in their prime,
All batsmen and bowlers of note, who terrified
     parishes.

        Frank Mansell

The Three Winds

The hard blue winds of March
shake the young sheep
and flake the long stone walls;
now from the gusty grass
comes the horned music of rams,
and plovers fall out of the sky
filling their wings with snow...
tired of this northern tune the
winds turn soft blowing white butterflies
out of the dog rose hedges, and the schoolroom
songs are full of boys' green cuckoos piping
the summer round....

    Laurie Lee *'The Sun My Monument'*

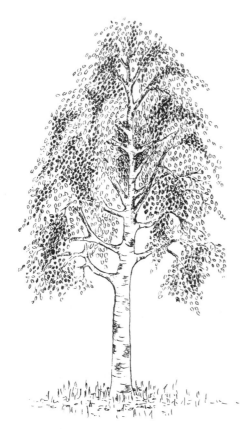

Child's Song in Spring

The silver birch is a dainty lady,
She wears a satin gown;
The elm tree makes the old church shady
She will not live in town.

The English Oak is a sturdy fellow,
He gets his green coat late;
The willow is smart in a suit of yellow,
While brown the beech trees wait.

Such a gay green crown God gives the larches –
As green as he is good!
The hazels hold up their arms for arches
When Spring rides through the wood.

The chestnut's proud, and the lilac's pretty,
The poplar's gentle and tall,
But the plane tree's kind to the poor dull city –
I love him best of all!

        E. Nesbit

Water, Water, Wallflower –
Ring Game

Water, water, wallflower, growing up so high,
We are all God's children
And we all must die.
Except for ..... and .....
The fairest of us all
They can dance and they can sing
And they can play the violin.
Fie! Fie! Fie! for shame
Turn your back to the ring again.

Ending:

Fie! Fie! Fie! for shame
Turn your face to the ring again.

Actions:

Walk round holding hands in a circle. Adult chooses two names of children next to each other and when they all sing 'Fie! Fie! Fie! for shame...' they all stand still and wag their fingers at the two, who then turn and face outward. The song is repeated as they all walk round holding hands with the two facing outwards and then two other children next to those two are named and have to turn outwards. The song is repeated until all the children are facing outwards. Then they sing

or 'They can hop and they can skip,
They can play the candlestick'

(from Lark Rise to Candleford by Flora Thompson)

'Fie! Fie! Fie! for shame
Turn your faces to the ring again'.

and all the children turn round and face the inside of the ring again.

Water, Water, Wallflower

Water, water, wallflower, growing up so high, we are all God's children, and we all must die, ex-

cept for — and — the fairest of us all, they can dance they can sing they can play the violin,

fie, fie, fie for shame, turn your face to the ring again.

5

Oats and Beans –
Ring Game

Oats and beans and barley grow,
Oats and beans and barley grow,
Do you or I or anyone know
How oats and beans and barley grow?

First the farmer sows his seed
Then he stands and takes his ease,
He stamps the ground and claps his hands
And turns around to view the land.

Waiting for a partner,
Waiting for a partner,
Open the ring
And let one in.

When you are married you must obey
You must be true to all you say
You must be kind, you must be good,
And help your wife to chop the wood.

Actions:

The children form a circle and holding hands they walk round the farmer who stands in the middle. During the second verse they stand still, sow the seed, place their hands on their hips, stamp and clap and then turn around. During the third verse they gently rock from side to side, holding hands in a circle. Then they open the ring and the farmer points to a child who is to be his wife and she joins him, in the middle. During the last verse they wag their fingers whilst the farmer and wife dance round together holding hands in the middle. They end by chopping wood.

Lady Spring
– Ring Game
Tune of 'Nuts in May'

Look who's here
It's Lady Spring
Lady Spring, Lady Spring,
Look who's here
It's Lady Spring
Lady Spring is here.

Who'll come into our wee ring ....repeat
..... And dance with Lady Spring?

'Mary' will come into our wee ring .... repeat
To dance with Lady Spring.

Actions:

Children stand in a circle – Lady Spring, wearing a spring crown, in the middle. Children all dance round singing. One child is chosen to dance with Lady Spring. Then *that* child is Lady Spring and so on.

6

1. Candlemas : February 2

Candlemas Day takes its name from the blessing of candles on this day for use in church throughout the coming year. It is the feast of the presentation of Christ in the Temple when Simeon hailed him as 'A light to lighten the Gentiles'. Christians used to light candles for Baby Jesus and Mother Mary and perhaps that is why in some areas today the snowdrops which are very much in evidence at this season are known as Candlemas Bells or Mary's tapers.

"If Candlemas Day be fair and bright
Winter will take another flight.
If Candlemas Day be cloud and rain
Winter is gone and will not come again."

If the weather is mild in February the blackthorn or wild plum may blossom. The white flowers appear before the leaves on the black branches, which is why it is called blackthorn. The cold spell which often follows is known as the 'blackthorn winter'.

"Candlemas Day stick beans in the clay
Throw candle and candlestick right away".

It was felt by the housewife of long ago that by 2nd February she shouldn't need to get up by candlelight. In the evening they would have supper by the firelight and go early to bed.

There is an old belief that all hibernating animals, and in particular the badger, (or in the case of America, the groundhog) wake up on Candlemas Day and come out to see if it is still winter. If it is a sunny day, the animals will see their shadows and go back to earth for a further 40 days. If it is cloudy they will not be frightened by their shadows and will stay above ground. Thus, if it is cloudy, people believe we shall have an early spring. The Americans actually call Candlemas GROUNDHOG DAY for this reason.

Candlemaking

The traditional materials for candlemaking (when it was a standard domestic task) were beeswax and tallow. Beeswax is the wax from the honeycomb of the bee. The honeycomb would be melted in hot water, strained, and the resulting liquid was allowed to cool. Tallow is a hard fat which can be produced from rendered suet or from the fruits of some trees such as the bay tree, Japanese sumach tree, or - appropriately, the Chinese tallow tree. One of the elements comprising tallow is called *stearin*, and if you go today to obtain paraffin wax for candlemaking, you'll find stearin a necessary additive. It helps in dissolving dye, hardening the wax and producing a longer-burning candle.

Beautiful and pleasing as it is, beeswax is both hard to obtain and often expensive today, while tallow has always had a reputation for acrid smoke. If you are able to find beeswax, then "dipping" is a simple method for making your candles. The wicks are dipped into the melted wax, removed, allowed to cool or dipped in cold water to cool and this process repeated until the desired thickness obtained.

For making candles in moulds to vary shapes you may wish to use one of the many kits now available, which provide you with wax, wicks, dyes, stearin and even mould-sealing agents. You may wish to obtain ingredients individually and perhaps use the melted remains of old candle bits for extra colour instead of dyes.

You will need your choice of moulds, an old saucepan or double boiler for gently melting the wax, wicks, and if you are colouring your candles, dye discs dissolved in stearin.

Mould possibilities are vast - old margarine tubs, a discarded tea cup, yoghurt cartons, half-empty egg shell, walnut shells, or folded cardboard supported in a bowl of sand. Sand will support moulds which might otherwise tip or fall over when you are pouring wax. We have even formed holes in the sand to be moulds in themselves - this creates an interesting candle with a sandy textured pattern on its outside. You may even use attractively shaped glass jars or bottles, but these must be carefully broken to remove the candle.

If you have or can borrow a wax thermometer, you'll want your melted wax to reach about $180°F$ before pouring into moulds. The finish of the candle is enhanced if you can weight your mould in a container of water, such that the water is level with the surface of the wax. Your wick should be suspended before pouring the wax. Tie one end of the wick to a wire or hairpin, anything that will span the top of the mould. Weight the other end of the wick so that it hangs straight - a small metal nut or washer will do nicely.

Pour wax slowly and carefully, and when the mould is full, allow it to cool *slowly*. When the candle has started to set, it is a good idea to poke a stick or knitting needle down the centre near the wick. The wax shrinks slightly as it cools, so add a little more wax each hour just to keep the top level.

Allow the candle to set completely. It should be possible to lift or slide it from the mould - if it doesn't come out smoothly then chill the set candle in the mould in the refrigerator for half an hour. The cold should cause the set wax to contract slightly, enabling easier release.

Enjoy your finished candles!

Decorating Finished Candles

Whether you choose to decorate candles which you have made yourself or plain ones which you have bought, this is a simple activity which may be enjoyed by all age-groups. You can transform even the plain household candle into an attractive gift or decoration. Brightly coloured beeswax is available in some shops for modelling purposes, and this works well for shaping and applying pictures, seasonal or simply imaginative. One friend often makes little people forms with arms seeming to clasp around the candle. Flower shapes, stars, geometric patterns, tree motifs, simple bird or butterfly forms; whatever you choose will be original. Our little boy took to making little candle shapes on top of his candles, complete with carefully applied red flame, which he found fun. If you cannot obtain such modelling wax, use left over bits of candles or there is an obvious alternative which will be possible in any household where children use wax crayons. Hopefully you have not thrown away the left over little bits of various colours. Scrape away the discoloured bits and gather your colours together. The idea is to melt them down over boiling water, (the double boiler principle) and then apply while very soft either by hand or with an improvised stick applicator. If you have several colours, simply place them several inches apart on an old plate and put this atop a large saucepan of boiling water. If you keep an eye on them, they are not going to melt so quickly as to all run together. If just experimenting with one colour, use a saucer over a smaller pan. The picture making session can be as long or as short as you wish to make it.

Sometimes children like to apply glitter to candles. If so, choose your glue carefully so as to have a non-flamable one for sure. Place the candle on its side on a piece of newspaper or scrap paper. Apply the glue, either generally or in a pattern, then sprinkle the glitter generously over the glue on the candle. It will adhere to your desired pattern, and the extra (there will be lots of that) will fall to the paper, ready for saving and using again.

Big, thick candles may be painted without affecting their burning qualities. The best paint is that which is natural and shellac based. Avoid painting thin candles, for the proportion of paint to wax can disturb the capacity of the wick.

You may wish to apply dried flowers or paper cut-outs to candles for decorative effect. Apply with gum arabic, but do experiment to see that the candle can still burn well before 'mass-producing' these.

2. Valentine's Day : February 14

Good Morrow to you, Valentine.
Curl your locks as I do mine,
Two before and three behind.
Good Morrow to you, Valentine.

Long before St. Valentine became the patron saint of lovers, a festival was held in ancient Rome during February in honour of the great god Pan. The festival was called Lupercalia, and one of its customs was for the names of young men and women to be shaken in a box and then drawn in lottery fashion to choose token sweethearts. It happened that in the 3rd Century the Bishop Valentine of Rome was martyred on the eve of the feast of Lupercalia. A man noted for his goodness and chastity, it was fitting that the day eventually acquired his name. The element of chance and theme of love remain, as a Valentine is still known as an anonymous declaration of affection usually sent in card form. Flowers, red heart shapes, lace and birds are the images of the festival, the latter because of an old belief that birds also chose their mates on this day for spring nesting.

For children today it is the surprise element of a pretty card rather than romantic notions which holds enjoyment of the day. With white and red paper, a bit of old lace or even left-over frilly paper doiley and some glue they can make cards to send to friends, or leave on the breakfast table for a family member. Interesting two-dimensional cards are made by cutting out a centre shape, then cutting this again to a new pattern and hanging in back in the card with cotton thread. See below.

I sent a letter to my love –
Ring Game

Tune of Yankee Doodle

I sent a letter to my love
And on the way I dropped it,
A little puppy picked it up
And put it in his pocket.

Actions:

Children sit in a circle on the floor. One of them walks round the outside whilst they all sing the song and then drops a handkerchief when they say "dropped it" behind a child. At the end of the song both children, the one who dropped the handkerchief and the one who had it dropped behind him, run round the ring in opposite directions and try to reach the empty place first. The one who loses his seat then takes the handkerchief round and the verse is sung again.

I sent a letter to my love and on the way I dropped it, a little puppy picked it up and put it in his pocket.

9

Valentine Tea

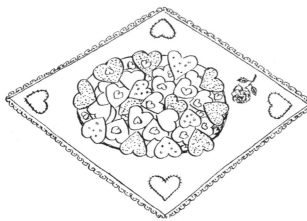

6 oz butter or margarine
6 oz sugar
8 oz flour
a pinch of bicarbonate of soda
¼ teaspoon salt
2 eggs
1 lemon

If you have a heart-shaped cake tin this is a good time to use it. Paper bun cases filled with a few old fashioned heart-shaped sweets (remember the ones with little fortunes on them?) and nuts or raisins are nice surprises set by children's places at tea. Try the following recipe for heart-shaped biscuits. As children we used a particularly revolting reddish pink icing for these, and thought they were splendid. Try them with the icing of your choice:

Cream the butter or margarine with the sugar, add the eggs then the flour sifted with the salt and the bicarbonate of soda, the grated rind of the lemon and 1 tablespoon of its juice. Roll out thinly, cut into heart shapes and bake in a moderate oven, 355°F (Reg. 4) for about 10 minutes. When they have cooled, decorate with a soft royal icing (see page 26) Pipe round the outside and write your loved one's name in the middle, your children could each have one with their names on too.

For biscuits you can hang by ribbons, see (see p.136)

3. Shrove Tuesday and Shrovetide

Once, twice, thrice,
I give thee warning,
Please to make pancakes
'Gin tomorrow morning.

Shrove Tuesday or Pancake day is the day before Lent begins. Eggs and fat were not eaten during Lent so they had to be used up and pancakes were the traditional way of doing this. It was often a time of great festivity before the fasting and penance during Lent.

Pancakes with lemon and sugar or honey

8 oz flour
4 eggs
1 pt milk
A little butter and salt.

Put the flour into a basin and make a well in the middle; gradually whisk or beat in the milk and eggs and when all the flour is mixed in, add the butter and salt. Leave to stand for ½ hour.

Use a little oil in frying pan (a brush is helpful) and thinly spread the batter over the hot pan. Turn or toss and when the pancake is ready you can either serve immediately with accompaniments or stack them and keep warm in the oven.

Professor Branestawm's machine

The process of pancake-making should hopefully not be as complicated as *Professor Branestawm's machine.*

"Whizizizzi, POP" went the machine and a larger and thicker pancake than any shot out of the machine higher than it was supposed to, turned over eight-and-a-half times and dropped on the Professor's head, where it enveloped him like an unreasonable hat ten sizes too large....

'Whiz, POP' went the machine and out shot another pancake which made straight for the Mayor but missed him and stuck to the wall .... Faster and ever so much faster flew the pancakes. Thicker and thicker. Bigger and bigger. They came out flatways and edgeways. They shot high in the air and stuck to the ceiling. One sailed across the room and hit the Vicar in the waistcoat Pop, poppety, pop. It was like a machine-gun but much more sploshy.

The Professor struggled out of his pancake just in time for another one to drop over him. Two pancakes were on the clock, four were draped over the light. The Mayor was eating his way through a complete set of pancakes of varying sizes that had fallen in front of him. The four firemen put their helmets on and brandished their axes but only succeeded in smashing two cups, one saucer, and the sugar basin. Mrs Flittersnoop put her head gingerly out from under the table and was immediately gummed to the carpet by a three-foot pancake two inches thick that had just shot out.

(Taken from *Pancake Day at Great Pagwell*)

by Norman Hunter

"Mix a pancake
Stir a pancake
Pop it in the pan.
Fry a pancake
Toss a pancake
Catch it if you can."

Try and make up your own simple tune to go with this.

Fastnachts – A 'Pennsylvania Dutch' Shrove Tuesday doughnut tradition of German origin.

1 pt milk
1 tablespoon dried yeast dissolved in a cup of warm water
7 oz sugar
pinch of salt
1½ lbs flour
3 well beaten eggs
½ teaspoon nutmeg
2 oz melted butter

Scald milk and set aside to cool. Add a cup of the flour to the dissolved yeast and mix to a batter. When the milk is lukewarm, add to it the yeast and flour froth, then stir in 1 teaspoon of the sugar and 12 oz flour. Set in a warm place to rise overnight. The following morning, add well beaten eggs, nutmeg, sugar and salt and mix well. Stir in enough flour until the batter cannot be mixed by a spoon, then set aside to rise until light. Roll on a well floured board and cut with a round cutter first, using a smaller cutter to create a hole in each centre. Let rise a final time, then fry in hot oil until golden brown.

Sour Milk Pancakes

4 oz sifted self-raising flour
1 tablespoon sugar
1 teaspoon salt
½ teaspoon bicarbonate of soda

Beat until light
1 egg
Add 8 oz sour milk.

Combine sifted and liquid ingredients with a few swift strokes. Beat in 1 or 2 tablespoons veg. oil or melted butter until the batter is smooth.
Because of the oil or butter in this mixture, you should need very little oil when frying. Fry in rounds or pour Pancake Men shapes to fry until golden brown.

These are good with savoury or sweet fillings or plain with lemon as above. In America they would be eaten with butter and maple syrup - a sweet but delicious combination if you can get the genuine syrup.

4. Mothering Sunday

It is the day of all the year
Of all the year the one day,
And here come I, my Mother dear,
To bring you cheer,
A—mothering on Sunday

In a past age of few holidays the middle Sunday in Lent was one when young people working away from home were given the day off to visit their mothers. From the 16th Century on, girls "in service" would bake to show their mothers their new skills in the form of a gift. This traditional gift was a Simnel Cake which is a rich fruit cake with a layer of marzipan in the middle and another on top.

Simnel Cake

8 oz plain flour
pinch salt
large pinch of baking powder
2 oz rice flour
8 oz sultanas
4 oz currants
4 oz glace cherries, (chopped and washed)
1 oz candied peel (finely chopped) optional
8 oz butter
grated rind of 2 lemons
8 oz caster sugar
4 eggs (separated)
beaten egg (to decorate)
3-4 tablespoons warm glace icing (see p.14)

Almond Paste

8 oz ground almonds
10 oz caster sugar
6 oz icing sugar (sifted)
2 egg yolks, or 1 whole egg
juice of ½ lemon
1-2 teaspoon orange flower water

To make the almond paste, place the almonds, caster sugar and sifted icing sugar in a bowl and mix them together. Whisk egg yolks (or whole egg) with the lemon juice and flavourings and add this to the mixture of ground almonds and sugar. Pound paste lightly to release a little of the oil from the almonds. Knead paste with the hands until smooth. Store in cool place until needed.

Prepare the cake tin and set the oven at 350°F (Reg. 4).

Cake Mix

Sift the flour with the salt, baking powder and rice flour into a large basin. Mix together the sultanas, currants, cherries and peel. Cream the butter with the lemon rind until soft, add the sugar and continue creaming until mixture is light and fluffy, then beat in the egg yolks. Whip egg white until stiff. Fold one-third of the flour into the mixture, then fold in the egg whites alternately with remaining flour and fruit. Put half the mixture into prepared tin spreading it a little up the sides.

Take just over one-third of the almond paste, roll it into a smooth round, place it in the tin and cover with the remaining cake mixture. Bake in the pre-set oven for 2 hours, then reduce heat to 300°F (Reg. 2), cover cake with a double thickness of greased paper and continue cooking for about 30 mins, or until a skewer inserted in the cake comes out clean. Allow the cake to cool a little, then remove it from the tin and slide it on to a baking sheet.

Decoration

Divide the remaining almond paste in two, shape one portion into a number of even-sized balls and arrange them round the top edge of the cake. Brush the paste with a little beaten egg, put the cake under the grill for a few minutes to brown. When the cake is cold, pour a little warm glace icing on the centre of the cake. Arrange a group of marzipan fruits, made from the last portion of almond paste on the icing and tie a ribbon round the cake.

Marzipan fruits

A wide variety of fruits can be made most successfully if you try to keep the shape and size of the different fruits in your mind. The remaining almond paste can be used and colour only small piece at a time, adding the liquid colouring from the point of a skewer. Mould the fruits with the fingers, colour them and leave to harden before arranging on the cake.

Instead of almond paste you can use boiled marzipan.

1 lb granulated sugar
6 fl oz water
¾ lb ground almonds
2 egg whites (lightly beaten)
juice of ½ lemon
1 teaspoon orange flower water
3-4 tablespoons icing sugar

Place the sugar and water in a saucepan and dissolve over gentle heat: bring it to the boil and cook steadily to 240°F. Remove the pan from the heat and beat the syrup until it looks a little cloudy, stir in the ground almonds, add the egg whites and cook over a gentle heat for 2-3 minutes. Add the flavourings and turn on to a cold surface dusted with icing sugar. When the marzipan is cool, knead it until quite smooth, colour and shape as required.

A simple alternative to Simnel Cake

Caraway Angel Cake

5 oz flour
4 oz caster sugar
2 oz butter
¼ pt milk
2 egg whites
1 teaspoon baking powder
2 oz finely sliced candied peel
1 large teaspoon caraway seeds

Beat the butter and sugar to a soft cream and gradually stir in the milk. When the mixture is quite smooth, add the stiffly whipped whites of egg until all is stirred together. Sieve flour with a pinch of salt and the baking powder; add to mixture, stirring lightly. Add candied peel and caraway seeds. Bake in greased tin 1¼ hrs. in a moderate oven, 325°F (Reg. 3).

Glace Icing

8 oz icing sugar
1½-2 tablespoons warm water
A little lemon juice

Sift the icing sugar into a bowl and gradually add the water. The icing should be thick enough to coat the back of a spoon thickly. Add the lemon juice and use immediately. (Reduce the amount of glace icing by half if it is just required for the top of the Mother's Day Cake). Other flavourings can be added for different cakes, for example, coffee, orange or chocolate.

5. Good Friday – Easter

Hot-cross buns, hot-cross buns;
One a penny poker,
Two a penny tongs,
Three a penny fire shovel,
Hot-cross buns.

By Christian tradition, the day of the crucifixion of Christ, the Friday immediately preceding Easter which celebrates the Resurrection. Ideally this is a day to make hot-cross buns at home, and to find some time to paint eggs if children have been blowing and saving them for a week or two beforehand.

Apart from the obvious symbolism of the cross on these spicy buns, carried over from pre-Reformation days, there is also a school of thought which sees it as a picture of quadrants showing the four seasons.

Hot-cross buns! Hot-cross buns!
One a penny, two a penny,
Hot-cross buns!
If you have no daughters,
Give them to your sons,
One a penny, two a penny,
Hot-cross buns!
But if you have none of these little elves,
Then you may eat them all yourselves.

Hot Cross Buns

1 lb plain flour
½ teaspoon salt
½ teaspoon mixed spice
scant ½ pt milk
¾ oz yeast (fresh)
2-4 oz butter
2 oz caster sugar
2 eggs (beaten)
6 oz currants
1 oz finely chopped candied peel (optional)
sweetened milk for finishing.

Put the flour, salt and mixed spice into a bowl. Warm the milk carefully to blood heat and add the yeast and butter. Stir until yeast is dissolved, then mix in the sugar and eggs. Make a well in the flour and tip in the liquid and beat until smooth.

Turn dough onto floured board and work in currants and candied peel. Knead dough until it is elastic and not sticky, then place in warmed greased bowl and sprinkle with a little flour, cover and leave for 1½ hours until doubled in bulk. Knock it down once if you like and allow to rise again. Shape the dough into about 16 buns and arrange on a greased baking sheet and allow to prove until twice their size,

about 15 minutes. Brush the tops with some sweetened milk.

For the crosses, make a small quantity of short-crust pastry with white flour and roll out and cut into strips which you can fix on to the buns in crosses.

Put in hot oven 425°F (Reg. 7) for 15 mins. Put a tray of water in the bottom of the oven to provide a steamy atmosphere.

Flower Seeds for Eastertime

Here are some seeds which are easy to grow and which will give a great deal of pleasure:

candytuft
cornflower
godetia
clarkia
nasturtiums
marigold
scabious
love in a mist

Seeds make a good little present for children at Easter if you feel they are likely to receive plenty of sweet things anyway: put a few into a blown egg (see later).

Planting Seeds on Good Friday

Traditionally, Good Friday was the time to plant seed potatoes. In the morning we usually clear some ground and plant seeds as a family tradition. Sometimes, the children have already put seeds in a dish a couple of weeks before Easter. If watered every day, these come up and can make an Easter basket. Some seeds can also be put into an eggshell and watered.

15

6. Eastertide

Here's two or three jolly boys
All of one mind,
We've come a pace-egging,
And hope you'll be kind;
We hope you'll be kind
With your eggs and your beer,
And we'll come no more pace-egging
Until the next year.

Daffodillies yellow,
Daffodillies gay,
To put upon the table
On Easter Day.

Easter

The festival of Easter drives its name from pre-Christian goddess symbols of rebirth, fertility and Spring; the Saxon Eastre and Old German Eostre. The ancient symbols of hare and egg, both known as signs of the return of life after Winter's sleep, today carry the Christian association of the Resurrection of Christ. When we exchange Easter eggs as gifts we are re-enacting an ancient wisdom – that which appears to be still and dead in fact contains new life.

For an Easter tree, cut down a really large branch and anchor it firmly in a heavy plant pot full of earth or sand. Any branch which is just beginning to sprout young green leaves is beautiful but if you know where to find catkins or pussy willows or if you have a forsythia or flowering cherry available then you have the makings of a memorable Easter tree. The children can decorate this with blown eggs which they can either paint or dye and hang with pretty ribbon or wool. (See below)

There is a lovely tradition for children, brought to us by Dutch friends, of making "Easter Poles" for the week between Palm Sunday and Easter. They may be walked with in simple procession, or more simply used as decoration, as when stood in a bowl of blossoming hyacinths. A slender green branch is formed and tied to form a hoop shape which is then tied with ribbons or lengths of wool to hang from the top of a larger sturdier stick or pole. Crepe paper streamers of varying colours are hung from the hoop, and at the top of the pole may sit a fine bread hen or chicken shape with raisins for eyes - to be eaten, of course, after festivities! The hoops may be decorated as you wish - with bells, flowers, paper egg shapes, etc. But the small child will probably feel the streamers and bread chicken are most important.

16

To blow Easter Eggs

Eggs which have been soaked in a solution of vinegar and water *should* be easier to paint with ordinary water-colour or even felt tip pens. Soak them overnight before blowing. Make a tiny hole at either end of the egg, blow slowly and steadily until the yolk emerges, and save this for baking! Rinse under cool water, dry, and decorate. Blown eggs which will hang from a branch for decoration are effective when done in three ways. They may be simply painted; they may have tiny beads, dried flowers, shells, sequins, lace etc. glued on them as well as added colour; or they may be made into tiny hanging windows by removing one side. What you place inside is up to your imagination. A marzipan or felt chick, a tiny red paper heart or flower, a sweet or beautiful pebble are a few suggestions.

Blown eggs needn't be soaked beforehand. But if you wish to do intricate detailed painting which will last for a long time and make a beautiful gift, you may wish to try applying a light clear varnish to the blown eggs before painting with the paints of your choice. To do this, tie a short match-stick to a piece of cotton and insert the match-stick in one end of the egg so that you can hang it (this is the same method for hanging them from Easter trees) for varnishing. Try the rungs on an upside down kitchen stool or chair to hang a line of eggs from. Varnish lightly and carefully, leave to dry, and later you can hold and turn the eggs individually for intricate decorating.

Hard-boiled Eggs

Eggs may be boiled plain colours or with initials, names or designs drawn on beforehand with melted candle wax. Again, either soaking in vinegar before boiling or adding a spoonful of vinegar to the coloured water used seems to make the shell more receptive to colour. You may wish to use vegetable colour dyes for boiling; otherwise try concocting your own. Onion skins produce beautiful deep golden yellow, and if you deliberately wrap some eggs inside skins you will find beautiful delicate patterns on them when they are cool. Try beetroot juice for pink, moss or birch leaves for green. If you tie a leaf or tiny branch to an egg with cotton, the pattern of the same should remain in picture form after removing the string when the egg has cooled.

Hide the finished boiled eggs carefully for a 'hunt' on Easter morning, out in a garden if possible. When gathered in they make a colourful breakfast!

17

Easter Baskets

Our little girl brought this method for a simple basket home from school. It is easy to make and effective.

Begin either with a plain piece of drawing paper, or one which has been painted with water colour. Cut even slits from the bottom edge, between one third and one half the way up. Now staple the paper into a round and simply fold the under edges in to make a bottom to the basket and glue. Add a paper handle, and fill with straw or grass for Easter.

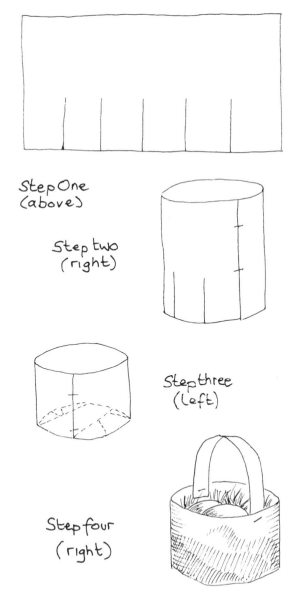

Step One
(above)

Step two
(right)

Step three
(left)

Step four
(right)

The Easter Hare –
a German Legend

Long, long ago, there was a village where the people were very poor. One Easter time the mothers had no money to buy the presents of sweets they usually gave their children on Easter Sunday. They were very sad for they knew how disappointed the children would be.

'What shall we do' they asked each other as they drew water from the well.

'We have plenty of eggs' sighed one.

'The children are tired of eggs' said another.

Then one of the mothers had an idea, and before dinner-time all the mothers in the village knew about it but not a single child.

Early on Easter morning, the mothers left their homes and went into the woods with little baskets on their arms. It was quite impossible to see what they had in the baskets as they were covered with coloured cloths. When the mothers returned home, the cloths were tied about their heads like head-squares, and the baskets were filled with wild flowers.

'My mother went to pick flowers for Easter this morning' said one child, as they all walked together to church.

'So did mine' said another.

'And mine too' said all the others and laughed for they were happy and it was Easter Sunday.

When they came out of church, the children were told to go and play in the woods before dinner. Off they ran, laughing and talking. The girls and boys picked flowers and climbed trees when someone shouted 'Look what I've found'.

'A RED egg'.

'I've found a BLUE one'.

'Here's a nestful, all different colours'.

They ran about searching in the bushes and filling their pockets and hats.

'What kind of eggs are they?' they asked each other.

'They're too big for wild birds' eggs.'

'They're the same size as hens' eggs.'

'Hens don't lay eggs these bright colours, silly.' Just then a hare ran out from behind a bush.

'They're hares' eggs,' cried the children. 'The hare laid the eggs! Hurrah for the Easter Hare.'

The Easter Hare

In the time when the Jesus Child lived among men, the earth was beginning to die; the stout oaks could no longer withstand the storm; the delicate aspens shook as with an ague, and the flowers opened their blossoms only to gaze at the sun and wither away. Men and women wandered over the earth with sad hearts and listless eyes.

Only the Jesus Child knew that the earth would not die for he had come to bring life and hope. So he called the animals to him and said, "Which of you will be my messenger and journey through the world saying to everyone you meet, 'The earth will live anew, for the Christ Child has come'."

Then all the animals pressed around him saying, 'Send me, send me.' The Jesus Child saw that it would be difficult to choose so he said, 'The one who can most quickly circle the earth and return shall be my chosen messenger.'

Then the wild stag thought 'I am the fleetest afoot - I shall win the race.' And he went bounding over the hills. But when he came to the rocky highlands, he could not resist leaping over crag and burn and so

happy was he in his game that he forgot the passing of the hours.

The salmon said to himself 'I can dart through the water, and float with the tide - I shall far outstrip the heavy-footed beasts.' But when he saw the sunbeams sparkling on the stream, he thought they were golden flies. All day long he lept, hoping to catch the bright winged vagrants. And so the day turned to its close.

The hawk exulted 'I am the swiftest of all who circle the earth.' And he shot like an arrow through the blue. But suddenly his keen eye saw a tiny field mouse creeping among the corn. Straight as a plummet, he swooped - his journey was forgotten in the joy of the chase.

Only the hare kept quietly on his way. Turning neither to right nor left, gazing ever before him, he steadfastly held his course, and just as the sun was setting, he completed the circle of the earth. Thus it was that the hare became the messenger of the Jesus Child.

But when our Lord told him to bear the good

tidings to all mankind, the hare was overcome with fear. 'How shall I make them believe me?'. Then the Jesus Child asked the raven for the gift of one of his eggs. "Show them this egg," said our Lord "and say, 'Just as the golden yolk shines in the egg, so the child who has come from heaven, has brought the light of the sun to earth and the earth will not die but live anew'." Then the hare set forth upon his way with joy.

For many years the hare journeyed from place to place telling the glad news and at last he come back to the hills of Palestine. But when he returned he found that Christ had already died upon the cross and his body had been laid in the dark earth. But the hare knew the wonderful truth. He knew that just as the golden yolk is hidden within the egg, so the light of heaven was now to be found in the innermost heart of the earth.

So it is that every Spring the hare is still the messenger of joy and brings us the Easter egg.

The Egg Hunt

If well planned and organised, the Easter Egg Hunt can be an enjoyable activity for family and friends, or even a large group of children and adults. If you live in the City or have no garden whatsoever, you may wish to team up with several others for an outing to either the park or wood or common land in your area. You will want one person to be 'Hare' and secretly hide the eggs well, so that they need genuine looking for. Use both hard-boiled coloured eggs and any assortment of little sweet (there are some lovely speckled ones available as well as the more usual jelly bean ones) eggs or chocolate ones wrapped in pretty paper. The 'Hare' should have enough time to make a little nest for some of the individual eggs, perhaps even having a sack of straw or cut grass for this purpose. If you can keep the half-egg shells from previous baking sessions (rinsed out) they make containers for the tinier eggs.

Each child participating will need a container, ideally an Easter basket which he or she could make beforehand of strong paper, or a small wicker basket or even a bowl. They mustn't begin looking until everyone is ready to start at the same time. Eggs may be behind bushes, amid clumps of daffodils, up in the forks of tree branches, in high grass, under a drain pipe if it is a garden hunt, or somewhere in an innocent looking rose bush. The fun is in the finding them, as much as in enjoying them later.

Very young children are sometimes happy to bring their findings to a large communal Easter basket, and we know one 'Hare' who surreptitiously re-hid the eggs while the toddlers were still hunting, thus extending the time of the whole exercise, and without their noticing!

Egg Rolling

A race in which participants must roll eggs (hard-boiled ones are strongly recommended) down a stretch of field will be more challenging and fun for older children and adults! Everyone will need a long stick to roll with - golf clubs are not fair! - or you can improvise with relay races, or having each person return to the starting point to begin again with another, etc. If it all seems like a terrible waste of eggs, gather appropriate egg-sized stones and pebbles for the exercise and present the winner with a genuine Easter egg.

Marzipan Easter Symbols

Amongst the flowers and pretty eggs that decorate the table on Easter Day our children like to make little marzipan symbols of Easter which they give to the friends and relatives who have tea with us that day. These range from little chicks, eggs in nests, baskets with eggs in, ducks, bunnies and hares and they decorate them with little pieces of glace cherry, angelica and melted chocolate which they put on with a brush.

A trick they play is to make biscuits in patty tins so that they come out in the shape of a tart with sides. They turn these upside down on a plate and hide a little Easter egg underneath each.

Rolled biscuits (see p. 126) cut into egg, rabbit, duck or chick shapes are tasty and appropriate as little gifts.

Easter Egg Cosies

Take some different coloured felt pieces and make three shapes as below: sew together with blanket stitch using pretty thread or wool and stitch around the base.

Make a little chick out of yellow felt (or indeed a little hare) and stuff with wool and fix on the top. Give a different colour to each of the children on Easter morning.

Easter Nests

1 lb pastry
10 oz marzipan
whites of 2 eggs
any jam
little sugar

Roll out pastry and cut into rounds to fit into patty tins. Put rice or beans in them to 'bake blind' until nicely browned, then take cases from tins and empty. Smooth jam in the bottom of each pastry case. Beat eggs to a stiff froth, add a little sugar and put meringue in cases to line them like little nests. Shape marzipan like eggs, roll in cocoa if you wish, and put one in each nest.

Nests

Our children make their own little nests at Easter using sticks and straw, sometimes putting this into a little box made of paper or cardboard which they have decorated and on Easter Saturday evening they go and find a special place to hide it in the garden. They sing 'Easter Hare, Easter Hare, come into our Garden'. In the morning, they race out in bare feet to see if he has been and find two or three little eggs and sometimes find a simple pom-pom chick or little hare or a pretty dyed feather lying in the nest. The magic of this time is very special.

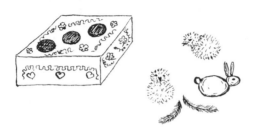

Making Chicks, Hares & Lambs

One can make chicks, hares and lambs by using two pom-poms, one for the head and one for the body and tied together. Use felt for beaks, ears etc, and pipe cleaners for legs.

Hares and rabbits can be made by cutting out a piece of card four inches across, modelling the body and head with sheepswool - and then sticking this to the base. Ears and eyes can be made with a different colour of wool.

Columba di Pasqua

Traditional Italian Easter/Whitsun Dove Cake

12 oz flour
4oz butter
¼ oz salt
3 oz sugar
6 egg yolks
3 oz sultanas
2 oz candied peel
1 oz yeast
grated lemon rind

Sift flour and make a well in the middle. Dissolve the yeast in warm water and pour into the flour together with 5 of the egg yolks and the sugar. Add the salt and knead lightly - the dough shouldn't be too smooth. Soften the butter and work into the dough. Again, do not handle it too much. Then add the sultanas, the peel and the grated lemon rind. Shape into the form of a dove and put onto a greased and floured baking sheet. Leave to rise until doubled in bulk. Then brush with beaten egg yolk and if you like add bits of almond for eyes. Bake in a moderately hot oven - about 400°F (Reg. 6) for 10 minutes, then reduce temperature to 350°F (Reg. 4) and bake for about ½ hour, until cooked.

Russian Paskha Easter Cake

3 lb cottage cheese
½ lb unsalted softened butter
2½ oz chopped candied fruits and rinds
½ teaspoon vanilla essence
⅜th pint double cream
4 egg yolks
7 oz caster sugar
2¼ oz finely chopped blanched almonds
1½ - 3 oz whole blanched almonds, toasted
1¼ - 2½ oz candied fruits and rinds

Drain the cottage cheese of all moisture by setting in a colander, cover with greaseproof and put a saucer on top for 2-3 hours. Meanwhile put the candied fruits and vanilla essence into a small mixing bowl, stir thoroughly and let mixture rest for 1 hour. Rub cheese through fine sieve or blender and put into large bowl. Beat softened butter thoroughly into cheese and set aside. Heat the cream in saucepan over high heat until small bubbles form around the edge of the pan. Set aside. Beat eggs and sugar together in mixing bowl with a whisk until they thicken enough to run sluggishly off the whisk when lifted out of the bowl. Slowly add hot cream in thin stream still beating, then return mixture to pan. Cook over a low heat, stirring constantly until the mixture thickens to a custard-like consistency. Do not allow it to boil or it may curdle. Stir in candied fruits, off the heat, and set the pan in a large bowl filled with ice cubes and covered with 2″ water. Stir the custard constantly with a metal spoon until completely cool, then mix it thoroughly but gently into the cheese mixture and stir in the chopped almonds.

The Russians use a special Paskha mould, you can use a 3-pint clay flower pot with an opening at the bottom. Set the pot in a shallow soup plate and line it with a double thickness of damp cheesecloth, cut long enough so that it hangs at least 2″ over and around the top of the pot. Pour in the batter and fold the ends of the cheesecloth lightly over the top. Set a weight on top of the cheesecloth and chill in fridge for 8 hours until firm. To turn out, unwrap the cheesecloth from the top, invert a flat serving dish on top of the pot, and grasping the two firmly together turn them over. The Paskha will slide out easily. Gently peel off cheesecloth and decorate with almonds and candied fruit. This can be served alone or with a Madeira Cake. It will keep in the fridge for up to one week before serving.

(Surrounded by dyed eggs and with a candle on the top, it is blessed in Russian Churches at Easter)

Madeira Cake
to go with Russian Paskha Cake

8 oz butter
grated rind of lemon
10 oz caster sugar
5 eggs
13 oz plain flour
pinch salt
1 teaspoon baking powder
1 teacup milk

Cream the butter with the grated lemon rind and add the sugar gradually and continue beating until the mixture is light and soft. Beat in the eggs one at a time, adding a little flour each time. Then sift remaining flour, salt and baking powder and fold into the mixture with the milk. Put into prepared tin and bake at 350°F (Reg. 4) for 1½ hours. After 1 hour reduce heat to 325°F (Reg. 3). To check if the cake is cooked press lightly with fingertips and if it springs back it is ready. May be served with a sprinkling of icing sugar over the top.

Easter Biscuits

8 oz flour
4 oz butter
4 oz sugar
Handful of currants
½ teaspoon mixed spice and cinnamon
Squeeze of lemon
Beaten egg with tablespoon of brandy

Rub the butter and flour and add the sugar, currants, spices and lemon. Mix in the egg and brandy and form a paste. Place on a floured board and roll out thinly and cut into 5″ rounds. Bake in a quick oven 375-400°F (Reg. 5-6) but watch carefully as they should not be over-cooked – they should be sweet and crisp. They look pretty if served with a little bunch of primroses or violets in the middle.

Easter Cake

9 oz flour
pinch bicarb of soda and teaspoon baking powder
6 oz margarine
6 oz brown sugar
1 teaspoon mixed spice
1 lb almond paste
2 eggs
white icing
1 oz glace cherries
2 tablespoons apricot jam
¾ gill milk and 1 tbs. coffee essence
(or ¾ gill cold coffee).

Prepare a moderate oven 350°F (Reg. 4)
Grease three 8″ sandwich tins. Cream the fat and sugar and beat in the eggs. Fold in the flour, baking powder, bicarb of soda and spices. Mix to a soft dropping consistency with the liquid. Divide the mixture into three tins and bake for approx. 25 mins. Then divide the almond paste into three and into two of the thirds knead the glace cherries. Roll these two pieces into rounds, the size of the cake. When the cakes are cold sandwich the three cakes together by spreading each cake with some jam and topping with the round of almond paste and cherries. Make the remaining third of the almond paste into 12 egg-shapes and arrange these around the edge of the cake. Grill the top of the cake to give the eggs a toasted appearance. Coat the centre with white icing and complete by placing an Easter chick in the middle. If you find almond paste a little too sweet just add some lemon juice to it.
(See recipe for Mother's Day Almond Paste and Glace Icing).

And the May month
Flaps its glad green leaves
Like wings ....

Thomas Hardy

24

7. May Day

Good morning, Mistress and Master,
I wish you a happy day;
Please to smell my garland
'Cause it is the first of May.

A branch of May I have brought you
And at your door I stand;
It is but a sprout, but it's well budded out
The work of our Lord's hand.

May day was in ancient tradition the celebration of the beginning of summer or Beltane in Celtic lands, and by Roman tradition sacred to Flora, the goddess of Spring. The May queen is still representative of Flora, or Persephone her Greek counterpart. In Shakespeare's "The Winter's Tale" there is a scene where the young heroine takes on the role of Flora, speaking of her native flowers:

> "... daffodils,
> That come before the swallow dares and take
> The winds of March with beauty; violets, dim,
> But sweeter than the lids of Juno's eyes,
> Or Cytherea's breath; pale primroses, ... bold oxlips, and
> The crown-imperial; lilies of all kinds,
> The flower-de-luce being one."

If the wreath of flowers goes back to Spring goddess symbols, the Maypole itself represents, most probably, the tree of life and fertility. In the modern context both are just good, festive fun, and a reminder that warmer days are ahead.

There are country districts where the young maidens rise early on May Day and wash their faces in the dew. In some areas it is thought that this will ensure a beautiful complexion for the rest of the year and in others it is believed that if a girl washes her face in the morning dew she will marry the first man she meets thereafter.

Children may not get the chance at school today to enjoy the tradition of a May Pole with flowers on the top and pretty ribbons dangling from it and the very simple skipping dances which can be done around it, either to the accompaniment of music or singing. But they can enjoy making little May Poles.

Use the inside cardboard roll of some foil or clingwrap and paint it with bright colours. Then take long strips of crepe paper in various colours and glue these into one end. When it is dry you can decorate the top of the pole with a flower.

Children and adults have traditionally worn flowers when dancing around the May Pole. A single blossom in the buttonhole or hair, or an actual 'May Crown' or wreath of flowers for the head symbolize the full arrival of spring and new growth.

"Where are you going to, my pretty maid
Where are you going to, my pretty maid?"
"I'm going a-milking, Sir", she said,
"Sir" she said, "Sir" she said,
"I'm going a-milking, Sir", she said.

"May I go with you my pretty maid,
May I go with you my pretty maid?"
"Indeed you may, kind Sir," she said,
"Sir", she said, "Sir", she said,
"And it's dabbling in the dew that
makes milkmaids fair".

May Day Baskets

When we were children, we had a custom of making May Day baskets for our neighbours and friends, and leaving them at their doors in secret early in the morning. This would give them a surprise on opening their doors!

May Day Cake

Make a Victoria Sponge Cake and use a lemon butter cream icing in the middle with a lemon soft royal icing over the whole of the outside. Alternatively, have the inside filled with jam and whipped cream and the whole cake covered with lemon soft royal icing.

For the Maypole, you can either attach ribbons to one end of a piece of barley sugar which you then press into the middle of the cake, allowing the ribbons to fall over the outside of the cake and decorate the top of the Maypole with a few small flowers, or, you can wind coloured ribbons round a knitting needle and create a similar effect.

Victoria Sponge Mix

6 oz margarine
6 oz caster sugar
6 oz flour
Pinch bicarb. of soda
Teaspoon baking powder
3 beaten eggs
2 tablespoons warm water

Cream together margarine and sugar, then add the flour, bicarb. and baking powder. Slowly beat in the eggs and water. Grease and flour 2 tins and cook at 425°F (Reg. 7) for 20 minutes. Cool on racks.

Soft Royal Icing

1 lb icing sugar
2 egg whites
1 teaspoon lemon juice or orange flower water
½ teaspoon glycerine

(Add minute amounts of colouring on a skewer if desired)

Pass the icing sugar through a sieve, whisk egg whites to a froth, add icing sugar, a tablespoon at a time, beating thoroughly. Stir in flavouring and glycerine and continue beating until icing will stand in peaks.
Keep bowl covered with a damp cloth when using icing. Alter quantities for the amount you need for a particular cake.

Butter-cream Icing

4 oz butter, soft
6 oz icing sugar (sifted)
flavouring:
2 tablespoons lemon juice
2 tablespoons cocoa
2 tablespoons coffee
2 tablespoons orange juice, etc.

Cream together with wooden spoon or with electric whisk.

Crullers
A Scandinavian Treat for May Day

1½ tablespoons lukewarm water
⅓ oz active dry or compressed yeast
¾ cup milk, heated to lukewarm
2 eggs
1¼ teaspoons caster sugar
2 level teaspoons salt
½ lb flour
Vegetable oil for deep–fat frying
icing sugar

Put the lukewarm water into a bowl and sprinkle in the yeast. Let it stand for 5 minutes, then stir until yeast is dissolved. Put the bowl in a warm, draught-free place for 5 minutes or so, until the yeast bubbles and mixture doubles. Now stir in the milk. In another bowl, stir the eggs and sugar together and pour in the yeast mixture, stirring briskly: add the salt. Mix in the flour, ½ cup at a time, beating vigorously until a soft batter is formed. Cover with a kitchen towel and put in a warm place for one hour, until the batter has doubled in bulk but do not let it stand longer.
Pour enough oil into a deep-fat fryer to have about 2″ depth, and place this over a medium-high heat until the oil is very hot. Put a cup of the batter into a pastry bag fitted with a plain ¼″ tip. Squeeze the batter into the hot fat making 3″-4″ circles, moving the bag in a circle to build a bird's nest of 2 or 3 rings more or less on top of one another. Deep fry several at a time, turning them over after a minute when golden brown. When they are ready, drain them on kitchen paper and when they are cool, sift icing sugar over them and serve immediately.

Maypole Song

Here's a branch of snowy may,
A branch the fairies gave me.
Who would like to dance today
With the branch the fairies gave me?

Dance away, dance away,   *Dance away, dance away,*
Holding high the branch of may.   *Holding high the branch of may.*

May Song

Here's a branch of snowy May, a branch the fairies gave me. Who would like to dance to day with the branch the fairies gave me. Dance away, dance away, holding high the branch of May.

'Now we go Round the Maypole High': Song

(Sung to the tune of *'Here we go round the Mulberry Bush'*)

Now we go round the Maypole high,
Maypole high, Maypole high,
Now we go round the Maypole high,
Let coloured ribbons fly.

See lasses and lads go tripping by,
Tripping by, tripping by,
See lasses and lads go tripping by
Let coloured ribbons fly.

In rainbow hues make garlands gay,
Garlands gay, garlands gay,
In rainbow hues make garlands gay,
Let coloured ribbons fly.

Let coloured ribbons fly.

Morwenna Bucknell

The Lark in the Morn – Folk Song

As I was a walking
One morning in the Spring
I met a pretty maiden
So sweetly she did sing.
And as we were a-walking
These words she did say,
'There's no life like the ploughboy's
All in the month of May.'

The Lark in the morn
She doth rise up from her nest,
And mounts upon the air
With the dew all on her breast.
And like the pretty ploughboy
She doth whistle and doth sing,
And at night she doth return
To her own nest back again.

The Lark in the Morning

'May Day' from 'Lark Rise to Candleford'

'On the last morning of April the children would come to school with bunches, baskets, arms and pinafores full of flowers – every blossom they could find in the fields and hedges or beg from parents and neighbours. On the previous Sunday some of the bigger boys would have walked six or eight miles to a distant wood where primroses grew. These, with violets from the hedgerows, coswlips from the meadows, and wallflowers, oxlips, and sprays of pale red flowering currant from the cottage gardens formed the main supply. A sweetbriar hedge in the schoolmistress's garden furnished unlimited greenery.

Piled on desks, table, and floor, this supply appeared inexhaustible; but the garland was large, and as the work of dressing it proceeded, it became plain that the present stock wouldn't 'hardly go nowheres', as the children said. So foraging parties were sent out, one to the Rectory, another to Squire's, and others to outlying farm-houses and cottages. All returned loaded, for even the most miserly and garden-proud gave liberally to the garland. In time the wooden frame was covered, even if there had to be solid greenery to fill up at the back, out of sight. Then the 'Top-Knot', consisting of a bunch of crown imperial, yellow and brown, was added to crown the whole, and the fragrant, bowery structure was sprinkled with water and set aside for the night.'

All hail gentle spring
With thy sunshine and showers,
And welcome the sweet buds
That burst in the bowers;

Again we rejoice as thy light step and free
Brings leaves to the woodland and flowers to the
bee,

Bounding, bounding, bounding, bounding,
Joyful and gay,
Light and airy, like a fairy,
Come, come away.

Come see our new garland so green and so gay;
'Tis the first fruits of spring and the glory of May.
Here are cowslips and daisies and hyacinths blue,
Here are buttercups bright and anemones too.

Flora Thompson

The Cuckoo and the Donkey – Ring Game

The cuckoo and the donkey
They quarrelled one fine day,
As to who could sing the better,
As to who could sing the better,
In the lovely month of May
In the lovely month of May.

The cuckoo said 'Hear me sing'
And so began to call
'But I can do it better
But I can do it better'
Said the donkey with 'Eeyore'.
Said the donkey with 'Eeyore'.

They sang so bright and loudly
One heard them far and wide
They sang so well together
They sang so well together
'Cuckoo, cuckoo', 'eeyore'
'Cuckoo, cuckoo', 'eeyore'.

Actions

Two lines of children face each other holding hands
and in the *first* verse they both advance and retreat.
In the *second* verse, the side who are the Cuckoo
step forward (up to the fence) and then the Donkey
side advances too. When he says 'But I can do it
better ...', and pushes the Cuckoo backwards a little.
In the *third* verse both sides advance and retreat but
at the end, the Cuckoo side sing 'Cuckoo, cuckoo'
and step forwards so that the others have to step
back but then when they sing 'Eeyore' and step
forwards the Cuckoos have to step back.

The Cuckoo and the Donkey

The cuckoo and the donkey, they quarrelled one fine day , as to who could sing the

better, as to who could sing the better, in the lovely month of May, in the lovely month of May.

Here we come gathering nuts in May
– Ring Game

Here we come gathering nuts in May,
Nuts in May, nuts in May,
Here we come gathering nuts in May
On a cold and frosty morning.

Who will you have for nuts in May,
Nuts in May, nuts in May,
Who will you have for nuts in May
On a cold and frosty morning?

We'll have ...... for nuts in May, etc...
Who will you send to fetch her away, etc...
We'll send ...... to fetch her away, etc...

Actions:

Form two lines of children.
In the *first* verse the two lines skip forwards and backwards, facing each other. In the *second* verse, one line advances and then in the *third* verse the other side advance, choosing the name of one child in the opposite line. In the *fourth* verse the first side again advance and ask and in the *fifth* verse, the other side choose one from their own side. The two named children step forward from the two lines and put their right feet on a marked line and try to pull the other one across with the right hand. The successful one takes the other onto his side and the game continues until one side has won all the other team members.

* One version of this song goes, 'Here we come gathering *Knots of May'*, which is seasonally more appropriate than *'nuts in May'!*

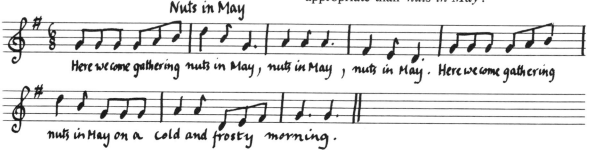

Nuts in May

Here we come gathering nuts in May, nuts in May, nuts in May. Here we come gathering nuts in May on a cold and frosty morning.

Dough Sculpture for May Baskets –
Activity

This is an effective, inexpensive way to make baskets of the size and shape of your choice. You will need oven-proof moulds as the baskets need baking. Choose baking tins or dishes in shapes that you like.

For the dough

1½ teacups of standard cooking salt
1½ lbs plain flour
14 oz hot water
1 egg for glazing the finished basket

You will need

Baking dish (for this example, one which is 12″ around and 2″ deep.

Pastry brush or small paint brush
Wooden skewer or sharp pencil
Clean damp cloth
Aluminium foil
Baking sheet
Clear varnish

1. Cover the outside of the baking dish with foil, turning any excess into the inside of the dish.

2. In a medium size bowl, add water to the salt and stir gently until salt is dissolved. Leave to cool.

3. Gradually add dissolved salt to the flour, mixing with your hands as dough will be very stiff.

4. Knead the dough until it is smooth and pliable. If

it seems too wet for easy kneading, add flour. If it is too dry, or stiff, add a few drops of water. Work fairly quickly as the dough soon dries out, and keep damp cloth handy for covering unused dough.

5. Take ¾ of the dough and roll it out on a lightly floured surface into a rectangle abour 14″ x 18″ and ⅛″ thick.

The idea now is to cut strips of corresponding lengths for 'weaving' a basket in lattice fashion. The strips should be about ¾″ wide for easy handling and your longest ones will be about 17″ long.

6. Place a square of foil on a table top and position half the strips as above, leaving about ¾″ between, Begin to weave with one of the longer strips through the centre of the strips on the foil. Brush occasionally with water to secure your weaving.

Try not to stretch the strips as you weave. If they break, mend with a little water.

7. Turn the baking dish upside down. Lift the foil with the lattice work on it, holding flat and place over the upside-down dish. Gently lower it over the dish.

8. Lift dish, tucking excess foil to the inside, and trim the strips even with dish edge. Mould the lattice

to the shape of the dish by pressing lightly with your hands. Place the upside-down dish with lattice shape moulded over it on the baking sheet, cover with damp cloth.

9. Now take left-over scraps and your reserved ¼ of the dough and knead together. When smooth, roll on your palms to form two ropes. Wind together, one over the other to form a twist.
Attach the twist to the basket edge by dampening the strip ends with water and pressing the twists against them, wrapping it around the edge and wetting the overlapping ends of the twist to finish.

10. Bake at 325°F (Reg. 3) for 30 minutes. While it is baking, prepare a glaze by mixing the egg with a teaspoon of water. Take the basket from the oven and remove baking dish by pulling up foil edges. Return the basket now to the baking sheet, turning it over to its actual basket position and brush over with egg glaze. Bake for 15 minutes and glaze again. Repeat this until basket is golden brown and dry. Leave to cool on wire rack.

When your basket is completely cool you may apply a coat of varnish.

Finished baskets may be given bright ribbon handles and filled with fresh flowers for May Day. Later they are useful for use in the home, for bread, rolls or biscuits at table.

If you adapt the above to form two smaller baskets on pudding bowl moulds or similar, do watch your baking time accordingly.

Growing Things

From the Garden: *Pressing Flowers*

A flower press is a very useful item to have throughout the year. Whenever there is an opportunity to collect a few flowers and especially wild flowers, or leaves, they can be put into the press for later use. It should also be mentioned at this point, that using blotting paper pressed between a couple of heavy books can serve the job as efficiently as a bought press.

Pansies, montbretia, buttercups, cow parsley, Michaelmas daisies, leaves, delphinium petals, celandine, clover, are just a few that press well, and it is worthwhile experimenting.

On rainy days or perhaps when a child is in bed, they will enjoy making the pressed flowers into pretty designs which can be used for:-
Christmas or birthday cards
St Valentine Day cards
Gift tags
Calendars
Book Marks

or simply into a beautiful picture to put up in their bedroom, to remind them of some favourite outing in the spring or summer. Seasonal pictures with flowers for each of the months can be very informative too.

It is possible to buy from a good stationers most of the items you will need to make these things:
1) stiff card or paper, coloured or white.
2) clear, sticky-backed plastic sheet if you want to cover the picture i.e. book marks.
3) rubber-based adhesive; also a small paint brush to put the glue on the flowers.
4) calendar booklets.
5) some pretty ribbon will add the finishing touches.

Spring Greens
Common Sorrel

One of the first green plants in the Spring is Sorrel. The leaves may often be picked as early as February when other fresh greens are scarce. Sorrel doesn't flower until between May and August, bearing spikes of tiny red and green flowers on a smooth stem which can be between 6″ and 2′ tall. The leaves are shaped like little arrows. They are cool, and somewhat sharp when eaten raw, often reminding children of pickles or lemons, and for some tastes, excellent in salads. In France the chopped leaves are added to potato, lentil or bean soups. It is sometimes added to egg dishes.

To make sorrel soup, take about a pound of the leaves and chop them with a large onion and a sprig of rosemary. Sauté the mixture in 3 oz melted butter or margarine, stirring in a tablespoon of flour and simmering for ten minutes. Stir frequently, allowing

for the juices to extract without burning. Then add 3 pt boiling water, two tablespoons of breadcrumbs and mixed herbs to your liking. Simmer for one hour. When well cooked, remove from the boil and just before serving stir in mixture of two well-beaten eggs and half a cup of top-of-the-milk or cream.

Stinging Nettle

Nettles appear each spring abundantly in environments both urban and rural. The stem is coarse and covered with stinging hairs. The leaves are heavily veined and almost heart-shaped. They should be used as greens for eating only in the spring, for by the beginning of June the leaves are very coarse, bitter and potentially hard on the digestion! In the novel *Rob Roy,* by Scott, an old gardener is described as raising nettles under glass as 'early spring kail' and they are certainly a traditional source of green vegetable before the usual planting season.

It is best to pick the young shoots when they are only a few inches high. If you gather later in the spring, choose the tops and young pale green leaves. It's probably advisable to wear gloves, but it is said that a firm grasp of young leaves should leave no sting. Before cooking remove the stem and wash the leaves well. Here are two recipes for nettle soup, depending on your taste and need.

Hearty Nettle Soup

Fill a saucepan with washed nettles and boil gently, with lid on pan, in no more water than has remained on the leaves after washing. Cook for ten to fifteen minutes, then strain off water and add a knob of butter and some chopped onion. Cook five more minutes, then sieve or blend to a purée. Add well-cooked mashed potato and mixed herbs with salt to taste. This provides a thick, hearty soup which is a meal in itself and is particularly nice with grated cheese when served.

Cream of Nettle Soup

Prepare your nettle puree as above. Then melt an ounce of butter in a pan and stir into it an ounce of flour and a pinch of salt and pepper. Remove from heat and stir in a pint of hot milk, beating until the sauce is smooth. Now boil up the sauce and simmer for five minutes, stirring all the time. Then pour on the nettle purée and mix well.

II. HERBS

Scarborough Fair

"O, where are you going?" "To Scarborough Fair",
Parsley, sage, rosemary and thyme,
"Remember me to one who lives there,
For once she was a true love of mine".

"Tell her to make me a cambric shirt",
Parsley, sage, rosemary and thyme;
"Without any seam or needlework,
For once she was a true love of mine".

"Tell her to wash it in yonder well",
Parsley, sage, rosemary and thyme;
"Where never spring water nor rain ever fell,
For once she was a true love of mine".

"Tell her to dry it on yonder thorn",
Parsley, sage, rosemary and thyme;
"Which never bore blossom since Adam was born,
For once she was a true love of mine".

"Now he has asked me questions three",
Parsley, sage, rosemary and thyme;
"I hope he will answer as many for me,
For once he was a true love of mine".

"Tell him to find me an acre of land",
Parsley, sage, rosemary and thyme;
"Betwixt the salt water and the sea sand,
For once he was a true love of mine".

"Tell him to plough it with a ram's horn",
Parsley, sage, rosemary and thyme;
"And sow it all over with one peppercorn,
For once he was a true love of mine".

"Tell him to reap it with a sickle of leather",
Parsley, sage, rosemary and thyme;
"And bind it up with a peacock's feather,
For once he was a true love of mine".

"When he has done and finished his work",
Parsley, sage, rosemary and thyme;
"O tell him to come and he'll have his shirt,
For once he was a true love of mine".

Marjoram

Thyme

Scarborough Fair

Oh where are you going? To Scarborough fair. Parsley, sage, rosemary, and thyme. Remember me to one who lives there, for once she was a true love of mine.

Herb Song

Summer time, stretch our in the sun,
Spread out your arms, feel the earth is breathing.
Light in the air, pours copper on your hair,
Gold on your arm and shoulder gleaming.

Chorus:

Parsley, tarragon, fennel and savory,
Lavender baskets for the making,
Rosemary, marjoram, dill and sweet cicely,
Lemon balm when your heart is aching.

Down in the stream, the water is cool,
Rats go scudding in the lush green rushes
Shrimps and shiny black water bugs tickle you.
Brace your legs where the current is strong.

Chorus:

Take my hand and we'll walk out in the sun,
Spread out your soul and you'll feel it floating.
Harvest the sky-scents and colours on the wind.
Store the seeds carefully for next year's sowing.

Chorus:

Sylvia Mehta
Stroud Folk Singer.

Herb Song

Summer time, stretch out in the sun, Spread out your arms feel the earth is breathing, Light in the air pours copper on your hair, gold on your arm e your shoulder gleaming. Chorus: Pursley, tarragon, fennel and savory, Lavender baskets for the making, Rosemary, marjoram, dill and sweet cicely, Lemon balm when your heart is aching.

Growing and using basic culinary herbs

The beauty of herb-growing is that you can do it in very little space, or in old tubs or pots. We once lined the steps to our basement flat with pots of herbs, and managed to grow everything from borage to savory and parsley for kitchen use. A strong clump of chives will do well in a pot of even rocky soil, offer bright greenery, and make all the difference to baked potatoes or salad.

Mint

Angelica
Seeds germinate slowly; keep in moist peat or sand until sowing in August, or use straight from plant. The stems are used candied for decoration and flavouring. This is a good flavour with rhubarb.

Anise
Needs a warm, sheltered area, kept if possible on the dry side. Sow as early as possible under glass, allow almost a month for germination. Plants will need a light soil. Chopped leaves may be used in salad, or added to the cooking of strong greens. Anise-tea is soothing to the digestion, and the seeds are used in baking.

Basil
Sow on a warm day in March, plant out in June or grow in pots. Use in soups, sauces with tomato or with spaghetti dishes.

Borage
Sow in April, and use the leaves when young and tender. Will grow 2-3 ft. and produce delicate sky-blue and pink flowers. The fresh young leaves of Borage are used mainly in salads and cold drinks, and the flowers make an attractive and tasty garnish.

Caraway
Sow seeds in autumn or spring, harvest in July and remove the seeds at once. The seeds are used in bread, cakes and biscuits, and for both red and green cabbage recipes.

Chervil
May be sowed several times during the year, from March through to the autumn, needing extra water in dry spells and able to withstand winter weather. The leaves have a sweet smell and savoury flavour, making a good addition to soups, herb and cheese sauces, sandwich spreads, and salads.

Chives
Divide clumps every spring or autumn and try to lift and replant every two years if possible. Chopped chives are delicious in cream cheese, soups, salads, egg dishes and on potatoes or rice as garnish.

Coriander
Should be sown early in the spring and likes a sunny position, preferably in the company of Dill, Chervil or Fennel. The seeds add flavour to bread and cakes, curries, stews and also in pickling and preserving fruits. (Cut down the plant when the seeds begin to ripen, dry and remove seeds.)

Dill
Sow seeds in March, thinning out the plants as they grow. The leaves add a fresh taste to salads, new potatoes, or cucumber dishes, and the seeds in making pickled gherkins.

Fennel
Sow seeds in April or May; if possible allowing a sunny place for this tall and stately plant. The seeds, like those of Anise, make a tea known to be particularly good for the digestion, and a traditional remedy for windy babies. Use the leaves for salads, fish and pickles. The lower stalk or thick stem section just above the root is prized for its subtle flavour when cooked and served in a white or cheese sauce.

Garlic
Plant Garlic cloves in autumn or spring in good, rich soil and a sunny spot. Long regarded as a vital

medicinal plant, the use of Garlic is beneficial in all manner of cooking. Use it in salad dressings, tomato sauces, stews, and with pulses. Add it to melted butter for 'garlic bread'.

Hyssop
An evergreen-like shrub, mainly propagated by division, but you may get a good plant by sowing when the seeds have just ripened in late summer. The young leaves make a good addition to soups, gravies, stews, stuffings, salads, pickles, onions and red cabbage.

Lavender
Commonly associated today with scent, the traditional uses of Lavender placed it in the kitchen as well, with the flowers a source of flavouring for sweets, drinks and teas. When added to teas it has a soothing quality.

Lemon Balm
Likes a sunny position, offering prolific heart-shaped bright green leaves. The leaves are at their best before the flowers develop, and may be used for a lemony drink either fresh or dried. Steep them in water on their own, or with a slice of real lemon and some honey. They are also nice added to sandwich spreads, salad dressings or cooked vegetables.

Lovage
A large vigorous plant which rather resembles overgrown celery (gone slightly wild). Lovage needs plenty of water, and sends out an impressive root system in search of it. The leaves add a celery-like flavour to soups, casseroles and stews, while having their own distinct refreshing taste when eaten fresh in mixed salads or sandwiches.

Marjoram
Sow seeds indoors in March and transfer young plants to the garden after frosts have ceased. The leaves are excellent in soups, stews and as an addition to pulses and bean dishes in general.

Mint
There are dozens of varieties of mint, but round-leaved Lamb mint is probably the best for sauce. Mint roots spread rapidly; use the leaves in garnish form for new potatoes, in mint sauce or for jelly.

Parsley
Old wisdom held that it was best to plant parsley on Good Friday. Soak the seeds overnight and sow in the open ground or in pots; germination is slow. Plants like a semi-shady position. Parsley is probably the most popular flavouring and garnishing herb. Use it chopped and fresh to add to soup just before serving, on potato dishes, in salads, cooked in white or cheese sauce, baked in flans, with pulses, etc.

Rosemary
Grow from cuttings (taken in August) in well-drained, sheltered soil. A sprig of Rosemary has traditionally been added to meat dishes, but its flavouring is equally welcome in pulses, dumplings, rissoles, mixed vegetables and egg and cheese dishes.

Sage
Grow from seed or root division. There are both silver and red varieties which make beautiful plants. A traditional ingredient for stuffing and meat dishes, sage gives flavour to soups, stews, broad beans and gravies. The dried leaves make a tea in their own right, particularly good for throat conditions.

Savory
Winter Savory is a perennial, evergreen in winter, but summer Savory is an annual raised from seed and offering a subtler flavour. Does well in poor stony soil but needs a sunny position. In both Dutch and German the name for Savory means Bean Herb. Add it to cooked dried bean dishes or use with broad beans.

Sweet Bay
A bush which grows best in fairly dry, half-shady conditions. Young Bay plants do not like frost, but may be kept in a pot in the greenhouse during winter. As trees they become hardier. Main uses are with soups, stews, fish, egg custards and milk puddings.

Tarragon
Grow from cuttings or root division; French Tarragon is seemingly the most popular for flavour. Tarragon does not dry well and is best used fresh as a mild seasoning for chicken, fresh salads or cooked root vegetables.

Thyme
Sow indoors in March, or outside only when the frosts have ceased. A mature plant benefits from root division. Use on egg dishes, in soups and stews.

Drying herbs

Herbs for drying should be picked just before they come into flower, preferably on a dry day before the sun is hot. Ancient country traditions hold that it is preferable to pick by hand or with an implement which is not made of steel and there are still teachers (in Oriental cooking particularly) who maintain that tearing by hand saves flavours which a knife blade will dull. Remove the leaves from stalks of large varieties and tie smaller herbs into sprays. Place on shallow trays in thin layers and leave in an airing cupboard, on a cooker rack or in a cool oven (125°) until dry. This gives clean freshly-coloured and tasty herbs. Drying them in the sun or hanging them in the window is more picturesque, but colour and flavour do fade a bit. Parsley is difficult to dry and seems to retain moisture. Try placing it in a hot oven (400°) for one minute only, and then move to an airing cupboard or dry shelf for as long as necessary. It should retain its colour this way. Alternatively, parsley freezes well.

When your herbs are dry, remove from the stalks and rub down with a rolling pin. Put into small tins or jars and store in a cool dry place. If you've an abundance of them, they make delightful gifts, and should be used within a year if possible.

Note: Marigolds and Nasturtiums are easily grown flowers that have an important place in the kitchen. The dried centres of marigolds may be used instead of saffron for colour, and the young leaves are good in salad or when dried for herbal teas. Nasturtium flowers, seeds and leaves are all used as flavourings. The leaves and yellow/orange flowers are fine in salads, while the seed pods can be pickled.

Potato Hotpot with Rosemary

2 lbs potatoes
1 lb onions
salt and pepper
Sprigs of Rosemary
2 oz butter
½ pint milk

Dishes using herbs

Sweet Mixed Herb Seasoning

2oz parsley
2 oz marjoram
2 oz chervil
1 oz thyme
1 oz basil
1 oz savory
pinch of tarragon (optional)

Dry the herbs when they are in season, weigh them when they are dry. Rub each to a fine powder and sift through a strainer. Mix together and keep in a bottle or jar with a tight lid. Use for the general seasoning of soups, sauces, etc.

Rosemary or Lavender Sugar

Sprigs of fresh Rosemary or Lavender
Caster sugar

Clean and dry the rosemary or lavender. Place in a screw-top jar and fill with sugar. Shake well and leave for twenty-four hours. Shake again and leave a week before use. Use the sugar in milk puddings or to sprinkle on cakes or biscuits.

Parsley Sauce

1 tablespoon butter
1 tablespoon flour
½ pint milk or stock
3 tablespoons fresh parsley

Melt the butter, gradually add flour and stir well. Add milk slowly, cook gently for five minutes and add chopped parsley just before serving.

Peel the potatoes and onions and slice them thinly. Place in a buttered casserole in alternate layers, seasoning well with salt, pepper and finely chopped Rosemary leaves. Dot with butter, finish with a layer of potatoes. Pour on milk. Put on the lid and bake at 350°F (Reg. 4) for 1½ hours until the milk has been absorbed. Remove the lid for the last 15 minutes to brown the top of the potatoes.

Fennel Sauce

1½ oz butter
1 heaped tablespoon chopped fennel
1 oz plain flour
¾ pint water

Melt 1 oz of the butter and cook the fennel in it for half a minute or so. Blend in the flour and then gradually add the water, beating smoothly over a low heat. Cook gently until the sauce is creamy, season to taste with salt and pepper and add the remaining butter.

Baked Fennel

This is an aromatic dish, nice served with a blander food; fish, rice, or potatoes.

1½ lbs fennel
3 oz butter
1 large lemon with thin yellow rind skinned off
Salt and pepper

Trim the base and top stems of the fennel. Keep some of the feathery green tops. Cut into long thick pieces and blanch in boiling, salted water for 5 minutes. Melt butter in shallow oven-dish or casserole. Remove from heat and grate in the white of the lemon, then add about 2 tablespoons of its juice. Place fennel in dish, add salt and pepper and turn in the butter. Cover tightly with lid or foil and bake at 300°F (Reg. 2) for about an hour. Garnish with snipped fennel tops.

Sage and Onion Tart

8 oz short crust pastry
3 medium sized onions
1 oz butter
¼ pint creamy milk
1 egg
1 tablespoon chopped fresh sage
1 teaspoon chopped fresh parsley
4 oz rindless bacon, chopped
salt and pepper

Line a pie plate with the pastry. Chop the onions and sauté in hot butter until soft. Mix with the milk, egg, herbs, bacon and seasoning and pour into the pastry case. Bake at 400°F (Reg. 6) for thirty-five minutes.

Herb Cream Cheese

4 oz Cream Cheese
a clove garlic
1 tablespoon chopped parsley
1 tablespoon chopped thyme
1 tablespoon chopped chives
salt and pepper

Cream the cheese with a fork. Work in the crushed garlic clove and chopped herbs, season well with salt and pepper, roll cheese into a ball and chill if possible before serving. Delicious with dark wholewheat or rye bread.

Herbed Green Beans

1 lb fresh green beans
1½ oz butter
¼ cup chopped onions
¼ cup chopped celery
1 garlic clove, crushed
1 teaspoon dried rosemary
1 teaspoon dried basil

Cut the beans into 1 inch lengths and cook in a very little water about ten minutes, then drain. Stir in butter, onion, celery, herbs and garlic; let this cook gently for a further ten minutes until the beans are tender. Season to taste with salt.

Herb Dumplings
(with soup or in stew)

A ratio of 2 to 1 for flour and fat, such as:

4 oz self-raising flour
2 oz margarine
salt

generous amounts of chopped dried herbs:

parsley, thyme, marjoram, and basil,
water

Rub fat into flour, add salt, herbs, and enough water to mix and form into little balls. Drop into boiling soup or stew, allow to simmer 15-20 minutes until cooked.

Herb Soda Bread

8 oz wholewheat flour
8 oz unbleached plain flour
pinch of salt
1 teaspoon baking powder
2 teaspoons cream of tartar
1 teaspoon honey or brown sugar
½ teaspoon dried marjoram
½ teaspoon dried basil
½ teaspoon dried thyme
2 oz soft margarine or butter
½ pint plain yoghurt or sour milk

Place all the above ingredients, except the milk or yoghurt, into a large mixing bowl. Rub the fat into the mixed dry ingredients until well blended with them. Now add the yoghurt and stir to form a soft dough. Turn out, knead lightly, and shape into a round. Score the top of the bread in criss-cross fashion. Leave for five minutes. Bake at 375°F (Reg. 5) for 30 minutes. When cooked, the bread should be well risen and sound hollow if tapped at the base.

Serve warm if possible. This bread is of the 'quick' varieties – good if you need a loaf straight away and haven't time for a yeast process. It is best eaten on the day of baking, but will keep longer if wrapped in a clean tea towel. It can be toasted if there is some left over.

Some of the seeds may be used instead of the above herbs. Try coriander, fennel, caraway or dill.

Some teas and medicinal uses of herbs in the home

Peppermint makes a wonderful tea, especially good for indigestion or a cold – just pour boiling water on some leaves.

Use **sage** in the same way and add some honey for coughs, colds and sore throats.

Cheering Tea

This is an ancient recipe, fun to prepare in late summer, pretty to look at, and surprisingly refreshing to drink.

Take a handful each of:

lavender, corn flower, marigold, lime blossom, plus a half-handful fennel seeds, a pinch of poppy seeds.

Dry the herbs (in trays or hanging). Mix them, rub petals free of flowers, blend in seeds and mix well. Store in a glass jar to appreciate the colourful mixture, and prepare for tea as usual.

Sleepy Tea

Dry gathered meadowsweet and lime blossom, mix well. Add a bit of honey when brewed, and sleep well!

Use an infusion of **rosemary, parsley** or **thyme** over the hair after washing it to prevent dandruff.

An infusion of **marjoram** leaves and tips, or **thyme** or **basil** cures nervous headaches.

Rub teeth with **sage** leaves which whitens the teeth, hardens the gums and freshens the mouth.

Apply crushed **mint** leaves to cuts and bruises.

Rub **lemon balm, rosemary** or **mint** on a nettle sting for quick relief. In fact many aromatic herbs are good for this.

Winter **savory** or **basil** gives instant relief from wasp and bee stings.

Some Household uses for Herbs

Insects dislike the smell of sage, rosemary and pennyroyal, so hang bunches up in the house to keep flies and mosquitoes at bay.

Apart from smelling sweetly, rosemary branches and bunches of thyme can be placed between blankets and sheets in the linen cupboard to keep moths away. Woodruff, lavender, rosemary and dried rose petals can be put loose in the bottom of chests or cupboards or put into sachets to make them smell good.

Pot-Pourri

Pot-pourri is very pleasant to have in a bowl and will scent a room beautifully. If you only want to use it for some occasions you can leave a lid on and just take it off when you want to scent the room and mix the flowers around with a spoon: it will last right through the winter. If you find the smells are wearing off, then just add a little more of the essential oil.

Start during the summer by picking any of the following on a warm, dry day:-

rose petals and buds at their best
lemon verbena
scented geranium
forget-me-not
pinks
basil
lavender
thyme
bay
marigold
delphinium
wallflower
rosemary
marjoram
lily of the valley

Pomanders.

jasmin	thyme
narcissus	camomile
pansies	marigold
violets	sage
honeysuckle	hyssop
peonies	cornflowers

It is a question of experimenting to your own taste. (Only use the flower heads).

Lay these out on newspaper, muslin or net curtaining, in a dry, dark place, such as an airing cupboard (not too hot) for a few weeks until they are crisp.

Mix them in a large bowl with orris root powder which helps to preserve the herbs and flowers: add common salt. Grate in some allspice and nutmeg, bruised cloves, dried orange and lemon peel and add some concentrated oil of your choice such as lavender, bergamot or rose, which you can usually get from a good health food store, chemist or herb shop, or add some good rosewater, and a little brandy. Keep covered for at least a month. It should not be too moist. When it is ready add a little more essential oil if you feel it is needed.

Pomanders.

Choose a firm-skinned orange or lemon and either stick the cloves straight into the skin, which can be a bit hard on the thumb so a thimble can be useful, or use a skewer to make holes all over the orange first. The orange needs to be closely covered with the cloves then roll it in a mixture of orris root, ground cinnamon and allspice.

Wrap individually in tissue paper and leave in a dry,

dark warm place for several weeks (i.e. airing cupboard). When it is ready, tie up with a ribbon - velvet looks very pretty - with a loop at the top so that it can be hung in a room or a wardrobe. They can keep for years if they are made carefully.

Pretty Moth Sachets.

There are some herbs that moths don't like such as mint, mugwort, thyme, sage, sweet marjoram and rosemary. Mix these dried herbs together and place a tablespoon or two into little muslin bags, whatever shape you like, and sew the top. You can put this into a prettily designed piece of material and trim the edge with lace. You can put a little loop on one corner so that it can be hung on a hanger.

Another old recipe suggests a mixture of cinnamon, cloves, nutmeg, caraway seed, mace, camphor and orris root.

You can also make sweet smelling sachets to put into clothes either with lavender, pot-pourri (see p.39) or a combination of dried lemon verbena, pinks, lavender, wallflowers, rosepetals, allspice berries crushed and other dried herbs that you can experiment with.

Bouquet Garni

Mix together some crushed dried thyme, bay leaves, parsley, basil, sage and tarragon and place a teaspoonful in the centre of a round of muslin the size of a tumbler. Gather it up in a little bag and tie it securely with thread making a loop at the top so that the bag can be taken out of the casserole when the food is cooked. Fill a pretty jar with the bags and tie with ribbon for a present.

These are extremely useful to add to soups, stews and pies.

Tea-cosy

Try helping the children to make a pretty tea-cosy and place herb sachets on each side of the cosy along with the wadding.

You can use such herbs as lemon verbena, rosemary, lavender, bergamot, rose petals, allspice berries and grated nutmeg and whenever the warmth of the teapot filters through to the herbs, the air will smell sweetly around it.

SUMMER DAYS

III. SUMMER DAYS

Summer Sayings

Cut thistles in May
They grow in a day;
Cut them in June,
That is too soon;
Cut them in July,
Then they will die.

A Cherry year,
A merry year;
A Pear year,
A dear year;
A Plum year,
A dumb year.

A swarm of bees in May
Is worth a load of hay;
A swarm of bees in June
Is worth a silver spoon;
A swarm of bees in July
Is not worth a fly.

St. Swithin's Day if thou dost rain,
For forty days it doth remain.
St. Swithin's Day if thou be fine,
For forty days the sun will shine.
(July 15)
If it rains on St. Swithin's Day it is said that
"St. Swithin is christening the apples".

A sunshiny shower
Won't last half an hour.

Bed in Summer

In winter I get up at night
And dress by yellow candle light.
In summer, quite the other way,
I have to go to bed by day.

I have to go to bed and see
The birds still hopping on the tree,
Or hear the grown-up people's feet
Still going past me in the street.

And does it not seem hard to you,
When all the sky is clear and blue,
And I should so much like to play,
To have to go to bed by day?

Summer Sun

Great is the sun, and wide he goes
Through empty heavens without repose;
and in the blue and glowing days
More thick than rain he showers his rays.

Though closer still the blinds we pull
To keep the shady parlour cool,
Yet he will find a chink or two
To slip his golden fingers through.

The dusty attic, spider-clad,
He, through the keyhole, maketh glad;
And through the broken edge of tiles,
Into the laddered hayloft smiles.

Meantime his golden face around
He bares to all the garden ground,
And sheds a warm and glittering look,
Among the ivy's inmost nook.

Above the hills, along the blue,
Round the bright air with footing true,
To please the child, to paint the rose,
The gardener of the world, he goes.

42

It was Long Ago

I'll tell you, shall I, something I remember?
Something that still means a great deal to me.
It was long ago.

A dusty road in summer I remember,
A mountain, and an old house, and a tree
That stood, you know,

Behind the house. An old woman I remember
In a red shawl with a grey cat on her knee
Humming under a tree.

She seemed the oldest thing I can remember,
But then perhaps I was not more than three.
It was long ago.

I dragged on the dusty road, and I remember
How the old woman looked over the fence at me
And seemed to know

How it felt to be three, and called out, I remember
"Do you like bilberries and cream for tea?"
I went under the tree

And while she hummed, and the cat purred, I remember
How she filled a saucer with berries and cream for
                                        me

So long ago,

Such berries and such cream as I remember
I never had seen before, and never see
Today, you know.

And that is almost all I can remember,
The house, the mountain, the grey cat on her knee,
Her red shawl, and the tree,

And the taste of the berries, the feel of the sun I
                                        remember,
And the smell of everything that used to be

So long ago,

Till the heat on the road outside again I remember,
And how the long dusty road seemed to have for me
No end, you know.

That is the farthest thing I can remember.
It won't mean much to you. It does to me.
Then I grew up, you see.

Eleanor Farjeon

43

The Flowers

All the names I know from nurse:
Gardener's garters, Shepherd's purse,
Bachelor's buttons, Lady's smock
And the Lady Hollyhock.

Fairy places, fairy things,
Fairy woods where the wild bee wings,
Tiny trees for tiny dames --
These must all be fairy names!

Tiny woods below whose boughs
Shady fairies weave a house;
Tiny tree-tops, rose or thyme,
Where the braver fairies climb!

Fair are grown-up people's trees;
But the fairest woods are these;
Where, if I were not so tall,
I should live for good and all.

Robert Louis Stevenson

The Lavender Bush

At her doorway Mrs. Mayle
Grows a bush of lavender,
Large, and round, and silver-pale,
Where the blooms, a misty blur,
Lift their purple spikes on high,
Loved of butterflies and moths,
And on these, to bleach and dry,
Mrs. Mayle spreads little cloths.

Tray cloths, mats of cobweb-weave,
All of them too fairy-fine
For a careful soul to leave
Dangling on a washing-line,
Mrs. Mayle lays softly there
Till she brings them in once more,
Sweet with blossom-scented air,
From the bush beside the door.

Elizabeth Fleming

Daddy fell into the Pond

Everyone grumbled. The sky was grey.
We had nothing to do and nothing to say.
We were nearing the end of a dismal day.
And there seemed to be nothing beyond,
Then
        Daddy fell into the pond!

And everyone's face grew merry and bright,
And Timothy danced for sheer delight.
'Give me the camera, quick, oh quick!
He's crawling out of the duckweed!' Click!

Then the gardener suddenly slapped his knee,
And doubled up, shaking silently,
and the ducks all quacked as if they were daft,
And it sounded as if the old drake laughed.
Oh, there wasn't a thing that didn't respond
When
        Daddy fell into the pond!

Alfred Noyes

From Cider with Rosie

When darkness fell, and the huge moon rose, we
stirred to a second life. Then boys went calling along
the roads, wild slit-eyed animal calls, Walt Kerry's
naked nasal yodel, Boney's jackal scream. As soon
as we heard them we crept outdoors, out of our
stifling bedrooms, stepped out into moonlight warm
as the sun to join our chalk-white, moon-masked
gang.

Games in the moon. Games of pursuit and
capture. Games that the night demanded. Best of all,
Fox and Hounds – go where you like, and the whole
of the valley to hunt through. Two chosen boys
loped away through the trees and were immediately
swallowed in shadow. We gave them five minutes,
then set off after them. They had churchyard,
farmyard, barns, quarries, hilltops, and woods to run
to. They had all night, and the whole of the moon,

44

and five miles of country to hide in .....

Padding softly, we ran under the melting stars, through sharp garlic woods, through blue blazed fields, following the scent by the game's one rule, the question and answer cry. Every so often, panting for breath, we paused to check on our quarry. Bullet heads lifted, teeth shone in the moon. 'Whistle-or'oller! Or-we-shall-not-foller!' It was a cry on two notes, prolonged. From the other side of the hill, above white fields of mist, the faint fox-cry came back. We were off again then, through the waking night, among sleepless owls and badgers, while our quarry slipped off into another parish and would not be found for hours.

Round about midnight we ran them to earth, exhausted under a haystack. Until then we had chased them through all the world, through jungles, swamps, and tundras, across pampas plains and steppes of wheat and plateaux of shooting stars, while hares made love in the silver grasses, and the large hot moon climbed over us, raising tides in my head of night and summer that move there even yet.

by Laurie Lee

Poor Jenny is a-weeping – Ring Game

Poor Jenny is a-weeping
A-weeping, a-weeping,
Poor Jenny is a-weeping
On a bright summer's day.

Pray tell me who you're weeping for,
Who you're weeping for, who you're weeping for,
Pray tell me who you're weeping for,
Pray tell me who you're weeping for,
On a bright summer's day.

I'm weeping for my true love
My true love, my true love,
I'm weeping for my true love
On a bright summer's day.

Stand up and choose your true love
Your true love, your true love,
Stand up and choose your true love
On a bright summer's day.

Now Jenny choose your bridesmaids ....
Now Jenny choose your page-boys ....
Now Jenny choose your Parson ....
Now Jenny shall be married ....

Jenny sits in the middle of the ring and the others dance round her, changing direction after each verse. She chooses a child/children at the end of the appropriate verses, who join her in the ring. During the last verse they form a procession with the parson in the front, then Jenny, her true love, bridesmaids and page-boys. then the game can be repeated with a new child playing Jenny.

Poor Jenny

Poor Jenny is a weeping a weeping a weeping, poor Jenny is a weeping on a bright summers day.

45

The Pedlar's Caravan – Song

I wished I lived in a caravan,
With a horse to drive, like a pedlar-man,
Where he comes from nobody knows,
Nor where he goes to, but on he goes.

His caravan has windows two,
With a chimney of tin that the smoke comes
                                        through,
He has a wife, and a baby brown,
And they go riding from town to town.

Chairs to mend and delf to sell
He clashes the basins like a bell.
Tea-trays, baskets, ranged in order,
Plates, with the alphabet round the border.

The roads are brown, and the sea is green,
But his house is just like a bathing-machine.
The world is round but he can ride,
Rumble, and splash to the other side.

With the pedlar-man I should like to roam,
And write a book when I come home.
All the people would read my book,
Just like the Travels of Captain Cook.

W B Rands.

I wish I lived in a Caravan

I wish I lived in a caravan with a horse to drive like a pedlar man, where he comes from nobody knows and where he goes to I just don't know.

Summertime – Song

This can be done with single hand movements

Over in the meadow in the sand in the sun
Lived a dear mother turtle and her little turtle one.
'Dig' said the mother
'I dig' said the one
So he dug and he dug
In the sand, in the sun.

Over in the meadow, where the stream runs blue
Lived a dear mother fish and her little fishes two.
'Swim' said the mother
'We swim' said the two
So they swam and they swam
Where the stream runs blue.

Over in the meadow in a hole in a tree
Lived a dear mother robin and her little robins
three.
'Sing' said the mother
'We sing' said the three
So they sang and they sang
In the hole of the tree.

Over in the meadow in the reeds on the shore
Lived a dear mother water rat and her little ratties
four
'Dive' said the mother
We dive' said the four
So they dived and they dived
In the reeds on the shore.

Over in the meadow in a snug beehive
Lived a dear mother honeybee and her little honeys
five.
'Buzz' said the mother
'We buzz' said the five
So they buzzed and they buzzed
Near the snug beehive.

Over in the meadow in a nest built of sticks
Lived a dear mother crow and her little crows six.
'Caw' said the mother
'We caw' said the six
So they cawed and they cawed
In their nest built of sticks.

Over in the meadow where the grass is so even
Lived a gay mother cricket and her little crickets
seven.
'Chirp' said the mother
'We chirp' said the seven
So they chirped and they chirped
In the grass soft and even.

Over in the meadow by the old mossy gate
Lived a brown mother lizard with her little lizards
eight.
'Bask' said the mother
'We bask' said the eight
So they basked and they basked
By the old mossy gate.

Over in the meadow where the clear pools shine
Lived a green mother frog and her little froggies nine.
'Croak' said the mother
'We croak' said the nine
So they croaked and they croaked
Where the clear pools shine.

Over in the meadow in a soft shady glen
Lived a dear mother firefly and her little flies ten.
'Shine' said the mother
'We shine' said the ten
So they shone and they shone
In the soft, shady glen.

47

I. Whitsun

Spring goeth all in white
Crowned with milk-white may:
In fleecy flocks of light
O'er heaven the white clouds stray.

White butterflies in the air;
White daisies prank the ground;
The cherry and the hoary pear
Scatter their snow around.

Robert Bridges

Whit Sunday is the seventh after Easter, the Church day of Pentecost, recalling the manifestation of the Holy Spirit to the Apostles. By tradition the appearance of the white dove at Pentecost lends itself to the theme of a 'white' Sunday, as did the white gowns worn by newly baptized converts. In northern Europe the connotation is also a natural one, with the blooming of white May, Hawthorn and Lilac at this time. For children this can be a time to celebrate the blossoms, bringing a few into the home if possible, or finding white daisies to place on a saucer of water for the table or weave into chains. have a cake with white icing for tea, perhaps with an icing dove nesting on it. (See modelling icing recipe.) One friend says that she and all the family try to wear something white, blouse, shirt or scarf, etc., and that they always have milk and coconut macaroons.

Macaroons

1 cup desiccated coconut
3 tablespoons flour
¾ cup honey
3 egg whites
¼ teaspoon vanilla or almond essence

Beat the egg whites until stiff. Add the honey and vanilla, pour in the coconut and flour and stir well with a wooden spoon. Form into balls, place on an oiled baking tray and bake for ten minutes at 350°F (Reg. 4). Take out while still moist. (Instead of an oiled baking tray you can place a sheet of rice paper on a tray.)

Modelling Icing

1 egg white
1 rounded tablespoon liquid glucose
A little cornflour
500 gm./1 lb icing sugar
Few drops of colouring when needed.
(A little lemon juice if you like.)

Mix the egg white and glucose together in a basin. Gradually add enough icing sugar to form a stiff paste. Turn onto a surface sprinkled with cornflour and knead until smooth. Wrap in cling film and keep in a plastic bag to prevent from drying – it can keep up to six weeks in the fridge.

'Little White Doves' – Song

Little white doves
So white and so free
In the dovecote nest I see,
Look up to the bright blue sky
Spread your wings and gently fly.

Fluttering, fluttering, all around
Lighting gently on the ground
Back into the dovecote fly
Fold your wings and gently sigh.

Morwenna Bucknell

White Dove Song

White dove is flying through the sky,
Bring us a golden ray from on high
White dove has something wise to say,
Just flown out of the sun today.

Little white dove, what news I pray,
Open up your heart so bold
To receive the glittering gold.

Little white dove,
Little white dove.

49

White Whitsun Bird

Cut out of stiff white paper any appropriate bird shape. Glue on white streamers for a tail out of crepe paper. Make wings of soft white paper and fold as for a fan. Fold in half and slip through a hole in the bird's body until half-way point. Thread string through a hole where the bird will balance when hung from the string.

White Whitsun Bird

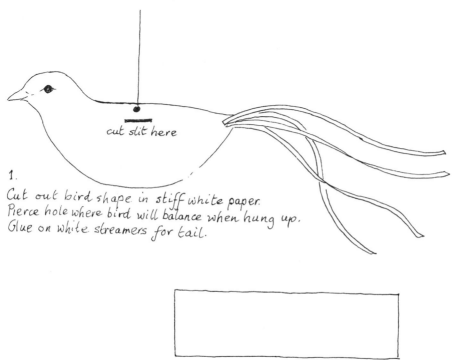

cut slit here

1.
Cut out bird shape in stiff white paper.
Pierce hole where bird will balance when hung up.
Glue on white streamers for tail.

2. For wings use thinner white paper (N.B. not drawn to scale)

x

3. Fold like a fan. Fold in half at x and slip through slit in bird's body.

2. Midsummer

The celebration of the summer solstice may be June 21, the longest day of the year, or June 24, the official calendar Midsummer Day and the feast of St. John the Baptist. Ancient peoples, watching the sun reach its highest point at this time, lit evening bonfires to encourage it to shine and ripen their crops. In many parts of the country bonfires still blaze at this time, songs are sung and the half-way point of the year marked. For many people the day is associated with fairies, as immortalized by Shakespeare in *A Midsummer Night's Dream.* In the play, Puck speaks of " ... we fairies, that do run, By the triple Hecate's team, From the presence of the sun, Following darkness like a dream", while Oberon and Titania follow on:

'Through this house give glimmering light
By the dead and drowsy fire:
Every elf and fairy sprite,
Hop as light as bird from brier;
And this ditty, after me
Sing, and dance it trippingly.'

'First rehearse this song by rote:
To each word a warbling note,
Hand in hand, with fairy grace,
Will we sing, and bless this place.'

'The Joyful Feast of St. John'

'Then doth the joyful feast of St. John the Baptist
take his turne,
When bonfiers great with loftie flame, in every
towne doe burne;
And yong men round with maides, doe daunce in
every streete,
With garlands wrought of Motherwort, or else with
Vervain sweete,
And many other flowre faire, with Violets in their
handes,
Whereas they all do fondly thinke, that whosoever
standes,
And thorow the flowres beholds the flame, his eyes
shall feele no paine.
When thus till night they daunced have, they
through the fire amaine
With striving mindes doe runne, and all their
hearbes they cast therein,
And then, with wordes devout and prayers, they
solemnely begin,
Desiring God that all their illies may there
consumed bee
Whereby they thinke through all that yeare from
Augues to be free .....'

From a 16th Century poem by Thomas Kirchmeyer.

Midsummer Night

The sun goes down,
The stars peep out,
And long slim shadows
Flit about.

In velvet shoes
The quiet dark
Comes stepping soft
O'er wood and park.

And now the world
Is fast asleep;
And fays and elves
Their revels keep.

They fly on the backs of the grey-winged moths,
They skim on the dragon-flies green and gold
On shimmering dew-wet grass they alight,
Tiny petal-skirts whirl, gauzy wings unfold.

The fairies are dancing beneath the moon
Hush! See the shimmer of their twinkling shoon!

Elizabeth Gould

51

Haytime

It's Midsummer Day
And they're cutting the hay
Down in the meadow just over the way,
The children all run
For a frolic, and fun –
For haytime is playtime out in the sun.

It's Midsummer Day,
And they're making the hay
Down in the meadow all golden and gay,
They're tossing it high
Beneath the June sky,
And the hay rakes are spreading it out to dry.

Irene F. Pawsey.

Tales from the End Cottage

Mrs. Apple's Birthday

'What's special about today?' asked Black Dog. 'Time of year,' said a big black and white cow gazing at a buttercup. 'Comes only once, like Christmas', said another, staring away over the field, and chewing. 'Time of year,' mooed several cows together, 'Time of year.'

Black Dog looked mystified. 'Whatever do they mean?' he asked.

'Black Dog!' exclaimed Tooty suddenly. 'I understand! Once a year, like Christmas. It's Midsummer Day! The special day for fairies and magic. Cows know all about that. There's a fairy called Robin Goodfellow who looks after cows. He keeps away the bad magic which turns their milk sour.'

'Of course' said Black Dog 'I remember when I lived with the gipsies they tied the horse up very carefully on Midsummer Night in case he went away with the fairies. They used to shut their caravans up extra carefully too, in case the fairies took a fancy to one of their babies and gave them a fairy child in exchange. No wonder we're going to have a picnic'

By and by it began to be dusk. The cats sat staring about them with brilliant eyes. The Pekes lay with their noses on their paws, ears forward, listening, bright eyes watching.

'What's that' said Tooty quickly. At the same moment Black Dog gave a little whickering growl.

Rex looked at them 'You two are seeing things' he said and rolled on the grass.

The cats said nothing. They went on staring into the dusk with shining eyes. Browny came trotting over the brow of the hill. He stopped, looked over his shoulder and whinnied gently. Wild roses were twisted in his mane. He stood listening, his head held high.

The cats got up and walked over the grass towards Browny. Soon they began to run. The Pekes jumped up and followed, Black Dog running with his nose to the ground. Tooty just behind him. Browny kicked up his heels and galloped away. The cats and the Pekes ran faster, and faster and faster, and they all swept over the curve of the land and disappeared.....

Mrs. Apple glanced over her shoulder rather uneasily 'I think we ought to be getting back home' she said. 'Where have they all got to?' So she and Farmer Parsloe stood up and called all the animals by name ....

The animals came quietly over out of the dusk. It was as if they had never been away. Browny's roses had gone, but one pink petal clung to Black Dog's ruff ....

The Pekes trotted along quietly, side by side. 'Only once a year' said Black Dog.
'Yes' said Tooty. She sounded a little sad.

Midsummer in Bullerby

And now I want to tell you what we did on Midsummer Eve, the 23rd of June. In the South Farm meadow we had a Midsummer pole (we always have one in Sweden). Everybody in the whole village helped to make it.

First we rode way out into the forest in our wagon to pick leaves that we were going to use. Father drove, and even Kerstin was allowed to come along. She was so happy that she laughed and laughed. Olaf gave her a little branch to hold in her hand, and she sat and waved it back and forth ...

When we came home from the forest, Agda, Britta, Anna and I picked a big bunch of lilacs from the bushes behind our woodshed. Then we took them over to the South Farm meadow, where Oscar and Kalle had already cut the pole. We tied the leaves all round the pole and hung two big wreaths of lilacs from the crossbar at the top. Then we raised the pole and danced round it ...

Then we all sat down in the grass and drank coffee that Mother and Aunt Gretta and Aunt Lisa had made. We had buns and cake too. Grandpa drank three cups of coffee, because that's something he really likes.

'Coffee is something I have to have,' he says.

I don't like it at all, but when you drink it while sitting in the grass at Midsummer, it tastes much better than usual.

We played 'The last pair out' and a lot of other games. It's such fun when the mothers and fathers play with us. It would probably not be so much fun if we had to play with them every day, but when it's Midsummer, I think they should be allowed to play too.

Svipp ran round and barked while we played. I think he thought it was fun too.

We were allowed to stay up just as long as we wanted to that evening. Agda said if you climbed over nine fences before you went to bed, and if you picked nine kinds of flowers and put them under your pillow, you'd dream at night about the one you would marry.

Britta and Anna and I thought it would be lots of fun to climb over nine fences, although we already know who we are going to marry.

Astrid Lindgren

Gifts for the Fairies

On Midsummer night, our children sometimes put little cakes or biscuits out for the fairies. They put them into a corner of the garden which they believe is special to the fairies and next morning when they go there they find that they have been painted in different coloured icing and a few have been taken away. (Make butterfly shaped biscuits with the recipe for Christmas hanging biscuits which can easily be iced p.135 .)

Other times they make a little tray of tiny things to eat, cut up nuts and raisins, etc., and they put them on their dolls house plates and tables. They leave these out for the fairies and gnomes and in the morning they find the food gone and a little crystal in its place.

These are very magical moments.

53

3. Picnics

Holiday Memory

August Bank Holiday

And if you could have listened at some of the open doors at some of the houses in the street you might have heard:
'Uncle Owen says he can't find the bottle-opener...'
'Has he looked under the hallstand?...'
'Willy's cut his finger ...'
'Got your spade?'
'If somebody doesn't kill that dog ...'
'Uncle Owen says why should the bottle-opener be
under the hallstand?'
'Never again,
never again...'
'I know I put the pepper somewhere ...'
'Willy's bleeding ...'
'Oh come on, come on ....'
'Let's have a look at the bootlace in your bucket ...'
'If I lay my hands on that dog .....'
'Uncle Owen's found the bottle-opener....'
'Willy's bleeding over the cheese ...
And the trams that hissed like ganders took us all to the beautiful beach.

There was cricket on the sand, and sand in the sponge cake, sandflies in the watercress, and foolish, mulish, religious donkeys on the unwilling trot.

Dylan Thomas

On the Beach

A time for relaxing, playing games, splashing in the water and collecting things. Look out for a variety of pretty stones and shells: the large stones can be decorated with paints or pressed flowers, varnished and used as paperweights or decorative items, and the shells can be collected and later identified and spread out on the windowsill. They look very pretty in a dish of water on the table (add some salt to stop the water growing algae), or the little shells can be stuck on to boxes to make little holiday gifts for relatives.

A friend once made a pretty mobile by collecting small pieces of driftwood on the beach, the shapes they made were very unusual. Bigger pieces of driftwood can be worked with linseed oil to make a pretty decorative object.

Don't forget to hang some seaweed outside your front door to tell you what the weather will do the next day. If the seaweed is wet so will the weather be, if it is dry, the day will be fine.

Cherry Stones

Tinker, Tailor, Soldier, Sailor,
Rich Man, Poor Man,
Ploughboy, Thief -
And what about a Cowboy,
Policeman, Jailer,
Engine-driver,
Or Pirate Chief?
What about a Postman - or a Keeper at the Zoo?
What about the Circus Man who lets the people
through?
And the man who takes the pennies for the round-
abouts and swings?
Or the man who plays the organ, and the other man
who sings?
What about a Conjuror with rabbits in his pockets?
What about a Rocket Man who's always making
rockets?
Oh, there's such a lot of things to do and such a lot
to be
That there's always lots of cherries on my little
cherry tree!

A.A. Milne

Pip-Counting
– for Cherry or Plum Stones, or the seeds of
Watermelon

Tinker	A Laird
Tailor	A Lord
Soldier	A Cooper*
Sailor	A Thief
Rich Man	A Piper
Poor Man	A Drummer
Beggar Man	A stealer of Beef
Thief	

Wedding Counts

This year	Coach	Gold
Next year	Carriage	Silver
Sometime	Wheelbarrow	Copper
Never	Dust cart	Brass

Silk	Big box
Satin	Little box
Cotton	Band box
Rags	Bundle

Boots	Church	Big House
Shoes	Chapel	Little House
Slippers	Cathedral	Pig sty
Clogs	Abbey	Barn

One, Two, Three, Four, Mary at the cottage door.
Five, Six, Seven, Eight, Eating cherries off a plate.

* The Cooper was the maker of wooden barrels.

Picnics

What would the summer be without the occa-
sional picnic and sometimes it's nice to get away
from the conventional sandwiches: here are some
other ideas for such times. Make up a box of salad-
stuff – besides chunks of cucumber, tomato, lettuce,
chicory and endive, try some slices of raw carrot,
kohl rabi (which is rather like radish) and some cold,
cooked chunks of corn on the cob.

Also, plenty of fruit is good on a picnic – chunks
of melon or watermelon, a bowl of strawberries or
raspberries, some grapes or plums.

To do with Stones or Petals from a Daisy

One I love, two I love,
Three I love, I say,
Four I love with all my heart,
Five I cast away;
Six he loves, seven she loves, eight both love,
Nine he comes, ten he tarries,
Eleven he courts,
Twelve he marries.

Traditionally when you see magpies, but also to do
with Cherry stones:-

One for sorrow, two for joy
Three for a girl and four for a boy
Five for silver, six for gold
Seven for a secret never to be told.

Picnic–time

Here's a tree in summer
(hold a piece of grass with
seed head in your hand)

Here's a tree in winter
(slide your hand up the grass
and pull off the seed heads,
leaving grass bare)

Here's a bunch of flowers
(holding out seed heads
in other hand)

And here's the April showers
(sprinkle seed heads on ground)

Here's a tree in summer   Here's a tree in winter   Here's a bunch of flowers   And here's the April showers

Flans

These are so useful because you can use all kinds of ingredients. Line a greased flan dish with short-crust pastry – this is quite a good one to use:

6 oz plain flour
2-3 oz oats
1 oz sesame seeds
5 oz margarine or mixture of fats
4-5 tablespoons cold water
Pinch of salt

Cook this blind for ten minutes, 375°F (Reg. 5), and then tip in the following mixture. In a bowl mix 3 large eggs, 6 oz of good cheese (Emmenthal or Gruyere is best), ½ pt milk (and cream), a few herbs i.e. chopped chives, parsley, basil or a little mint, salt and pepper. This is the basis for the flan but to this you can add:

a layer of cooked ham or bacon;
cooked and chopped cauliflower, carrot,
French beans, peas, sautéed onion, leek,
mushrooms, peppers or courgettes.

In fact it is worthwhile experimenting with what is in season.

Spread the mixture into the flan base and cook at 375°F (Reg. 5) for 30 mins, or so, until brown on top.

Instead of one large flan, try making little individual ones in patty tins; these require less cooking time.

Pizza Flan

For this you can use the following pastry:

½ lb plain flour
pinch salt
1 level tablespoon icing sugar
5 oz soft butter
1 egg yolk
4 tablespoons cold water

Line a greased flan dish with this pastry and prick the bottom. Allow to chill for 1 hour in fridge and then cook blind for 10 mins. 375°F (Reg. 5).

For the filling heat some olive oil in a pan and add 6-8 large tomatoes which have been peeled, chopped and drained. Add 2 tablespoons of tomato concentrate and cook until the excess moisture is evaporated and mash to form a purée. Slice 3 large onions and simmer in butter until soft and golden and add some fresh rosemary or tarragon. Combine the onion and tomato mixture and stir in 2-4 tablespoons of Parmesan or grated Emmenthal or Gruyere. Fill the pastry case and you can arrange anchovies and black olives across the top if you like these and cook for 30 mins. 375°F (Reg. 5).

Pizza and Dough

1 lb flour
1 oz yeast (½ oz dried yeast)
¼-½ pt water
1½ teaspoon salt
3 tablespoons olive oil

Dissolve the salt in ½ pint of warm water. Put the flour in a bowl and make a well in the centre and pour in the yeast (which has been allowed to dissolve in about 2 tablespoonsful of warm water and a little sugar for 10 mins). Mix with one hand and gradually add more water with the other. It should end up elastic, springy and not too wet. Wash, dry, and flour your hands. Place the dough on a floured board and knead well, working in the olive oil, a small quantity at a time. The dough should now be pliable and not sticking to your hands – this is something you have to practise a few times. Cut into three or four pieces and make into pizza rounds and place in greased and floured tins and allow to prove for 20 mins. Then add the sauce. Alternatively put the sauce on before proving – you will have to decide which you prefer.

You need about ¾ pt. well seasoned tomato sauce as below (use tinned or fresh tomatoes).

First, chop 2 onions and some garlic and soften them in some oil for 10 mins. without browning. Add 1½ lbs. tomatoes skinned and roughly chopped, season and add sprigs of thyme, rosemary and a bay leaf. Simmer uncovered for 30 mins. and then remove the sprigs of herbs. If the mixture appears too runny add 2 tablespoonsful tomato concentrate.

Spread the dough with this tomato and onion sauce and lay little slices of Mozzarella or Bel Paese cheese over the top (otherwise ¼-½ lb. good grated cheese). To this you can add anchovy fillets and black olives and sprinkle the top with oregano, basil or marjoram, and olive oil – 1 dessertspoonful for each pizza. Allow the pizza dough to prove if not already done so and then cook for 15 mins. at 400°F (Reg. 6) then 375°F (Reg. 5) for a further 15-20 mins.

Other variations include adding slices of red or green pepper sautéed in oil, or mushroom sautéed in butter.

It is advisable not to go to the very edge of the dough with the mixture as it forms a kind of bank.

Cold Chicken Pieces

Buy some drumsticks or small chicken pieces and cook them in the oven with different flavourings.

For example, mix together:
6 tablespoons vinegar
6 tablespoons soy sauce
Some garlic
1 teaspoon mustard
¼ pt tomato sauce
2 oz brown sugar

and marinate the chicken pieces in this before cooking.

Alternatively, make a marinade of little lemon and a carton of yoghurt, salt and paprika, garlic and a little tomato puree.

Cook both these in a slow oven 1-1½ hours. These are all delicious when eaten cold on a picnic.

Meat Loaf

1 lb minced beef
1 lb sausage meat
Handful of fresh breadcrumbs
2 chopped onions
salt, pepper, a little garlic
basil or oregano
3 or 4 tablespoons tomato ketchup

Mix all the above ingredients together in a bowl and add 2 beaten eggs. Put into a prepared loaf tin and place bacon on the top. Cook for 2 hours 350°F (Reg. 4) for 1 hour, then cover with foil and cook for 2nd hour at 300°F (Reg. 2).

Scotch Eggs

Flour peeled hard-boiled eggs and wrap them in some sausagemeat to which you have already mixed in a little salt, pepper and mixed herbs. Brush with beaten egg and roll in breadcrumbs and deep fry for 10 minutes.

Allow to cool and drain on wire rack.

Spinach Tart

Make your pastry base as for the Pizza Flan then line the flan dish and prick the pastry. Cool for 1 hour in the fridge before placing in oven for 10 mins. or so 375°F (Reg. 5).

Cook 1 lb. spinach with some butter and salt and drain well and chop up finely. Allow to cool. Add ground pepper, a little garlic salt, and ½ lb. cottage cheese, 3 beaten eggs and 1-2 oz. grated Parmesan. Add 6 tablespoonsful double cream and a little freshly grated nutmeg.

Spread this mixture into the pastry shell and bake at 375°F (Reg. 5) for 30 mins, until the crust is brown, and the cheese custard set.

Cornish Pasties

12 oz shortcrust pastry (makes about 6 saucer rounds)
A mixture of:
Chopped up potatoes
　　”　　”　　swede
　　”　　”　　carrot
　　”　　”　　onion
　　”　　”　　peas
　　”　　”　　sweetcorn or other suitable vegetables.
½ lb minced meat (or grated cheese if you prefer)
One beaten egg with a little milk

Roll out the pastry and cut into rounds using either a side plate or saucer. Mix the other ingredients together, adding salt, pepper, oregano and a little tomato sauce if you like. Add some of the beaten egg and a little butter and put a reasonable amount onto each round. Dampen the edges of each pasty with milk and egg mix and draw the edges together on top of the filling to enclose it completely. Crimp the edges using finger and thumb. Put the pasties on a prepared baking sheet and brush over with remaining beaten egg and milk. Bake at 400°F (Reg. 6) for 15 minutes, then reduce the temperature to 325°F (Reg. 3) for a further 30 mins. or more so that they are tender in the middle when pricked with a fork. Excellent either hot or cold.

Popcorn

Our children love popcorn at any time but it is especially good freshly made on a picnic.

You can buy popping corn from a health food shop. Take a large pan with a lid and put enough good oil at the bottom to cover 4 oz. of corn. When the oil is hot drop in the corn and cover with a lid. When it starts popping shake the pan and you will know when it is all cooked because the popping will die down. You can either throw some salt over the corn, mix it in and put in a dish to cool, or you can stir in a heated mixture of butter, golden syrup, honey or brown sugar which has been dissolved in the butter over gentle heat.

Dips

These are good either before a meal, or as part of a light summer meal or picnic. Foods which can be used to dip include:
crackers, crisps, toast sticks, cucumber strips, green pepper strips, cauliflower florets, carrot sticks, radishes, celery sticks, broccoli stems, etc.

Sour Cream Dip

Combine the following:
2 cups thick sour cream
2 tablespoons chopped parsley
2 tablespoons chopped chives
1 teaspoon dried herbs
⅛ teaspoon curry powder
½ teaspoon salt
¼ teaspoon paprika

Cheese Dip

Beat until smooth:
6 oz cream cheese
1½ tablespoons mayonnaise
1 tablespoon cream
¼ teaspoon salt
1 teaspoon grated onion or chives
1 teaspoon Worcestershire sauce

Cream Cheese Dip

Mix together a small carton of cream cheese, cottage cheese and sour cream with fresh herbs such as mint, parsley, chives, a little garlic, salt and pepper. Mix thoroughly and cool in fridge. A little blue cheese can be added to this if you like.

Avocado Dip

You will need:
2 ripe avocado pears
juice of ½ lemon
2 tomatoes, peeled and chopped
1 crushed clove of garlic
½ small onion, grated
pinch of salt and pepper
½ teaspoon Worcestershire sauce
4 tablespoons natural plain yoghurt

Halve the avocados, remove stones and scoop out the flesh: then use a fork to mash it before adding lemon juice. Add the other ingredients and beat well until smooth.

Picnic Sandwich Fillings

1. Mixture of mashed sardines, cottage cheese and good mayonnaise.
2. Mashed hard boiled eggs and chopped spring onions with a little mayonnaise.
3. Slice a French loaf lengthways and fill with an omelette which has been allowed to cool. Chop the French bread into manageable sections and eat with salad.
4. Grate some Cheddar cheese and apple and toss in a little lemon juice. Coarsely chop walnuts and mix all the ingredients together for a refreshing filling.
5. Cottage cheese, Marmite and tomato.
6. Broad Bean spread. (Cook broadbeans well, then drain and mouli or sieve to remove skins, add a bit of oil and vinegar, salt and pepper to the softened inner beans with garlic if you like, and mix to a smooth spread).
7. Sliced apple and peanut butter.
8. Cucumber and grated carrot.
9. Bacon, lettuce and tomato.
10. Sliced tomato and avocado.
11. Lettuce with mushroom sauce. (Sauté ¼ lb sliced mushrooms in 2 tablespoons butter, remove mushrooms when they have cooked and add to the pan one cup white sauce with a bit of yeast extract or tomato purée, when heated and thickened, add the sautéed mushrooms. Cool, and use to spread on bread.
12. Cream cheese and chopped green olives.

13. Chopped hard-boiled eggs with Marmite and lettuce or tomato.

Cake Trays

Make a sponge mix in the usual way:-
6 oz plain flour
6 oz margarine
6 oz sugar
pinch bicarbonate of soda
teaspoon baking powder
3 beaten eggs
3 tablespoons warm water

Grease and flour a baking tray which has 1″ sides and put the sponge mix into this. Cook at 375°-400°F (Reg. 5-6) for 20 mins. or so until springy to the touch.

When it is cool you can cover the whole cake with a butter cream mix (see p. 26) and dot with chopped cherries or mixed nuts and cut it into slices for the picnic.

Alternatively, with the basic sponge mix add the grated peel and juice of one lemon and after cooking mix the juice of another lemon with 3 tablespoonsful sugar or icing sugar and pour this over the cooked cake immediately on removal from the oven. Allow to cool in tin.

Another idea is to mix into the basic sponge mix some chocolate chips, chopped nuts, chopped cherries or sultanas. Make up your own combinations.

4. Other Summer Food and Drink
Soups, Salads, Puddings, Drinks

Cold Cucumber Soup

1½ pints good chicken stock
 (or vegetable stock if preferred)
2 onions
1 large cucumber
sprig of mint
1 dessertspoon arrowroot
a little milk
top with cream.

Fry the onions in a little butter and add the chicken stock and simmer for 10 minutes. Add the chopped cucumber to the soup and the sprig of mint and cook for a further 10 minutes. Now liquidise the soup and return to the saucepan. Blend the arrowroot with a little milk and mix this into the soup. Bring the soup to the boil stirring all the time and cook for ½ minute. Add seasoning to taste and a little cream. Allow to cool and refrigerate over night – serve with chopped chives and mint on top of each bowl and a little cream.

If you like a thicker soup, add a chopped up potato when you put the chicken stock into the pan.

Vichysoisse

1 lb leeks
2-3 potatoes
1 onion
1 pint chicken stock
1 pint creamy milk
seasoning, parsley, chives
thin cream

Fry the chopped leeks and onion in a little butter and add the chicken stock, chopped potatoes, herbs and seasonings. Simmer for about 20 minutes and then liquidise the soup. Add the milk - not too much otherwise the soup will be too thin - and allow to cool. Serve cold with chopped chives, parsley and a little cream.

Iced Tomato and Courgette Soup

1½ lbs peeled tomatoes*
1 lb steamed courgettes
4 ice cubes
seasoning
2 teaspoons finely chopped onion
lemon juice
1 flat teaspoon orange rind
small carton sour cream
1 teaspoon caster sugar

Liquidise the above ingredients except the cream and ice cubes. Stir in the cream and refrigerate. When serving, put the ice cubes into the serving bowl and pour on the soup and garnish with chives.

* *A simple method of peeling tomatoes is to prick them and put them in a dish of boiling water for a few minutes. Take out one at a time and the skins will come off easily.*

Cottage Pea Soup

1 lb green peas (and mange tout if you can get them)
½ oz butter
1 onion, thinly sliced
sprig of mint
sprig of parsley
1 pt chicken stock
2 teaspoons flour
4 tablespoons milk
1 tablespoon double cream

Shell the peas, and rinse them and the mange tout under the tap. Melt the butter in the pan and cook the onion until it is transparent. Stir peas into the butter and onion mixture. Add the chopped mange tout, mint, parsley, stock, salt and pepper and simmer for ½ hour or so. Now you can either thicken the soup with blended flour and milk, bring to the boil, stirring continually, adjust the seasoning and finally stir in the cream, off the heat, and serve at once **or** you can liquidise the soup and then thicken with blended flour and milk, adjust seasoning and stir in some cream before serving.

Pasta Salad

Cook some pasta shapes (shells, macaroni pieces or equivalent) in the usual way until tender and then rinse them under the cold tap in a colander.

Make a French dressing (p.137) and add some tomato purée, then cover the pasta with this. Mix in some chopped spring onions, celery and green peppers.

Whole Lentil Salad

This is a very satisfying salad. Use the whole lentils, not the split ones, and it is a good idea to let them soak for a few hours beforehand and then rinse them under the tap.

Put the lentils into some fresh water and cook them with a few mixed herbs, garlic, seasoning and perhaps a carrot and onion for flavouring. When they are cooked which takes about 20-30 mins. (taste one to make sure) strain off the liquid and rinse them under the tap and remove the onion and carrot. Allow them to stand for a few minutes until all the water is drained off and then put them into a large dish and mix with a good French dressing (see p.137) perhaps adding more olive oil than usual. Serve with thinly sliced onion, egg and tomatoes on top.

Leeks or Courgettes and Mushrooms à la Grecque

If you are using leeks try to keep them whole and blanch them in salted water for a few minutes, drain them in a colander. If you are using courgettes and mushrooms, or indeed little whole onions, steam them gently for only a few minutes and drain them - split the courgettes down the middle.

Now put the following ingredients into a pan:
4 tablespoons dry white wine or wine vinegar
1 oz sugar
3 tablespoons olive oil
salt, ground pepper, ground garlic, oregano
a little French mustard or tomato purée, and lemon juice

Bring this to the boil, stirring constantly, then put in your vegetables and simmer until they are tender. Bring out the vegetables into a dish and boil the liquid to reduce and thicken, then pour over the vegetables and allow to cool, sprinkle with chopped parsley.

Carrot Salad

4 large carrots
½ cup seedless raisins
chopped parsley
1 tablespoon lemon juice
1 cup sour cream or plain yoghurt

Grate the carrots, add raisins, parsley and lemon juice; mix in the sour cream or yoghurt. This may be served on lettuce leaves if you wish, or with sliced cucumber on top. Try your own variations, such as adding a bit of grated apple or nuts.

Celeriac Salad

The "ugly duckling" of vegetables, celeriac is a tough, knobby root, but is nicely and subtly flavoured and versatile. It is difficult to peel, so cut the outside the way you would a swede or old turnip. Scrub well. You may grate it raw for salad, or for better flavour slice thinly and simmer for 10 minutes or more with a dash of lemon juice to keep the white colour. Drain, allow to cool, then toss in either mayonnaise or a French dressing. You may add chopped spring onion, chives, chopped parsley, or tomato as you wish. Serve on watercress, endive or lettuce leaves.

Tomato and Lentil Salad

8 oz whole lentils, soaked for at least 1 hour
salt and pepper
chopped spring onions, celery and parsley
4 tomatoes, sliced

Drain the lentils, place in a pan and cover with cold water. Add a pinch of salt and simmer for 30 to 40 minutes until softened. While simmering, prepare the dressing:

½ pt tomato juice
1 tablespoon lemon juice
1 clove garlic, crushed
pinch of salt and pepper
chopped chives
2 tablespoons olive oil

Place ingredients in a jar or bottle with tight lid, shake well to blend.

Add the dressing to the cooked lentils while they are still warm so that they fully absorb the flavour. When the mixture is cool, add other salad ingredients, with salt and pepper to taste.

Cucumber Salad

Cucumbers may be sliced thinly, tossed in dressing and served with chopped parsley. But some people find the flavour slightly acrid. If an alternative is wished for a less bitter taste, try the following: Peel and slice cucumber into thin rounds, place on a plate and salt each layer. Put a weight, such as a heavy plate, over the cucumbers and refrigerate three to six hours. Drain, toss in sour cream and garnish with chopped dill, basil or tarragon. Serve at once.

Bean Sprout Salads

You may buy bean sprouts in many good markets or green-grocers, or you may grow them at home by exposing fresh beans to light and rinsing daily until they begin to sprout, the entire process taking anything from four or five to ten days for good sprouts. Use a jam jar, or one of the many special layered trays available for this purpose. Mung beans and alfalfa seeds (available in health food stores) or fresh wheat kernels are very successful for home growing and a delicious addition to any meal. They are also extremely good for you, and tasty when served plain.

Salad possibilities with beansprouts are many and varied. Toss them with peeled chopped mushrooms and tomato in a French dressing.

Serve beansprouts with thinly sliced red and green pepper and chopped spring onion.

Add them to a tossed salad of lettuce and other greens.

German Hot Potato Salad

In a covered saucepan cook until just tender:

6 medium-sized potatoes in their jackets
Peel and slice while they are hot.

Heat in a frying pan:
4 rashers of bacon, cut into small pieces, or 2 tablespoons bacon dripping.

Add and sauté until brown:
¼ cup each of chopped onion and celery
1 chopped dill pickle or gherkin

Heat to boiling point:
¼ cup water or stock
½ cup wine vinegar
pinch of sugar and salt
⅛ teaspoon paprika or ¼ teaspoon dried mustard

Pour the above in with bacon and onion, mix well. Combine this with potatoes and serve at once with chopped parsley or chives. This dish is equally good cold and may be made in advance for picnics or cold suppers.

Hungarian Potato Salad

Boil the potatoes and when they have been drained, cut them into small pieces. Whilst they are still hot mix them with the following:

Carton of yoghurt
Carton of sour cream
2-3 tablespoons olive oil
chopped gherkins (optional)
lemon juice
garlic
salt and pepper to taste

Allow to cool and before serving mix again and decorate with chopped chives and parsley.

Cold French Bean Salad

Cook the beans in a pan of salted water until tender and then drain them and put into a dish. Whilst they are still hot put a good French dressing over the top (see p.137) with a little cream added if you like and mix well.

Serve when cold with chopped chives over the top.

American Gingham Salad with Cottage Cheese

Place in a large mixing bowl and toss:

1½ cups coarsely chopped young spinach leaves or Swiss chard
2 cups shredded red cabbage
⅓ teaspoon salt
¼ teaspoon celery seed
about 3 tablespoons chopped olives or chives
1 cup cottage cheese

Place the mixture on a bed of large lettuce leaves and serve with mayonnaise.

Cold Ratatouille

Gently fry some chopped onions with chopped red and green peppers until tender. Add garlic. Meanwhile peel and cut into small pieces an aubergine or two, and chop some courgettes into thick slices. Blanch these in a pan of boiling water and simmer for two minutes and then drain – this helps to preserve their colour and removes any bitterness in the skins.

Add the aubergines and courgettes to the other mixture and cook for 20 minutes with a lid on the pan. Add some mushrooms, skinned tomatoes, salt, pepper and oregano. Cook for a further 10-15 minutes, mix well and allow to cool. Serve cold with a sprinkling of chopped parsley.

Cold Rice Salad

Boil your rice in salted water until tender. Then in order to avoid a sticky appearance rinse the rice well under the cold tap in a colander. Allow to cool and drain. Add Turmeric during cooking for a yellow appearance.

Then put the rice into a large bowl and add a variety of salad ingredients, for example:

chopped celery, peppers, spring onions

sliced raw mushrooms
chopped nuts
sultanas
a tin of sweetcorn
a few black olives

Now mix the whole salad with a good French dressing (see p.137) and add a little fresh mint.

Sprouting Salad

Mix together:

1 bunch of watercress, chopped
a cup of beansprouts
some chopped celery
1 cup alfalfa sprouts

Mix with a French dressing to which you have added some fresh herbs.

Gooseberry Cake

4 oz butter
5½ oz self-raising flour
large egg yolk
4 oz sugar
1 tablespoon dry white wine
1½ teaspoon orange flower or rose water
½ tablespoon aniseeds
⅓ nutmeg, grated
scant 3 oz gooseberries

Melt the butter and while still warm, not hot, stir in the flour, yolk, sugar, wine and flavourings. Beat well. Fold in the gooseberries – alternatively sandwich the gooseberries – between two layers of the mixture in a buttered and sugared tin or baking dish. Bake at 350°F (Reg. 4) until the top is golden brown and a skewer pushed into the centre comes out clean: from 40 minutes - depending on depth.

Note: For eating cold, make with two egg yolks.

Strawberry Cheesecake

2 oz butter or margarine, melted
4 oz digestive biscuits, crushed
(see Italian Cheesecake)
1 oz brown sugar
12 oz curd cheese, 5 oz yoghurt
about 4 tablespoons clear honey
½ oz gelatine, soaked in 3 tablespoons water
grated rind and juice of 1 lemon

3 egg whites
strawberries to decorate with, about ½ lb.

Combine the melted fat with the sugar and biscuit crumbs so that it is manageable for pressing over the base of an 8″ pie dish or the removeable base of a cake tin. Place in the refrigerator for 20 minutes until it is firm.

Meanwhile, place the cheese in a bowl and mix in the honey, lemon rind, yoghurt and juice. Beat until smooth. Put the soaked gelatine in a bowl over a pan of simmering water and stir until dissolved. Stir this into the cheese mixture. Whisk the egg whites until they are stiff, then fold them gently into the cheese mixture. Spoon over the biscuit base and chill for 2-3 hours until well set. Then remove from tin (if you are using the cake variety) and arrange the strawberries on top.

Italian Cheesecake

Crust:

½ lb plain digestive biscuits, crushed either in a liquidiser or in a polythene bag and rolled with a rolling pin.
4 oz butter

Mix the biscuit crumbs with the melted butter and line a loose-bottomed 7″ cake tin with the mixture. Put into a warm oven for 5-10 minutes and then allow to cool.

Filling:

2 teaspoons gelatine
½ lb curd cheese
3-4 oz caster sugar
6 fl oz double cream
2 eggs
juice of one lemon
1-2 oz sultanas (optional)

Add a little water to the gelatine and melt over a double saucepan of hot water stirring carefully and allow to cool. Mix the cheese, sugar, cream, egg yolks and lemon juice and beat until smooth (can be done in the liquidiser). Add the melted gelatine and mix in well. Now whisk the egg whites until stiff and fold them into the cheese mixture with the sultanas, if you wish. Pour the mixture into the tin on top of the crumb mix and refrigerate for several hours. Before serving, carefully remove the sides of the tin leaving the cake on the base of the cake tin.

Summer Pudding

1 lb raspberries
½ lb red currants
½ lb blackcurrants
6-8 oz caster sugar
slices of white bread

Simmer the red and blackcurrants with sugar to taste until tender, and simmer the raspberries separately as they take only a very short time. Cook all the fruit as briefly as possible. When the fruit is soft line a basin with strips of white bread (no crusts). The pieces must make a close-knit mould inside the bowl with no cracks. Pour the hot fruit into this and enough juice to keep the fruit fairly stiff and to saturate the bread. Put the red and blackcurrants in first with the raspberries on top. Cover the top with a lid of bread, using no crusts. Finally place a saucer on the top with a heavy weight. Leave the pudding all night in a cold place for the juice to permeate the bread and the whole pudding to congeal to firmness. The next day carefully turn it out and serve with thick cream or egg custard.

Vanilla Ice-cream

You can vary this vanilla ice-cream by adding different flavours, such as melted chocolate, nuts, coffee, soft fruits.

2 eggs
4 oz caster sugar
½ oz cornflour
1 pt milk
¼ pt double cream
1 teaspoon vanilla essence

Make the custard by whisking together the eggs and the sugar and stirring in the cornflour mixed with a little of the milk. Heat the rest of the milk and add to the mixture. Return it all to the saucepan and bring to the boil: boil for 3 minutes stirring all the time. Turn into a basin to cool and whisk it now and then to prevent a skin forming. When it is cold pour it into the freezing tray, cover and freeze for about 1½ hours. Turn out and beat well before stirring in the slightly whipped cream, flavoured with vanilla essence. Return to the freezer and freeze for a further hour.

63

Blackcurrant Ice-cream

1 lb blackcurrants
8 oz icing sugar
juice of ½ lemon
½ pt double cream

Use a fork to strip the berries from the stalks and then rinse them under the tap. Crush the berries in a sieve using a wooden spoon and retain all the juices in a bowl. Now add the sieved icing sugar and lemon juice and mix well. Whisk the cream until thick and fold into the blackcurrant mixture. Put the ice-cream into refrigerator ice trays and put into the freezer or into waxed cartons and cover. Ready in a few hours.

Mint Ice-cream

4 oz caster sugar
¼ pt water
1 teacup mint leaves, stripped from stem
juice from ½ lemon
½ pt double cream

Put the sugar and water into a saucepan and stir over a low heat until the sugar has melted, then bring up to the boil. Put the washed and dried mint leaves into a liquidiser and pour in the hot syrup and blend until the mint is finely chopped. Leave the mixture until quite cold then strain into a mixing bowl. Add the strained lemon juice and stir in the cream. Whisk lightly to blend the ingredients and add a little green colouring if you like. Put into a refrigerator ice tray, cover and place in the freezer. As the mixture becomes icy round the sides, turn the edges into the centre with a fork. When it is half frozen turn it out into a cold basin and give it a good mix and return it to the container to refreeze. Leave for several hours. Before serving, put into the ordinary part of the fridge for 30 mins. so that the ice-cream is not too hard.

Water Ices

Lemon	¾ pt water
	½ lb sugar
	⅜ pt lemon juice
Orange	¾ pt water
	6 oz sugar
	¾ pt orange juice
	juice of one lemon

Coffee	⅜ pt water
	4 oz sugar
	¾ pt strong coffee
Strawberry	⅜ pt water
	4 oz sugar
	10 oz fresh ripe strawberries, puréed through sieve or liquidiser
	1½ tablespoons lemon juice

Bring the water and sugar to the boil over a moderate heat, stirring only until the sugar dissolves. From the moment the sugar and water begin to boil, let the mixture cook for exactly 5 minutes. Immediately remove the pan from the heat and let the syrup cool to room temperature. Now stir in the flavouring of your choice and pour the mixture into refrigerator trays. Freeze for about 3-4 hours and stir the water-ice every 30 mins. and scrape into the middle the ice particles that form around the edges. The finished water-ice should have a fine, snowy texture.

Fresh Lemonade

3 lemons
4 oz caster sugar
1½ pts water

Wash the lemons and squeeze out the juice. Place the lemon rinds in a basin with the sugar and pour over the water which should be boiling: stir to dissolve the sugar and then allow to cool. When it is cold, strain the lemonade into a jug, add the lemon juice and chill well before serving.

An attractive way to serve this drink, or other summertime cooling drinks, is to rub some lemon around the tops of the glasses you are going to use. Then dip the glasses into some caster sugar and you have a very attractive frosted ring around the top which tastes delicious.

Also try putting glace cherries, a sprig of mint or a mandarin orange into each of the divisions of the ice tray before freezing and add them to your drink.

Orange and Lemon Squash

2 lbs granulated sugar
1½ pts water
juice and grated rind of 3 large lemons
juice and grated rind of 2 large oranges
4 level teaspoons tartaric acid

Dissolve the sugar and water in a pan, bring to the boil and simmer for about 10 mins. Place the lemon and orange rind in a bowl with the tartaric acid and pour in the sugar syrup, mixing well.

Cover and leave to stand for 24 hours, then strain in the lemon and orange juice. Pour the squash into bottles and seal. Store in a cool place and dilute to taste with water.

Lemon and Grapefruit Barley Water

4 oz pearl barley
2 pts water
4 oz sugar
2 large grapefruit
1 lemon

Put the barley into a pan with just enough water to cover it and bring to the boil, strain off the liquid and rinse the barley under the cold tap. Return the barley to the pan and pour in 2 pts. of water and bring to the boil again, then cover and simmer for 1 hour. Strain the liquid into a jug, adding the sugar and stirring well before allowing mixture to cool. Extract the juice from the grapefruit and lemon and strain this into the barley liquor. Store in a screw topped jar in the fridge. (Makes two pints)

Ginger Beer

2 lemons
1½ lbs sugar
1 oz bruised root ginger
½ oz cream of tartar
3 quarts boiling water
1 oz fresh yeast
1 slice toast

Pare off the yellow part of the lemon rind into a bowl and squeeze out the juice and add this, the sugar, ginger and cream of tartar to the bowl. Pour over the boiling water. When it is lukewarm add the yeast, creamed with a little of the beer and spread on the toast. Ferment for 24 hours, then skim, strain,

bottle and tie down securely. The beer will be ready to drink in three days.

Rosie's Elderflower Fizz

1 gal water
4 lbs white sugar
6 whole chopped lemons
6 heads of elderflower
4 tablespoons white wine vinegar

Put all the above ingredients into a large container for 24 hours. Strain, bottle and keep for two weeks before serving.

Summer Milk Shakes

These are made quickly with a liquidiser but if you don't have one use a container you can really shake well.

Chocolate

2 tablespoons crushed ice
½ pt milk
2½ tablespoons chocolate syrup or equivalent

Strain this into a glass after you have shaken it well and serve with grated nutmeg or a little chocolate powder on top.

Strawberry or Raspberry

This is made the same way but use strawberry or raspberry jam or syrup, or even ice-cream or water-ice. Place some chopped up strawberries or raspberries on top.

65

5. Harvest

At harvest time the growing year has come full circle, and the bringing in of the ripe grains, vegetables and fruits is cause for celebration. Throughout Europe the concept of a Demeterlike Corn Mother figure or spirit in the grain was retained for centuries, with counterparts in the Americas in the form of Indian Maize goddesses. Given the vital importance of the harvest for survival, this is understandable, but few of us today can realise the significance of the "corn dolly" before the advent of the threshing machine. In the north of England, for example, the last sheaf left standing in the field was plaited and made into a doll-like figure, the 'kirn-doll' and carried to the harvest supper to embody the elements needed for the next growing season. In some areas, whoever cut the last sheaf was killing the corn spirit and bound to have bad luck; therefore to spread the ill luck as widely as possible, all the reapers threw their sickles in turn so that all carried the responsibility. They would then make the corn dolly to keep until the following year when a new one could replace it. This was true in North Pembrokeshire where the doll was called 'the Hag'. In Poland it was called 'Baba' or old woman, and there it would be made by two girls who delivered it with a garland, to the farmer.

The Harvest

The silver rain, the shining sun,
The fields where scarlet poppies run,
And all the ripples of the wheat
Are in the bread that I do eat.

So when I sit for every meal
And say a grace, I always feel
That I am eating rain and sun,
And fields where scarlet poppies run.

Alice C. Henderson

Mother Earth

Mother Earth
Mother Earth,
Take our seed
And give it birth.

Father Sun
Gleam and glow
Until the roots
Begin to grow.

Sister Rain
Sister Rain
Shed thy tears
To swell the grain.

Brother Wind
Breathe and blow
Then the blade
Green will grow.

Earth and Sun
And Wind and Rain
Turn to gold
The living grain.

Eileen Hutchins.

'A-reaping'

'I will go with my father a-reaping
To the brown field by the sea,
And the geese and the crows and the children
Will come flocking after me.
I will sing to the weary reapers
With the wren in the heat of the sun,
And my father will sing the scythe song
That joys for the harvest done.'

S. Maccathmhaoil.

Harvest

The boughs do shake and the bells do ring
So merrily comes our harvest in,
Our harvest in, our harvest in,
So merrily comes our harvest in.

We've ploughed, we've sowed,
We've reaped, we've mowed,
We've got our harvest in.

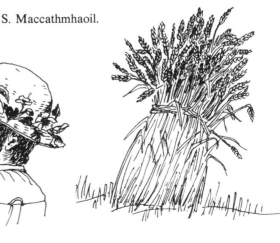

Lark Rise to Candleford

For a few days or a week or a fortnight, the fields stood 'ripe unto harvest'. It was the one perfect period in the hamlet year. The human eye loves to rest upon wide expanses of pure colour: the moors in the purple heyday of the heather, miles of green downland, and the sea when it lies calm and blue and boundless, all delight it; but to some none of these, lovely though they all are, can give the same satisfaction of spirit as acres upon acres of golden corn. There is both beauty and bread and the seeds of bread for future generations .....

With no idea that they were at the end of a long tradition, they still kept up the old country custom of choosing as their leader the tallest and most highly skilled man amongst them, who was then called 'King of the Mowers'. For several harvests in the 'eighties they were led by the man known as Boamer. He had served in the Army and was still a fine, well-set-up young fellow with flashing white teeth and a skin darkened by fiercer than English suns.

With a wreath of poppies and green bindweed trails around his wide, rush-plaited hat, he led the band down the swathes as they mowed and decreed when and for how long they should halt for 'a breather' and what drinks should be had from the yellow stone jar they kept under the hedge in a shady corner of the field. They did not rest often or long; for every morning they set themselves to accomplish an amount of work in the day that they knew would tax all their powers till long after sunset. 'Set yourself more than you can do and you'll do it' was one of their maxims, and some of their feats in the harvest field astonished themselves as well as the onlooker....

After the mowing and reaping and binding came the carrying, the busiest time of all. Every man and boy put his best foot forward then, for, when the corn was cut and dried it was imperative to get it stacked and thatched before the weather broke. All day and far into the twilight the yellow-and-blue painted farm wagons passed and repassed along the roads between the field and the stack-yard. Big cart-horses returning with an empty wagon were made to gallop like two-year olds. Straws hung on the roadside hedges and many a gatepost was knocked down through hasty driving ....

At last, in the cool dusk of an August evening, the last load was brought in, with a nest of merry boys' faces among the sheaves on the top and the men walking alongside with pitchforks on shoulders. As they passed along the roads they shouted:

"Harvest home! Harvest home!
Merry, merry, merry harvest home!"

As they approached the farmhouse their song changed to:
"Harvest home! Harvest home!
Merry, merry, merry harvest home!
Our bottles are empty, our barrels won't run,
And we think it's a very dry harvest home."

and the farmer came out, followed by his daughters and maids with jugs and bottles and mugs, and drinks were handed round amidst general congratulations .....

On the morning of the harvest home dinner everybody prepared themselves for a tremendous feast, some to the extent of going without breakfast, that the appetite might not be impaired. And what a feast it was! Such a bustling in the farmhouse kitchen for days beforehand; such boiling of hams and roasting of sirloins; such a stacking of plum puddings, made by the Christmas recipe; such a tapping of eighteen-gallon casks and baking of plum loaves would astonish those accustomed to the appetites of today.

Flora Thompson

Harvest Dollies

Wheat straw for corn dollies should be of the hollow, long-stemmed variety. Oat and rye straw is often suitable, but barley is not. Ideally it should be cut just before the crop is ripe, while the first joint just below the ear is still green. Ask permission of the farmer, and make sure that what little is taken is from the edge of the field. An alternative is to wait for the gleaning after the crop; if by then the straw seems brittle it may be damped down. First strip the side leaves to leave a clean stalk. To soften dry stalks, soak in warm or cold water, then stand straw on its end to let the surplus water drain away. Keep surplus material wrapped in a damp cloth while you are working.

Corn Dolly or Nek. This is a five straw plait made round a core of about 18 straws with good heads. Tie ends & plait 5 selected straws as shown. Width out gradually, then decrease & plait on beyond core. complete with 4 straw braid, tied & tucked in

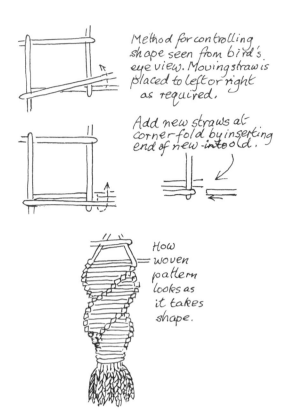

Method for controlling shape seen from bird's eye view. Moving straw is placed to left or right as required.

Add new straws at corner fold by inserting end of new into old.

How woven pattern looks as it takes shape.

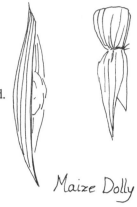

Head, arms and body are made separately and then fitted together. Fit a small ball of wool into one maize leaf and tie down, dampening and tucking in the sides to form the head.

Maize Dolly

Roll a long strip and tie off ends for arms.

For the main body, cut the narrow ends off a large leaf, form a slit in the centre to fit head 'neck' through, slide in arms and tie off to form a waist.

Experiment with straws, knotting and bending them towards your desired shape. Or try your hand at a harvest corn dolly in ribboned plait form. Choose 18 straws with good heads to be your core. Tie the end and begin plaiting 5 selected straws around the base, widening out, then decreasing. Bend the straws at right angles and outwards in the manner of a fan. Work anti-clockwise. See the diagram above, and think of numbering your straws 1-5. Straw no. 1 should be placed over 2 and 3 to lie between 4 and 5. Continue, adding new weaving straws when old ones become too short or tear. Cut the old straw off just before making a corner fold, insert the new one's thin end without splitting the old one, and proceed. Finish by tying off with a red ribbon.

For a dolly which will stand securely, use several thicknesses for the body to add weight and balance; snip the 'over' skirt for a frilly effect if you like.

The rest is up to your imagination. You may wish to create a maize bonnet, draw on a face, etc.

Children see all kinds of shapes in maize leaves if given the opportunity to play with them and form them. Whatever creature or dolly is formed, it should be allowed to dry completely, in a well-ventilated, open, dry space, for several days. Then it should retain its shape for a long time.

Maize Dollies

If possible, use the fresh maize leaves not long after they are stripped from the ear of corn. While fresh they have a moistness which allows for easy handling. Have a beige or light coloured cotton on hand for use in 'tying off', and some cotton-wool or sheeps wool for filling out.

Corn Cobs

In many cultures through the ages the 'cob' or empty ear of corn has itself been a dolly for children. Dry it off, and wrap in its own leaves or a little cloth blanket. You may add woolly hair and a tiny face, or leave it as it is.

Another playtime use of the cob is to make corn cob pipes. Cut the cob into 2″ or 3″ pieces and in one end of each piece dig out a hole with a knife blade. On the side make a hole just big enough to insert a twig or stick. Now dry off for several days. When dry, you will have a neat little pipe.

Little House in the Big Woods

'The attic was a lovely place to play, the large, round, coloured pumpkins made beautiful chairs and tables. The red peppers and onions dangled overhead. The hams and the venison hung in their paper wrappings, and all the bunches of dried herbs, the spicy herbs for cooking and the bitter herbs for medicine, gave the place a dusty-spicy smell.

Often the wind howled outside with a cold and lonesome sound. But in the attic Laura and Mary played house with the squashes and the pumpkins, and everything was snug and cosy.

Mary was bigger than Laura, and she had a rag doll named Nettie. Laura had only a corncob wrapped in a handkerchief, but it was a good doll. It was named Susan. It wasn't Susan's fault that she was only a corncob. Sometimes Mary let Laura hold Nettie, but she did it only when Susan couldn't see'.
Laura Ingalls Wilder

Harvest Recipes
Plaited Harvest Bread

1 lb flour
½ teaspoon salt
¼ pint milk
2 oz butter
1 egg, beaten
1 oz fresh yeast
1 oz sugar
1 tablespoon currants
pinch nutmeg
2 teaspoons grated lemon or orange rind

Place flour and salt in a warm bowl. Warm the milk to slightly over tepid, so that the butter will gradually melt in it while you stir. Allow the milk and melted butter mixture to cool, then stir in the egg. Mix the yeast with sugar and cream well, then set to let it froth. When the yeast mixture is bubbly, add it to the milk, mix, and add this to the flour. Stir gently, adding currants, nutmeg and rind, then leave in a warm place to rise. When double the original size, cut into three pieces, knead, then form three strips. Plait these, dampening the ends with milk to secure them. Place on a lightly greased baking sheet, let rise for 15-20 minutes. Bake at 425°F (Reg. 7) for about fifteen minutes.

Farmhouse Harvest Fruit Cake

5 oz butter
4 tablespoons golden syrup
2 tablespoons treacle or honey
¼ pt milk
¼ lb dates, chopped
¼ lb currants
¼ lb sultanas
½ lb chopped raisins
¼ lb mixed peel (optional)
¼ lb chopped nuts - hazels, brazils, etc
½ lb self raising flour
1 teaspoon mixed spice
1 teaspoon ground nutmeg
pinch of cinnamon
pinch of salt
2 eggs, beaten
½ teaspoon bicarbonate of soda

Use a 10″ round cake tin, lined with greased greaseproof paper.

Put the butter, syrup, treacle, milk, dried fruit, nuts, peel in a pan and heat slowly until the fat has melted. Gradually bring to the boil and simmer for 5 minutes, stirring occasionally. Allow the mixture to cool completely.

Sieve the flour, spices and salt into a bowl, and stir in the eggs. Add the bicarb. to the fruit mixture and pour this onto the flour. Beat well until all the ingredients are thoroughly mixed. Line the cake tin and pour in the mixture. Bake at 325°F (Reg. 3) for 1¾ hours, or until cake is well risen and cooked through.

Wheat Sheaf Harvest Bread

1 lb flour
1 teaspoon salt
1 oz fresh yeast
1 oz sugar   *Less then 1/4 c.*
½ pint tepid water or stock *1 c.*
1 tablespoon vegetable oil

Prepare yeast with sugar as above. Mix the flour, salt and oil together well, then add yeast and tepid water together. Stir well until stiff enough to be worked with the hands. Now knead well on a wooden board or table surface. When the dough seems smooth and pliable, press or roll ½ of it into a rough harvest sheaf shape to be a base for your modelling. Roll pieces of the remaining dough between the hands to form wheat stalks and bunch these together on top of your base; also model a binding rope for them if you wish, or apple, pumpkin or fruit shapes to decorate the base. Our children always enjoy making a tiny mouse to run up the wheat, and perhaps a cat on the other side. Remember either to model in small scale to allow for the dough rising, or to only let it rise for 15 minutes or so, so that your picture remains. Brush with milk or melted butter, and for extra effect, sprinkle wheat grains or oats atop the sheaf you have created before baking it. Bake at 425°F (Reg. 7) for the first ten minutes, then reduce heat slightly for a further 20-25 minutes.

For Harvest Festival

Use almond paste for modelling fruit and vegetables. Bought marzipan is very useful for this – break off the desired amount and mix it with the appropriate food colouring, a little lemon, and if your hands get sticky dab them in icing sugar. You can make little yellow bananas, lemons, corn, parsnips, pumpkins, green cabbages, peas, apples, grapes, red apples, strawberries, purple plums, grapes, etc., and use cloves for the stalks on apples. Make little trug baskets out of the marzipan and afterwards decorate the bananas and vegetables and baskets with melted chocolate put on with a paint brush. Children find this very absorbing work.

If you have time to make your own almond paste, this is a good recipe:
(Make only half the amount if you require only a small quantity)

1 lb ground almonds
½ lb icing sugar
½ lb caster sugar
2 small eggs
juice of half a lemon
1 tablespoon sherry or brandy (optional)
1 teaspoon orange flower water or rose water
A few drops of almond essence

Mix the sugar, icing sugar and almonds together, then add the beaten eggs and the other ingredients. Make into a smooth paste and roll out using extra icing sugar.

6. The Preserving Year

Bottling - The Oven Method

With the minimum of basic kitchen equipment it is possible to successfully bottle extra fruit with good results. You will need clean 1 or 2 lb. jars, either jam jars or special bottling ones such as Kilner jars.

Choose and prepare your fruits, washing, using pieces which are not bruised, 'topping and tailing' when necessary as with gooseberries, etc .. Cut pears or apples into even slices and keep in cold water and lemon juice to prevent discolouration. Plums, damsons, cherries, berries, currants, apricots, are best done whole.

Pack your jars with the prepared fruit. If you rinse the jars with cold water before you pack, the fruit seems to slide down better. A long-handled wooden spoon is useful for packing closely; jarring the bottle down on the hand several times also brings the fruit down. Pack as compactly and as close to the brim as possible.

Now lay patty pans, saucers or lids on top of the jars to prevent fruit scorching, place on the oven shelf so that the bottles or jars do not touch one another. Heat the oven **gradually** to 240°F (Reg. ¾) so that in 1 hour the fruit has slightly changed colour and shrunk down a bit in the bottle.
Note: ¾ hour is sufficient for berried fruit and softer varieties of apple.
     1½ hours for pears and tomatoes.
Have ready either boiling water or syrup (½ lb. sugar to the pint).

When the fruit is ready, remove each bottle out of the oven separately with bottle tongs or a dry tea-towel or cloth and fill with the boiling syrup up to within ¾ inch of the brim.

Fix the cover immediately and **air tight.** If you don't have special lids, porosan is excellent. Alternatively, try the time-honoured method of using a treble thickness of greaseproof paper, each piece stuck together with hot water starch and firmly tied down over the rim of the filled bottle. (Take care not to let the inside of such paper covers get wet by tipping or spilling.)

Store away in a dry, cool place. Fruit prepared this way may be used 'neat' as a pudding, or in pies, tarts, flans, etc...

Notes on testing jam

For testing whether jams or jellies are set before putting them into jars, put a small amount on a cold saucer and put in a cool place. When cool the jam should wrinkle and a skin form. Or dip the stirring spoon in the jam, lift it and hold horizontally: if the juice forms a heavy clot or flake as it drips from spoon, the jam is set.

Or: buy a sugar boiling thermometer. Before putting into the jam heat the thermometer by dipping in hot water. A good set should be about 220°F/110°C but more safely 222°F/111°C.

Lemon Curd
Can be made at any time

4 oz butter
juice and grated rind of 4 large lemons
4 beaten eggs
1 lb caster sugar

Melt the butter in a double saucepan and add the rind and strained lemon juice. Stir in the eggs and sugar mixing well until the sugar has dissolved. Continue heating, stirring occasionally, to thicken the lemon curd.

Pour into clean, heated jam jars, seal with pot covers and store in a cool cupboard. This should be eaten within a month.

This works equally well with 3 oranges and 1 lemon.

Marmalade
Beginning of the year

3 lbs Seville oranges
2 lemons
6 pints water
6 lbs preserving or granulated sugar

Wash the oranges and lemons and remove the peel carefully, making sure that you do not include any of the white pith. Shred the peel finely and put it in the preserving pan.

Squeeze the juice from the fruit, save the pips and pith and tie them up in muslin. Put this bag and the juice into the pan with peel, add the water and bring to the boil, then simmer gently for about 2 hours until the peel is really soft and the liquid in the pan has been reduced by half.

Remove the bag of pips and pith and squeeze it dry. Stir the sugar into the pan and dissolve it thoroughly, then boil rapidly until the mixture reaches setting point.

Cool for about 15 minutes, then pour the marmalade into the jars and seal with pot covers. Store in a cool place.

Orange and Lemon Marmalade

6 Seville oranges
2 large lemons
4 pints water
6 lbs sugar

Wash fruit well: cut into quarters, and remove centre pith. Put pith and pips into a small basin. Cut the fruit into thin slices and try to keep all the juice. Put the fruit as you cut it into a large bowl. Put 3½ pints of water over the fruit and the remaining water over the pips and pith. Leave to stand for 24 hours.

Pour fruit and water into preserving pan and strain water from pips into pan. Tie pips and pith into a piece of muslin and tie this to side of pan suspended in liquid. Simmer until liquid is reduced by half and peel tender. (1½-2 hours). Then remove pip bag and press out water into pan. Add heated sugar to the fruit stirring until dissolved. Then allow to boil only when all the sugar is dissolved and continue boiling for 10 mins: test for set and then allow marmalade to rest off the stove for a few minutes and stir really well. Pot in warm jars and cover in the usual way.

Elderflower Syrup

Try to gather your elderflowers from trees well away from busy roadsides or field borders where there has been spraying. It is said that early morning picking is best for fresh flavour. You'll want 1-1½ lbs elderflowers to 1 lb sugar.

Boil up one pint water to 1 lb sugar and pour this over as many flowers as can be covered by the liquid. Leave for 24 hours, covered with a clean cloth. Strain. Bring **just** to boiling point, then remove from heat. If you wish to store the juice for a long time, you may want to add a few citric acid crystals, to taste. Pour into hot, sterilised bottles, **right** up to the top. Screw on tops tightly so that no air space remains, and as it cools it ought to contract.

This is a beautiful drink, diluted, perhaps with a slice of lemon for hot summer days.

Gooseberry Chutney

8oz onions
3 lb green gooseberries
12 oz soft brown sugar
1½ pt spiced vinegar
½ oz mustard seeds
1 oz salt
6 oz seedless raisins

Peel and roughly chop the onions. Top and tail gooseberries and wash well. Place gooseberries and onions in preserving pan and add remaining ingredients and stir well. Simmer in uncovered pan for 1 hour until smooth and thick. Pour chutney into clean hot jars and cover in usual way. Store in cool, dark place.

Hodgkin

1 lb strawberries
1 lb raspberries
1 lb stoned cherries
1 lb halved apricots
1 lb sliced peaches
2½ lb granulated or caster sugar
1 bottle brandy

This beautiful conserve takes all summer to prepare and then should be allowed to mature until Christmas when it is delicious eaten with cream or ice-cream and the brandy can be served separately as a liqueur.

Place 1 lb strawberries in a large stone jar. Add 8 oz sugar and pour in enough brandy to cover, then seal. Add each fruit as it comes into season, 1 lb at a time, plus 8 oz sugar and brandy to cover, stirring gently with a wooden spoon on each occasion. Finish in Sept. and cover with tightly fitting plastic skin or a lid. Leave until Christmas to mature.

Gooseberry and Elderflower Jelly

Half fill a preserving pan with green sharp gooseberries. Barely cover with water. Simmer until the gooseberries have burst into a soft puree. Drain through a jelly or stockinette bag, without squeezing extra juice through. Measure the liquid.

Put the juice with warmed sugar back in the preserving pan, allowing ¾ lb to every pint. Boil until setting point is reached. Have ready half a dozen elderflower heads per litre (2 pts) of juice tied in a muslin or stockinette bag. Put it into the jelly when it is almost at setting point, and leave it there when you remove the pan from the stove. Taste occasionally and extract the bag when the muscat flavour is right: remember that flavours weaken as they cool. Pot in the usual way.

Raspberry Preserve

3 lbs raspberries
3 lbs sugar
1 oz butter

Warm a saucepan and rub it with the butter. Put in the raspberries and heat gently until the juice runs. Warm the sugar in a low oven, then add to the raspberries and beat over a low heat for up to half an hour. Pour into hot jars and cover.

Herb Vinegar

1 pt white vinegar
6 sprigs or so of mint, tarragon, sage, marjoram, thyme
    or basil (use your own combination)
½ teaspoon caster sugar

Put the vinegar into a saucepan and bring to the boil. Wash your herbs and put some into the vinegar, first crushing them slightly between your fingers. Add the sugar and stir well. As soon as the vinegar reaches boiling point, take off the heat. Allow the vinegar and herbs to become quite cold. Meanwhile wash and dry a few fresh sprigs of herbs and remove any faded leaves. Put the fresh sprigs into a bottle, strain the vinegar into it and cover with a screw top.

A mixture of mint, tarragon and sage is particularly good.

Mint Sauce

½ pt vinegar
6 oz demerara sugar
¼ pt freshly chopped mint

Boil the vinegar and sugar together for a minute, make sure that the sugar is dissolved. Add finely chopped mint, stir well and leave to go cold. Pour into screw topped jars – plastic, not metal. Put a waxed paper on the top of the sauce beforehand. Add a little extra vinegar and sugar when you use it.

Piccalilli

Late Summer

Cauliflower, cut into little pieces or florets.

2 green tomatoes chopped up
1 lb shallots, small as possible
2 larger onions chopped up
chopped up French or runner beans
some chopped up marrow
8 oz coarse kitchen salt
2 small cucumbers cut up
2½ teaspoons capers
½ teaspoon celery seed
4 oz butter

1 oz plain flour
¾ pt malt vinegar
4 oz sugar

2½ teaspoons turmeric
3 tablespoons dry mustard
few chillis, optional

Put the cauliflower, green tomatoes, beans, marrow and 2 kinds of onions into a pan and dissolve 8 oz salt in 6 pts of water and pour over vegetables. Set aside in cool place for 12 hours. Drain off liquid and add cucumbers, capers, celery seed, teaspoon salt and 2 pints of fresh water in the pan. Bring to boil over high heat stirring occasionally. Then reduce heat to moderate and cook uncovered for 10 mins. until vegetables tender. Drain into colander, discard liquid and place vegetables in a bowl.
Melt butter in heavy saucepan over moderate heat. Stir in flour and mix. Pour in vinegar and cook, stirring until sauce thickens and comes to the boil.

Reduce heat to low and simmer for 3 mins. then beat in the sugar, turmeric, mustard and chillis. Pour half the sauce over the vegetables and set the rest aside and cover. Marinate vegetables for 24 hours then stir in the reserved sauce. Pack into sterilised jars and cover tightly.

Country Chutney

3 lbs cooking apples
4 pts vinegar
1 lb brown sugar
4 oz coarse salt
1 tablespoon ground nutmeg
1 teaspoon ground cinnamon
½ oz mustard seeds
3 lbs stoned and quartered plums
2 lbs tomatoes, skinned and quartered
1 lb onions, peeled and chopped
3 ridge cucumbers chopped, not peeled
2 small pieces root ginger
12 peppercorns
12 cloves
6 chillis

Peel and slice the apples, remove cores and bruised parts. Boil vinegar with sugar, salt, nutmeg, cinnamon and mustard seeds, then add the fruits and veg. Put ginger, peppercorns, cloves and chillis in piece of muslin and tie to handle of pan suspended in liquid. Simmer gently until reduced to pulp – about 1½ hours. Pour into warm jars and cover in usual way.

Jean's Pickled Cucumbers

2 lbs of ridge cucumbers
2 onions
1 large green pepper
2 oz salt
1 pt cider vinegar (or stale cider)
1 lb brown sugar
¼ teaspoon ground cloves
1 dessertspoon of mustard seeds
½ teaspoon turmeric

Wash the cucumbers, don't peel them, slice thinly into a bowl and mix with peeled and sliced onions, shredded pepper and salt. Leave to stand for 3-4 hours, wash under the running water and then boil with vinegar for 20 mins. Add sugar, spices, stir well until boiling again. Cool in bowl, then pot and seal.

Crisp Pickled Onions

2 lbs shallots
2-3 tablespoons coarse salt
2 pts spiced vinegar

Spiced Vinegar:

1 oz peppercorns
¼ oz blade mace
¼ oz cloves
6 bay leaves
½ oz bruised ginger root
2 teaspoons mustard seeds
¼ oz whole allspice
¼ oz stick of cinnamon
4 chillis, crushed
1 tablespoon salt
2 pts malt vinegar

Boil spices and salt in a little vinegar to extract flavour then add remaining vinegar and boil for 3 mins. strain and cool.

Use hot vinegar if you want soft pickled onions but cold for crisp ones.

Peel onions and spread on a shallow dish, sprinkling with the salt. Peel onions under running cold tap to avoid your eyes running. Leave overnight. Put the onions in a colander and rinse under the cold tap, leave to drain well. Pack them not too tightly into jars and arrange with the handle of a wooden spoon. Cover with cold spiced vinegar and tie down – you can sprinkle a few spices on the top.

Grandma Maas' Best Dill Pickles

You will need:
Either large fresh cucumbers or the smaller 'ridge' variety
Sprigs of fresh dill
Some small onions, a few pieces of cabbage, carrot, green pepper
Pickling spices
3 tablespoons coarse (not iodized) salt
1 fluid oz wine vinegar
2 pts water, brought to the boil
Kilner jars, warmed

Wash and scrub the cucumbers thoroughly in cold water, slice lengthwise into pieces. Place in the bottom of each jar a sprig of dill, small onion, small pieces of cabbage, carrot and green pepper. Sprinkle in about ½ teaspoon mixed pickling spices. Add cucumber pieces until jar is almost full. Place a bit more dill or vegetables on top. Cover with a brine made from the salt, vinegar and water. Pour over the contents of the jars while the brine is hot, just off the boil. Seal tightly. Leave in the cupboard or larder for at least three months before use. Grandma Maas lined her cellar steps with them, made them in the autumn and brought them out for cold meals the following summer.

Green Tomato Chutney

1½ lbs green tomatoes
1 lb apples
8 oz sugar (brown)
12 oz sultanas
4 oz onions
salt
1 oz mixed spice
1 pt vinegar
pinch of dry mustard

Use an enamelled pan or casserole if possible. Chop the ingredients and cook slowly together until the colour deepens and the mixture gradually thickens. This will take a good two hours simmering. Pour into jars and seal.

Marrow Chutney

4 lbs marrow
½ lb onions
6 cloves
1½ lbs sugar
½ oz turmeric
9 chillis
1½ oz ground ginger
1½ oz mustard
2 pts vinegar
salt

Dice the marrow, lay on a large dish and sprinkle with salt. Leave overnight. Drain. Tie the cloves and chillis in a small muslin bag (if you wish) and boil with the other ingredients for 10 mins. before adding marrow. Boil for a further half an hour, until tender and put into jars.

Bean Pickle

6 lbs runner beans
6 large onions
1 quart white vinegar
4 oz plain flour
2 oz dry mustard powder
1 lb sugar
1 teaspoon each turmeric and black pepper

Slice the beans and onions thinly and cook in a little water until fairly tender. Drain well. Add a little vinegar to the flour to dampen it into a smooth paste. Then mix together in a large saucepan the vinegar, flour, mustard, sugar, pepper and turmeric. Bring to the boil and stir as it thickens; add beans and onions and continue stirring until the mixture boils again. Put into jars, and cover while hot.

Plum Chutney

6 lbs plums
½ lb onions
2 lbs sour apples
salt and allspice
1½ lbs dates
½ lb sugar
ginger (optional)
vinegar

Remove the stones from the plums, and cut all the ingredients into small pieces. Place the ingredients in a pan and cover with a pint of vinegar. Add 1 oz salt and spices, stirring well into the mixture. Simmer gently for a good 2 hours, or even longer. Put into warm jars and cover tightly.

Plum, Orange and Walnut Jam

3 lbs plums
2½ lbs sugar
2 oranges
½ lb shelled walnuts

Cut up the oranges with the peel on and put them through the mincing-machine. Stone the plums and tie the stones in a piece of muslin. Put the cut-up plums, stones and minced orange and sugar into the pan and simmer for about 1½ hours. Add the walnuts, roughly chopped and continue cooking for ¾ hour.
Test for setting in the usual way and put into pots

and cover. This is particularly good to eat around Christmas time.

Blackberry Cordial

Pour 1 pt white wine vinegar over 2 lbs ripe blackberries. Let it stand in an earthenware jar for up to seven days, stirring often to extract the juices. Strain well at the end of the week and bring the liquor to the boil along with 1 lb sugar and ½ lb honey – preferably in an enamel or stainless steel saucepan. Bring to a strong boil, then remove from the heat and allow to cool. Bottle, cork, and keep in a dark cupboard or the larder. This is said to be a good remedy for winter colds and sore throats, as well as a pleasant drink.

Apple and Cinnamon Butter

4 lbs cooking apples, peeled, cored and sliced
2 oz butter
7 oz sugar
3 teaspoons powdered cinnamon
4 whole cloves
½ pt water

Simmer all the ingredients in a covered saucepan until the apples are quite tender. Remove the cloves. Beat until creamy, heat until boiling and stir for a few minutes and then pour into heated jars and cover at once.

Hedgerow Jelly

3 lbs crabapples, windfalls, or cooking apples
2 lbs blackberries or rowan berries
2 lbs dark plums or damsons
Juice of 1 lemon
Sugar

Wash the apples and chop them up roughly. Wash and drain the blackberries or rowan berries. Wash and cut up the plums or damsons. Put all the fruit into a large pan with the lemon juice and add enough cold water to bring to the level of the fruit.
Bring to the boil and simmer until the fruit is tender and well broken down. Strain through a jelly bag overnight.
Measure the strained juice and weigh out 1 lb sugar for each pint. Heat the juice gently in the pan and add warmed sugar to taste, stirring until dissolved. Bring to the boil and cook rapidly until setting point, then skim, pot and seal in the usual way.

Apple and Blackberry Jam

3 lbs blackberries
1 lb green cooking apples, diced
4 lbs sugar
½ pt water

Cook blackberries and apples slowly until soft. Add sugar, boil to setting.

Beetroot Chutney

2 lbs beetroot
½ lb cooking apples (after peeling)
1 lb onions
½ lb brown sugar
1 pt spiced vinegar
salt and pepper to taste
1½ teaspoons cornflour

Cook beetroot and mince. Finely chop apple and onion and put in a saucepan with vinegar. Cook until tender, then add the cooked beetroot and sugar. Mix cornflour in a little vinegar and add to the ingredients, cooking gently until the mixture thickens. Put into warm jars and cover.

Blackberry Syrup

Stew blackberries, using about ¼ pint water to every 3 lbs fruit, until the juice is well drawn. Strain, then add for every pint of juice 6 oz sugar. Boil for 15 minutes, then bottle after cooling.

Elderberries and blackberries may be combined using the above recipe.

Elderberry Syrup

Rinse your gathered elderberries and remove the heavier stem and leaves. Add water and simmer slowly to extract the juices, using enough water to prevent burning. When cool, sieve through a cheesecloth, squeezing to give as much juice as possible. Take ½ gallon of the juice, put into a pan over a gentle heat and add to it the white of an egg, well beaten to a froth.

When it begins to boil, skim the froth as long as it rises; then for each pint add 1 lb cane sugar. Boil slowly until the syrup forms, then let stand until cool. Put into bottles, cover with paper pricked with holes.

Serve hot (diluted) on cold winter evenings, or when the children (or you!) have a sore throat or cold. For small children this is soothing for coughs in the night.

Quince and Apple (or Crabapple) Jelly

6 lbs cooking apples and quinces
3 cloves (optional)
sugar
juice of 1 lemon

Cut apples and quinces into quarters and cover with cold water in a saucepan. Add cloves. Bring to the boil and cook gently and well. Put apples and juice into strainer (a special jelly bag is best) and drain overnight.

Next day, measure the liquid and add about 1 lb sugar to every pint of liquid. Heat slowly to dissolve sugar, then bring to the boil and allow to boil rapidly until the jelly is set when tested.

During the time when boiling to make the jelly you can add some finely chopped mint from the garden and make your own apple or quince mint jelly which is delicious with lamb, poultry and game. (A few drops oil of peppermint may be added too).

Chestnut Jam

2 lbs sweet chestnuts
1½ lbs sugar
3 teaspoons vanilla essence
½ pt water

Prepare the chestnuts by cutting a small cross on both sides, as this means easy peeling later. Boil for half an hour, then peel and skin them. Put through a sieve or mouli. Now make a syrup by cooking the sugar in ½ pt water, adding the vanilla essence. When it thickens add the crushed chestnuts and cook gently until thick. Put in hot jars, cover.

IV. AUTUMN DAYS

Red in Autumn

Tipperty-toes, the smallest elf,
Sat on a mushroom by himself,
Playing a little tinkling tune
Under the big round harvest moon;
And this is the song that Tipperty made
To sing to the little tune he played.

"Red are the hips, red are the haws,
Red and gold are the leaves that fall,
Red are the poppies in the corn,
Red berries on the rowan tall;
Red is the big round harvest moon,
And red are my new little dancing shoon."

Elizabeth Gould

Harvest

Now all the farmers from far and wide
Have gathered their bounty of countryside:
Corn and barley from field and wold,
Honey from beehive and wool from the fold,
Fruit from the orchard all ripe, red and gold,
Log for the fire to keep out the cold.

Dorothy Hancock

Colour

The world is full of colour!
'Tis Autumn once again
And leaves of gold and crimson
Are lying in the lane.

There are brown and yellow acorns,
Berries and scarlet haws,
Amber gorse and heather
Purple across the moors!

Green apples in the orchard,
Flushed by a glowing sun;
Mellow pears and brambles
Where coloured pheasants run!

Yellow, blue and orange,
Russet, rose and red –
A gaily-coloured pageant –
An Autumn Flower bed.

Beauty of light and shadow,
Glory of wheat and rye,
Colour of shining water
Under a sunset sky!

Adeline White

Song

'The leaves be greene,
The nuts be browne,
They hang soe high
They will not come downe."

(Can be done as a 2 person round)

"The Leaves be Greene"
by the Consort of Musicke

The Leaves be Greene

The leaves be greene, the nuts be browne, they hang soe high, they will not come downe.

Autumn Leaves for Preserving

You can pick a variety of leaves which will do well when preserved – such as beech, maple, eucalyptus, hornbeam, laurel or lime. Pick branches of them when they have just turned and before the leaves start to fall.

Split the woody stems about 3″ up and stand them in a bucket of warm water for a few hours. If any of the leaves curl then throw them away as they will not last.

Make a solution of glycerine and water
1 part glycerine
2 parts water

Boil this together and put the mixture about 2″ deep in a container and stand the branches in this for several weeks until the glycerine solution has been soaked up. You can stand the glycerine container in a large bucket for convenience and put the branches into this to stand more safely. Now you can make decorative arrangements with the leaves.

Here are some useful flowers to dry in the autumn to liven up the home during the autumn and winter:

The straw daisy (or Helichrysum) – an annual
Chinese lanterns – perennial
Honesty – take off the outer leaves which leaves you with the silver pods – biennial
Achillea – perennial

Ripe seed heads of the **poppy** and **love in a mist**
Sea Lavender – perennial

To dry these, it is best to hang them in bunches upside down in a cool, dry, dark place.

Teasels, bullrushes, catkins, and pussy-willows also look beautiful indoors.

1. Michaelmas – September 29

Michaelmas is the feast of St. Michael, patron saint of the sea and maritime lands, of ships and boatmen, of horses and horsemen. As Michael nam Buadh, Michael the Victorious, he is known as conqueror of the powers of darkness; the Angel who hurled Lucifer down from heaven for his treachery. Folklore in England holds that the devil landed in bramble bushes, and therefore one must not pick blackberries after Michaelmas.

This festival was important in Celtic Christianity, particularly for the dedication of churches. From St. Michael's Mount in Cornwall to Mont St. Michel in France the importance of the saint is still signified. He is usually portrayed as riding a white steed and carrying a three-pronged spear in one hand and a three-cornered shield in the other. Because of the strong good vs. evil theme in this heritage, the story of a similar figure, St. George and the dragon, is appropriate at Michaelmas. The following verse, taken from the old Gaelic, uses the dragon symbol for evil.

MICHAEL THE VICTORIOUS

Thou Michael the Victorious,
I make my circuit under thy shield.
Thou Michael of the white steed
And of the bright, brilliant blade!
Conqueror of the dragon,
Be thou at my back.
Thou ranger of the heavens!
Thou warrior of the King of all!
Thou Michael the victorious
My pride and my guide!
Thou Michael the victorious
The glory of mine eye.

The Michaelmas Daisy takes its name from this festival and is in flower at this time. It is celebrated in similar fashion to the Harvest festival, and at one time this included the roasting of the annual Michaelmas Goose. Food given in the previous Harvest section and that suggested throughout Autumn can be adapted for any one of the festivals at this season.

St. George

There was a time when St. George came to the province of Libya, to a city which is said to be Silene. And by this city was a great lake wherein was a dragon which poisoned all the country. The people assembled to slay him, but when they saw him they fled. And when he came nigh the city he poisoned the people with his breath; and therefore the people of the city gave him every day two sheep to feed him, so that he should do no harm to the people; and when there were not enough sheep, there was taken a man and a sheep. Then was a law made in the town that there should be taken the children and young people by lot, and each one should be taken, were he gentle or simple, when the lot fell on him or her. So it happened that many of them had been taken, when the lot fell upon the King's daughter, wherefore the King was sorry, and said unto the people; "Take gold and silver and all that I have, and let me have my daughter". They said "How, Sir? Ye have made the law and our children be now dead and ye would do the contrary. Your daughter shall be given or else we shall burn you and your house."

Then the King began to weep and said to his daughter, "Now shall I never see thy marriage". Then he arrayed his daughter like as she should be wedded and kissed her and gave her his blessing and after led her to the place where the dragon was. When she was there St. George passed by on a white horse, and when he saw the young lady he asked what she did there, and she said, "Go your way, fair young man, that ye perish not also." Then he said, "Tell me what is the matter and why you weep". When she saw that he would know she told him that she was delivered to the dragon. Then said St. George, "Fair daughter, I shall help thee in the name of Jesu Christ". Then she said, "For God's sake young man, make your way and abide not with me, for you may not deliver me." Thus, as they spake together, the dragon appeared and came running to them; and St. George was upon his horse, and drew out his sword and made the sign of the Cross, and rode hardily against the dragon and smote him with his spear, and hurt him sore, and threw him to the ground. And St. George slew the dragon and smote off its head. Then returned they to the city, and all the people came to meet them rejoicing and the King offered to St. George as much money as there might be numbered; but he refused all and commanded that it should be given to the poor people for God's sake.

The Kite

Once upon a time there was a boy whose father helped him make a kite. They worked on it in the winter until its wooden cross was surrounded by transparent paper of yellow, red and blue.

In the summer, the boy flew his kite and the sun was so pleased with its colours that he sent his clearest rays of light. And so the kite looked like a flaming cross in the sky. The boy let his kite rise as high as it could until the string came to an end and the kite could go no farther.

Whoosh! There came a gust of wind! The string snapped and the kite went flying into the sky. The boy saw it rise higher and higher. Soon the kite had gone so high that he could hardly see it. Up there in the blue sky was much to be seen.

First the kite met a crow.

'Good morning', croaked the crow.

'Good morning', replied the kite.

'Are you a bird with your flaming wings and long tail?'

'No, I am not a bird.'

'What are you then and from whence do you come?'

'I come from the lad standing down there; he made me himself.'

'And where are you going?'

'That I do not know. I want to fly into the sky.'

'Then you do not belong here. Up here everybody knows whence he comes and where he goes. I fly every winter to the south and every summer to the north; I advise you to return to the human beings below, for if you do not know where you are going, you will lose your way in heaven.' But the kite was determined and rose further into the heights.

Then the kite met a seed.

'Good day', whispered the seed.

'Good day', replied the kite.

'Are you also a seed with your shoots and roots?'

'No, I came from the lad standing down there.'

'Where are you going?'

'I do not know. I want to travel into heaven'.

'Then you do not belong here. Up here everyone knows where he is going. I sail through the air and take in that which moves from the east to the west – the warmth of the sun. When I have it into myself I travel down again and bring it to the earth. The earth will make a flower grow out of me. If you do not know what to do, I advise you to descend to the earth or you will lose your way in these heights.'

But the kite did not hear and soared higher. Then he glided past a cloud.

'Good evening', murmered the cloud.

'Good evening', said the kite.

'Are you a cloud with your flaming sunset red?' asked the cloud.
'No, I was made by human beings. I come from the boy down there.'
'And where are you going?'
'Oh, only into the sky.'
'Then you do not belong here. Everyone here knows his purpose. I collect the lost red of the sunset and turn it into the red of the sunrise. I rain down with the red of the sunrise and bless the earth and when I have done that the sun carries me up once more so that the red of the sunrise can again be made. And so I travel up and down. I advise you to go back to the boy, for without a goal you will lose your way up here.' But the kite would not return and rose higher.

Then he came to the stars.
'Good night', sang the stars.
'Good night' sang the kite.
'What news do you bring to us, you comet of the earth?' sang the stars.
'I come from the boy who lies sleeping down there on the earth,' said the kite. He is waiting until I return but in the meantime he has fallen asleep and is dreaming about me.'
'We ask you to take our blessings back to the boy', sang the stars and everyone of them gave the kite some of their light.
Then came the Angel Michaël. He took a star and hurled it towards the strange newcomer. The kite burst into flames and like a torch plunged into the depths. The boy awoke from a dream. But when he looked around he realised that it could not have been an ordinary dream for next to him lay the cross of his kite and the coloured paper had been devoured by flames. And the cross was no longer wooden but was of bright, heavenly iron. The boy was astounded when he saw that. But he was also vexed because his beautiful kite was gone.

At home his father comforted him: 'Let us be glad. If your kite was not burnt, you would never have received this cross of heavenly iron. This iron is lighter than the lightest wood and stronger than the strongest steel. Let us use it to make a new kite.'

This they did, and next summer when the kite rose to the heavens he again met those who travelled from north to south, from east to west and from heaven to earth. And when he came to the stars he again met Michaël and again he plunged burning to the earth. But the cross of heavenly iron shone even more brightly than before. And this happened for many years and with every year the cross grew brighter and stronger. And when the boy had grown up, the cross took on a different form: it turned into a shining sword which gleamed with the light of the stars. With this sword the young man travelled through the world and he became a knight and servant of Michaël.

D. Udo de Haes

Simple Kite

You need: bamboo or very thin dowling
string, glue, tissue paper, line.

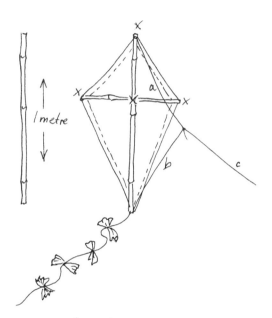

Note: line c should be knotted to string a b so that the lengths a and b are the same.

Split a piece of bamboo: the upright needs to be about 1 metre. ⅓ way down make a notch and fit another piece across which should measure same length between crosses (as indicated): tie in centre. Fix a piece of string round the whole of the outside and cut out the shape of the kite in tissue paper allowing an extra 1″ round the edges.

Do the same for both sides and glue together. Fix tail piece with string and pieces of tissue paper and attach the line as shown in diagram.

2. Halloween – October 31

Corresponding to the Celtic feast of Beltane or May Day which ushered in the heat and vegetation of summer, was the Eve of Samhain which marked Nov. 1 as the first day of Winter's cold and barrenness. The transition period from autumn to winter was thought in ancient times to include the return of the souls of the departed to the warmth and light they remembered from their former lives. Not only ghosts were anticipated, but general mischief, witchcraft, magic and hobogoblins of every sort. As a Christian festival, Halloween was first proclaimed within the Benedictine Order in the year 998, and later recognized by Pope John XIX in 1006. It is the eve of Hallowmass, now known as All Saints' Day which also honours and remembers the dead particularly the saintly.

There is an old saying in Cardiganshire that on Halloween a bogie sits on every stile. It is said that in Ireland on that night the fairy hills are thrown open and the fairies swarm forth; and any bold enough may peep in the open green hills to see their treasure, if he dare. From South Uist comes the saying:

> *'Halloween will come, will come.*
> *Witchcraft will be set agoing,*
> *Fairies will be at full speed,*
> *Running in every pass.*
> *Avoid the road children, children.'*

In the North of England a sprig of rowan was put above the door to ward off evil, and a bowl of oats in water or milk was left outside the door to appease any visiting spirits. To frighten away witches, people took to carving faces on hollowed-out turnips and placing candles inside. This custom has been handed down to present-day turnip lanterns and the New World pumpkin 'Jack-O-Lantern'.

As genuine fear subsided through the ages, the themes of the festival have been retained in playful fashion, and in many areas Halloween is a time for pranks and dressing up. One wonders if the party game of bobbing for apples might be reminiscent of the distant past, when suspected witches were 'bobbed' to test their innocence or guilt. At any rate, the mask, the black cat, the pointed black hat and the old-white-sheet-ghost help us face the coming winter darkness in bold and jovial fashion!

The Hag

The Hag is astride
This night for to ride;
The Devil and she together:
Through thick, and through thin,
Now out and then in,
Though ne'er so foul be the weather.

A Thorn or a Burr
She takes for a Spur:
With a lash of a Bramble she rides now,
Through Brakes and through Briars,
O'er Ditches and Mires,
She follows the Spirit that guides now.

No Beast, for his food,
Dares now range the wood;
But hushed in his lair he lies lurking:
While mischiefs, by these,
On land and on Seas,
At noon of Night are a working.

The storm will arise,
And trouble the skies;
This night, and more for the wonder,
The ghost from the Tomb
Affrighted shall come,
Called out by the clap of Thunder.

Robert Herrick

The Witch

I saw her plucking cowslips,
And marked her where she stood:
She never knew I watched her
While hiding in the wood.

Her skirt was brightest crimson,
And black her steeple hat,
Her broomstick lay beside her -
I'm positive of that.

Her chin was sharp and pointed,
Her eyes were - I don't know -
For, when she turned towards me -
I thought it best - to go!

Percy H. Ilott

The Witches' Spell

Double, double, toil and trouble;
Fire burn, and cauldron bubble.
Fillet of a fenny snake
In the cauldron boil and bake;
Eye of newt, and toe of frog,
Wool of bat, and tongue of dog,
Adder's fork, and blind-worm's sting,
Lizard's leg and owlet's wing,
For a charm of powerful trouble,
Like a hell-broth, boil and bubble.
Double, double, toil and trouble;
Fire burn, and cauldron bubble.

William Shakespeare.

There was an old woman toss'd up in a basket
Nineteen times as high as the moon;
Where she was going I couldn't but ask it,
For in her hand she carried a broom.

'Old woman, old woman, old woman', quoth I,
'O whither, O whither, O whither, so high?'
'To brush the cobwebs off the sky!'
'Shall I go with thee?' 'Ay, by-and-by.'

Three little ghostesses
Sitting on postesses
Eating butttered toastesses
Greasing their fistesses
Up to their wristesses
Oh, what beastesses
To make such feastesses!

Hey-how for Hallowe'en,
When all the witches are to be seen,
Some in black and some in green,
Heyhow for Hallowe'en!

'Trick'n and Treat'n'

It was Hallowe'en night: the moon was full, the air was cold, and the trees were craggy. The figures of two demons could be seen treading up a winding lane. One was a scaly red demon with a long floppy tail; he might have been a dragon or a devil, or perhaps one of those huge prehistoric lizards you sometimes see in museums. Only he wasn't; for one thing he was only three foot six inches tall. And his companion, a black demon with wings like a bat, was even smaller.

Both were carrying sacks. Occasionally they'd take things out of the sacks and gobble them up with a grin. What do you think they were gobbling?

Pieces of flesh? Magic herbs? No, not a bit of it! They were gobbling chocolate bars, toffee apples, liquorice - all kinds of candy. You see, the figures weren't really demons at all, they were two brothers called Richard and Paul, who had dressed up as demons for Hallowe'en night. For it's an old custom in our part of the world that on Hallowe'en night all the children put on disguises, and go from door to door demanding 'trick'n Treat'n'. This means 'Either you give me a treat, or I will play a trick on you'. Naturally most people prefer to give a treat, so that by the end of the evening, every child in the area has a big sack full of candy – enough to give him indigestion for a week.

Christopher Floyd

Trick or Treat

On Halloween it is a popular pastime for American and Canadian children to dress up and go to friends' houses on a 'Trick'n Treat'n' expedition. There is a tacit assumption that it is better to offer a treat to the children than suffer the trick!

Traditional Games for Hallowe'en

Hallowe'en is sometimes known as Nut Crack Night. Whisper you lover's name and throw a nut into the fire. If it burns quietly, all is well but if it cracks and bursts, your lover will not be true to you!

Apple Bobbing

Put some apples on strings and hang them from a line between two trees. Have the apples hanging at suitable heights for the children coming to the party. Each child has to try and take a bite out of their apple with their hands behind their backs.

If they manage it you can cut off the string and give them the apple. If they twist the stalk off and say the letters of the alphabet as they do so, the initial that fits with the number of twists indicates the initial of the one they will marry!

Have a bowl or tub of water and ask the participants to try and catch one of the bobbing apples with their teeth, not using their hands – this can be a bit wet so have a towel handy! When they have caught their apple, perhaps by the stalk, they can remove the peel in one long strip and throw it over their left shoulders. It is said that the one who catches the largest apple is in line for the largest fortune.

Stick two apple seeds on your cheeks and give the name of a suitor to each one – the one that sticks longest loves you the most.

If a girl sits alone and veiled before her mirror at midnight with a single candle burning she will see reflected in the mirror the face of her future husband looking over her left shoulder while the clock strikes twelve.

A game some of the older children would probably like to play is 'Hunt the Ghost'. Dress an adult or older child up in a sheet and then the children can give chase in the darkness, with or without torches.

Apple or Nut on the Mound

Find a very small apple (perhaps a crabapple), a nut or even a 10p. and place this on top of a large mound of flour. The best way to do this is to press as much flour as you can firmly into a large mixing bowl or tub, and then place a tray over the top and get someone to help you turn the whole thing over and carefully remove the bowl. Place the coin, nut or apple on top in the middle and then form a circle around it and when the music stops, the one who stands near the knife has to cut out a slice of flour without dislodging the apple. Continue with the

game; the one who dislodges the apple has to get it out with their mouth and you usually get a face full of flour but if you're lucky you also get a 10p! In some areas they use soot instead of flour!

Table Decorations

For simple but effective table decorations, try the following ghosts and witches. Even very small children are able to help with these.

Ghosts are easily done with white paper serviettes; place a smallish ball of wool or soft paper in the centre of the open serviette, gather it round and tie to give a 'head' impression. Place by each child's plate for Halloween tea – in a dimly-lit room they look happily 'ghostly' and after tea may be used for sticky faces and fingers!

Witches' hats may be made from small semi-circles of black paper and placed on satsumas or small oranges. Older children like drawing toothy faces on the satsumas with felt-tip pens!

You can make little witches out of pipe cleaners and felt, using wool for the hair and even make little broomsticks out of a little stick with twigs.

During the Halloween celebrations one of the special dishes is a large pot of mashed potato, which is brought in with lucky charms and 5p's mixed into it. Everybody has a spoon and takes it in turn to scoop some onto their plates. The lucky charm tells your fortune and the coins assure you of a fortune in life. Sitting round in candlelight, is the time for ghost stories and eerie happenings to be told.

Colcannon

Another traditional dish for Halloween is Colcannon. The Irish serve this with sausages or other cooked meat.

1 lb green cabbage or kale, chopped up.
1½ lb hot mashed potatoes
2 tablespoons chopped onion
a little milk, seasoning
2 oz butter

Cook the cabbage until tender but still crisp and then mix it with the mashed potato, onion and milk until it forms a smooth, firm mixture; add seasoning. Heat half the butter in a frying pan and add the mixture. Fry until the edges are crisp, dot with the rest of the butter and brown under the grill. (This is also delicious with a grated cheese and millet topping.)

Into this mixture you can add a button, silver coin, a ring, thimble and a horseshoe. Whoever finds the ring will marry within the year (or 'when young' if it is a child), the coin indicates riches and the horseshoe good fortune. The finder of the thimble or button will never marry! We didn't have all these things handy when we were doing it, so we made them out of small pieces of clay, allowed them to harden and wrapped them in silver foil, before they went into the mixture.

Jack O Lantern

Jack O Lantern, Jack O Lantern,
Your light it doth shine,
Sitting up upon the window
And your light it is mine.

Once you were a yellow pumpkin
Sitting on the sturdy vine,
Now you are my Jack O Lantern,
And in the night you will shine.

Sung to the tune of the Snow Song
– 'Oh where do you come from' (See p.119)

Cut the top off a turnip or swede – preferably in a flower pattern (zig-zag) and keep the top. Scoop out the inside vegetable and then make a face. Fix string on either side and place a night-light inside and put the lid back on. Now you have a Jack O Lantern.

Do the same with a pumpkin to shine in the house, perhaps as a table centre-piece.

Halloween Cake

Try making a Halloween cake. Make a victoria sandwich cake mix (see p. 26) and put into two greased and floured pudding basins. After cooling, sandwich together the two flat surfaces with a butter icing, and you have the round shape of a pumpkin.

Use orange modelling icing to cover the cake, dipping your hands in cornflour first and then decorate with green and orange modelling icing for the green leaves on top and the face. Stick the pieces on with butter icing and perhaps use liquorice for the eyes.

Farmer Boy

'....... And every morning he fed his pumpkin, that he was growing for the County Fair.

Father had shown him how to raise a milk-fed pumpkin. They had picked out the best vine in the field and snipped off all the branches but one, and all the yellow pumpkin blossoms but one. Then between the root and the wee green pumpkin they carefully made a little slit on the under side of the vine. Under the slit Almanzo made a hollow in the ground and set a bowl of milk in it. Then he put a candle-wick in the milk, and the end of the candle-wick he put carefully into the slit.

Every day the pumpkin vine drank up the bowlful of milk, through the candle-wick, and the pumpkin was growing enormously. Already it was three times as big as any other pumpkin in the field .....

At the County Fair

The tall judge had taken the red ribbon and the blue ribbon out of his pocket ....

He turned around slowly. Slowly he took a pin from his lapel and stuck it through the blue ribbon. He was not very near Almanzo's big pumpkin. He was not near enough to reach it. He held out the blue ribbon, above another pumpkin. He leaned, and stretched out his arm slowly, and he thrust the pin into Almanzo's pumpkin.

Father's hand clapped on Almanzo's shoulder. All at once Almanzo could breathe, and he was tingling all over. Mr Paddock was shaking his hand. All the judges were smiling. Ever so many people said 'Well, well, Mr Wilder, so your boy's got first prize!'

Mr Webb said, 'That's a fine pumpkin, Almanzo. Don't know as I ever saw a finer .....'
Mr Paddock said:
'I never saw a pumpkin that beat it for size. How'd you raise such a big pumpkin, Almanzo?'

Suddenly everything seemed big and very still. Almanzo felt cold and small and scared. He hadn't thought before, that maybe it wasn't fair to get a prize for a milk-fed pumpkin.

Maybe the prize was for raising pumpkins in the ordinary way. Maybe, if he told, they'd take the prize away from him. They might think he had tried to cheat.

He looked at Father, but Father's face didn't tell him what to do.
'I-I just - I kept hoeing it, and -' he said. Then he knew he was telling a lie. Father was hearing him tell a lie. He looked up at Mr Paddock and said 'I raised it on milk. It's a milk-fed pumpkin. Is-is that all right?'
'Yes, that's all right', Mr Paddock answered.

Father laughed, 'There's tricks in all trades but ours, Paddock. And maybe a few tricks in farming and wagon-making, too, eh?'

Then Almanzo knew how foolish he had been. Father knew all about the pumpkin, and Father wouldn't cheat.

Laura Ingals Wilder

Pumpkin Recipes

Pumpkin Soup

Melt ½ oz butter and add a large chopped onion and 2 teacups of cooked pumpkin. Stir in a little flour and then add 1 pt chicken or vegetable stock and milk to taste and bring to the boil, stirring. Add a pinch of ground cloves, ½ teaspoon sugar and 1 teaspoon lemon juice and a few drops of Tabasco, salt and pepper. Allow to simmer until well cooked, and then blend in the liquidiser or sieve. Bring back to the boil and stir in some double cream, check seasoning and serve with croutons.

or alternatively

Cut 2 lbs of pumpkin flesh into small pieces. Season with salt and pepper and put this into a saucepan with some chopped celery. Cover with 1½ pts milk and 1 pt vegetable or chicken stock. Simmer for about 30 mins. Sieve or liquidise and add chopped parsley and a lump of butter before serving.

Pumpkin Pudding

½ pt plus 3 tablespoons milk
¼ lb brown sugar
¼ teaspoon grated orange peel
¼ teaspoon ground ginger
scant ½ teaspoon ground cinnamon
scant ½ teaspoon salt
3 eggs lightly beaten
½ pt less 3 tablespoons freshly cooked puréed pumpkin

Preheat the oven to 350°F (Reg 4). Combine the

milk, brown sugar, orange peel, ginger, cinnamon and salt in a large mixing bowl. Stir thoroughly, then add the lightly beaten eggs and the puréed pumpkin. Beat vigorously with a spoon until the mixture is smooth and pour it into a 1½ pt shallow greased baking dish. Place the dish in a large pan in the middle of the oven and pour enough boiling water into the pan to come half-way up the sides of the baking dish. Bake the pudding for about 1¼ hours, or until a knife inserted in the centre of the pudding comes out clean. Remove the dish from the water and either cool the pudding to room temperature before serving, or refrigerate for at least 3 hours. If you like, the pudding may be made in six china or glass moulds, in that case, bake it for only 40 minutes until firm. Serve with whipped cream.

The Halloween Pumpkin
by the 'Pumpkin Pie' Folksingers

Pumpkin Pie Song

In the West there lived a maid,
She was a cook who knew her trade.
She baked sweet puddings and at harvest time,
She made delicious Pumpkin Pie.

CHORUS:
Pumpkin Pie, Pumpkin Pie,
She made a special Pumpkin Pie,
Pumpkin Pie, Pumpkin Pie,
You never tasted such Pumpkin Pie.

Now this young cook was in love with a man,
He was a gardener who worked the land,
He grew potatoes, beans and, O my,
Orange Pumpkins three feet high.

At the flower show he won the prize
For his Pumpkin of enormous size
He gave it to the cook to try,
So she made a very special Pumpkin Pie.

CHORUS

She used eggs and milk and sweet brown sugar,
Cinnamon, nutmeg and some ginger.
Special spices, for she would try,
To woo the gardener with Pumpkin Pie.

After one spoonful, his eyes began to glaze,
After two mouthfuls, he fell into a daze.
'My lovely cook, you're the apple of my eye,
I'd like to taste some more of your Pumpkin Pie.

CHORUS

Now the gardener and the cook, they're happy as
can be,
Living together with children three,
They'll be happy until they die,
With regular helpings of Pumpkin Pie.

CHORUS

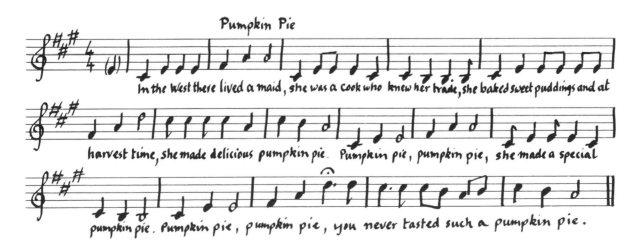

89

Pumpkin Bread

15 oz pumpkin
12 oz sugar
3 oz vegetable oil
2 eggs
7 oz flour
½ teaspoon baking powder
1 teaspoon bicarb of soda
1 teaspoon each salt, cloves, cinnamon and mixed
spice.
½ teacup raisins and nuts (optional)
2 oz water

Add sugar to oil and mix, then add eggs, pumpkin, spices sifted with flour, water and nuts or raisins. Bake an hour at 350°F (Reg 5).

Best Pumpkin Pie

1 unbaked pastry shell
15 oz pumpkin purée (thick)
3 eggs, slightly beaten
8 oz sugar
½ teaspoon salt
1 teaspoon (generous) cinnamon
¼ teaspoon cloves
½ teaspoon nutmeg
½ teaspoon ginger
1 cup top of the milk or evaporated milk
Juice and rind of lemon

Prepare pie crust. Combine eggs, sugar, salt, spices and lemon and beat well. Blend in pumpkin. Add milk and beat well. Turn into pie crust. Bake in hot oven (450°F, Reg. 8) for 10 minutes, then reduce heat and bake at 350°F (Reg. 4) for 40-45 minutes. Pie is done when tested by inserting a knife to see if it comes out clean (test centre). Serve with whipped cream.

Pumpkin Cookies

8 oz sugar
4 oz magarine
1 (small) egg
8 oz pumpkin
8 oz flour
half teacup each of walnuts and raisins
2 teaspoons cinnamon
1 teaspoon vanilla essence
1 teaspoon each baking powder and bicarb of soda
pinch of salt

Mix well, and drop on greased flat biscuit tin. Bake 8 to 10 minutes in 375°F (Reg 5) oven. These are good as they are, or may be iced if there are 'Sweet-tooths' in the family.

* Don't forget to save your pumpkin seeds and roast them. Place on well oiled baking dish, sprinkle with salt and put in a hot oven for ten minutes or until golden brown and crunchy. Delicious!

3. All Souls' Day

November 2 is by tradition the Day of All Souls, and it was long believed that the unhappy souls of the dead would return to their former homes. On the eve of All Souls it was customary to keep kitchens warm and leave food on the table overnight for the visiting spirits. Until 1850 the following 'Shropshire Soul Cakes' were distributed on All Souls' Day, and there is a similar 'soul cake' tradition in Belgium, Bavaria and the Tyrol.

Shropshire Soul Cakes

3 lbs plain flour
8 oz softened butter
8 oz sugar
1 oz yeast
2 eggs
1 teaspoon allspice
milk

Sift the flour and work in the slightly softened butter. Cream the yeast with a teaspoon of the sugar. Mix flour with the eggs, yeast and enough milk to make a light dough. Leave to rise, covered, in a warm place for about thirty minutes. Then work in the sugar and spice and form into flat bun shapes. Let rise for fifteen minutes, then bake at 425°F (Reg 7) for fifteen minutes.

Cakes were given to visitors, and distributed in particular to the poor, which meant that the latter by rights could ask for them. Hence, the origin of the custom of going 'souling' at the end of October or first day of November, still practised by children in parts of Cheshire and Shropshire. They go from house to house singing and collecting bits of food or money. This is no doubt also the origin of the American "trick'n treat'n" tradition, now associated more with Halloween.

Soul Cake Song

A soul, a soul, a soul cake,
Please good missus a soul cake,
An apple, a pear, a plum or a cherry,
Or any good thing to make us merry.
One for Peter, two for Paul,
Three for him who made us all.

The lanes are very dirty,
My shoes are very thin,
I've got a little pocket
To put a penny in.
If you haven't got a penny,
A half-penny will do,
If you haven't got a half-penny,
God Bless you.

Repeat first verse.

Soul Cake

A soul a soul a soul cake, please good missus a soul cake, an apple a pear a plum or a cherry, or

any good thing to make us merry. One for Peter two for Paul, three for him who made us all.

4. Guy Fawkes Night – November 5

On this English holiday bonfires are lit and effigies made of Guy Fawkes in memory of the day in 1605 when he was discovered in the cellars of Parliament preparing to blow it up. The 'burning of the Guy' and the great bonfires enjoyed on this night must surely go further back in origin, however, to the Celtic Samhain and the heralding of winter. In fact, Lancashire Parkin, now associated with Guy Fawkes night, was once called 'Harcake' or 'Soul Hars Cake', originally named for the Norse god Odin or Har and eaten on All Souls Day.

Lancashire Parkin

6 oz plain flour
1 teaspoon salt
1 teaspoon ground ginger
2 teaspoons ground cinnamon
1 teaspoon bicarb of soda
10 oz medium oatmeal
6 oz black treacle
5 oz butter
4 oz dark brown sugar
¾ pt milk
1 egg

Sift together the flour, salt, spices and soda, then add oatmeal and mix lightly. Heat the treacle, butter, sugar and milk together until the butter has melted. Cool slightly, add the egg and beat well. Pour these ingredients into the centre of the dry ones and stir rapidly until smooth. Turn into a greased and lined 7″ square tin. Bake at 350°F (Reg 4) for one hour. Store in an airtight tin for at least two weeks before using, as this mellows the flavour.

Lark Rise to Candleford

'Remember, remember, the fifth of November,
The gunpowder treason and plot.
A stick or a stake, for King James's sake
Will you please to give us a faggot?
If you won't give us one, we'll take two!
The better for us and the worse for you'.

The few housewives who possessed faggot stacks (cut from the undergrowth of woods in the autumn and sold at one and sixpence a score) would give the children a bundle or two; others would give them hedge-trimmings, or a piece of old line-post, or anything else that was handy, and, altogether, they managed to collect enough wood to make a modest bonfire which they lit on one of the open spaces and capered and shouted around and roasted potatoes and chestnuts in the ashes, after the manner of boys everywhere.

Flora Thompson

After the fireworks and bonfire come back into the house to a candlelit supper. Lots of hot soup or jacket potatoes are always favourites and you can decorate the table with Apple Pigs and gingerbread men.

Fried bread initials. Before the party, cut the children's initials out of rather stale, thickish bread with a sharp knife and fry quickly in deep fat until crisp and golden. Drain and keep crisp in an airtight tin and float them on top of each child's bowl of soup.

Mixed Vegetable Soup

At home we make a lot of soups in the autumn and winter months and really just use whatever vegetables we have in the house that are in season.

Start off by gently frying some onion in butter and oil and then mix in a little flour and some stock. Stir this well in: the stock can be made from a good chicken or vegetable cube. To this we add any of the following:
chopped celery, carrot, swede, Jerusalem artichoke, cabbage, curly kale, leek, mushrooms, potatoes, sweetcorn, some butter beans or other pulses which have been soaked overnight and cooked separately, or split lentils.
Little chunks of whole sweetcorn.

Your pot of soup will now be quite large and to this you can add tomato puree, seasoning, and herbs to taste. Bring to the boil and simmer gently for 20 minutes. A short while before serving you can add some cooked noodles, spaghetti or other pasta in small pieces or cooked rice. The same applies to the cooked pulses – you don't want these items cooking in the soup so long that they become disintegrated by the time you serve them.

Serve with grated cheese and bread and butter or garlic bread:-

Garlic Bread

Make a mixture of butter, chopped garlic, salt, pepper and a little lemon juice and mixed herbs and cut the French bread into sections placing some of this mixture in each cut. Wrap in tin foil and put in a low oven for 20-30 minutes.

Jacket Potatoes

These are lovely to have round a bonfire on Guy Fawkes Night, or at the supper table afterwards.

Here are some ideas for different ways to serve them after they have been cooked.

1. Simply cut in half and spread with butter, salt and pepper.
2. Cut the jacket potato in half and scoop out some of the potato from the middle. Mash this with some butter, salt and pepper and form a bank round the potato and then crack an egg into the middle. Put a knob of butter, salt and pepper and a little cream and Parmesan over the egg and bake in a hot oven for 10-15 minutes until the eggs are set.
3. Cut in half and serve with a mixture of cream cheese and chives in the middle.
4. Cut in half and put a mixture of grated cheese, millet, butter, salt and pepper on each half and then return to the oven or put under the grill to brown.
5. Cut in half and scoop out the potato and mash with butter, a little marmite, grated carrot, salt and pepper and return to the potato shell and reheat for a few minutes. Instead of grated carrot you can add sweetcorn and top with grated cheese which you brown under the grill.

Croutons

Fry little squares of bread in hot oil and garlic, then drain them on kitchen tissue. These are lovely on top of the soup with grated cheese.

Lentil Pottage

½ lb lentils
2 large onions, sliced into rings
2 carrots, chopped
2 sticks of celery, chopped
1½ pts stock
thyme sprigs
parsley sprigs
garlic (optional)
½ oz butter

Wash the lentils and soak overnight in a bowl. Drain off the water and place them in a large saucepan with the sliced onions, carrots and celery and garlic. Pour the stock over the vegetables and add the herbs, salt and pepper. Bring the soup to the boil and simmer for 1½ hours. Blend or sieve the soup and return the liquid to the pan. If the soup is too thick add some more stock to adjust. Before serving stir in the butter and serve very hot.

94

Gratin Dauphinoise

Butter a large dish and then alternate with layers of thinly sliced raw potatoes, chopped onion, sprinkle of grated cheese, salt, pepper, cayenne. Build up the layers and press them down firmly. Finish with a good grating of cheese and seasoning, some butter and a carton of cream and some milk. Cook in a slow oven for 2-3 hours.

Potato shapes

Boil some potatoes and when they are cooked allow them to dry out completely. Mash them with an egg yolk, a little butter, milk and some pepper. When they are cool shape them into pear shapes or balls and then egg and breadcrumb them. Fry in hot shallow fat for 4 minutes each side. You can use a piece of macaroni for a pear stalk.

Sweetcorn Fritters

3 eggs
1 tablespoon lemon juice
2 tablespoons oil
8 oz cottage cheese
1 oz flour
large can of sweetcorn
clove of garlic, crushed lemon and parsley for garnish
seasoning

Put the eggs, seasoning, lemon juice and oil into the liquidiser, (or whisk together). Then add the cottage cheese and flour and liquidise until smooth. Stir in the drained sweetcorn and the crushed garlic. Drop spoonfuls of this mixture into hot fat and fry until gold and crisp. Drain onto kitchen paper and then serve with lemon slices and parsley sprinkled over the top.

Autumn Dishes with Nuts

Nut and Rice Rissoles

2 oz rice
1 onion
1 oz margarine
4 oz ground nuts
1 egg

2 oz breadcrumbs
½ teaspoon sage
seasoning
4 oz cheese, grated
pinch of nutmeg

Peel and chop the onion finely, then cook in the margarine for a few minutes. Cook the rice until just tender; add the ground nuts, cheese, breadcrumbs, sage, nutmeg and seasoning to cooked onion and rice. Cool, add the egg and form into rissoles. Fry in hot oil until golden brown.

Savoury Nut Roast

6 oz ground nuts (mixed)
1 large onion, chopped and fried
1 large tomato
4-5 oz wholewheat breadcrumbs
1-2 beaten eggs
seasoning

Mix the nuts, breadcrumbs, onion and tomato and add seasoning to taste. Bind with the beaten eggs. Place the mixture in a greased ovenproof container with a lid and bake for 25 minutes in a moderate oven. Serve with a tomato sauce, mushrooms and potatoes.

Nut Balls for Soup

3 oz of any kind of ground nuts
3 oz brown breadcrumbs
1 teaspoon of chopped parsley (or more)
2 teaspoons grated lemon peel
¼ teaspoon celery salt
1 egg

Mix all together and bind with the beaten egg. If necessary, add a little stock or water, but the mixture should be stiff. Shape into small balls with floured hands and cook in a vegetable stew or thick soup for 35-40 minutes.

Best Nut Loaf

12 oz self-raising flour
6 oz sugar
1½ teaspoons salt
1 beaten egg
12 fl oz milk
2 tablespoons corn oil
¾ cup chopped walnuts

Sift together the dry ingredients. Combine egg, milk and oil, blending well. Add to dry ingredients and beat well. Stir in nuts. Turn into greased loaf tin, bake at 350°F (Reg 4) for 1 to 1¼ hours or until firm and done. Remove from pan, cool on rack.

Almond Rice Roast

1 lb brown rice
1 generous teaspoon yeast extract
4 oz ground almonds
1 large onion or two medium
3 teaspoons chopped parsley
1 teaspoon chopped marjoram
2 eggs, beaten
2 oz margarine
to garnish:
2-3 tablespoons blanched almonds (optional)

Cook the rice, simmering for a good fifteen minutes until all the water is absorbed, then add yeast extract to the hot rice. Cool, fork to separate grains, then mix with the ground almonds, grated onion, herbs and eggs. Grease a baking dish with half the margarine, put in the rice mixture and top with the rest of the margarine. Bake at 400°F (Reg 5/6) for 30 minutes. Top with blanched almonds and bake a further 5-10 minutes.

This is nice served with either a tomato sauce or stewed apple.

Date and Walnut Cake

12 oz flour
½ oz sugar
1 teaspoon baking powder
½ oz butter
4 oz walnuts
1 lb dates, finely chopped
1 teaspoon bicarb of soda in a teacup of cold milk
1 egg

Cream the butter and sugar, add the egg, then the flour, dates and walnuts. Mix with the milk and bicarb, beat well. Mix in baking powder. Bake in a moderate oven for 1 to 1½ hours.

Lentil and Walnut Roast

1 large onion, chopped
1½ oz margarine
4 oz lentils
3 oz ground walnuts
seasoning
1 teaspoon sage
1 level dessertspoon yeast extract
2-3 oz breadcrumbs

Wash the lentils and place in a pan; just cover with water. Cook until the lentils are just tender. Cook the onion in the margarine for 30-40 minutes until tender. Add the cooked lentils to the onion with the remaining ingredients. Place in a greased dish and bake in a hot oven for 40 minutes.

Nut and Grain Savoury

8 oz whole grain (wheat, pearl barley, millet etc)
¾ pt water
¼ pt milk
2 tablespoons corn oil
2 medium onions
2 tomatoes
4 oz mushrooms
2-3 oz cashew nuts or blanched almonds
1 teaspoon yeast extract
1 teaspoon chopped parsley

Soak the grain overnight. The following day, drain and then simmer in the water and milk for an hour. Prepare the other ingredients, wash, chop and fry the onions, tomatoes and mushrooms in the oil until just tender. Place in the bottom of an ovenproof dish, stir the nuts, yeast extract and parsley into the cooked grains and add salt to taste. Bake in the centre of a moderate oven, 350°F (Reg 4/5) for half an hour. Serve hot with a green salad or green vegetables.

Carrot Cake

This is a beautifully moist cake which keeps well stored in an airtight container for three to four days. It can be left plain, but the Cream Cheese Frosting is a popular addition to this recipe, in which case it is best stored in the refrigerator.

Makes 16 squares:

½ lb carrots
6 oz soft brown sugar
6 fl oz vegetable oil
3 eggs
5 oz plain flour, or:
3 oz plain flour and 2 oz wholewheat flour
1¼ level teaspoons bicarbonate of soda
1¼ level teaspoons baking powder
1 level teaspoon cinnamon
¼ level teaspoon nutmeg
¼ level teaspoon salt
1 oz walnuts (optional)
2 oz raisins (optional)

96

Cream Cheese Frosting:
3 oz full fat soft (cream) cheese
1½ oz soft margarine
¼ teaspoon vanilla essence
5 oz icing sugar

Walnut pieces to decorate (optional)

Prepare a moderate oven, 350°F (Reg 4). Brush a 8″ square cake tin with melted fat or oil. Line base with greaseproof paper; grease paper.

Peel and finely grate carrots. Place sugar and oil together in mixing bowl, beat together with a wooden spoon. Beat eggs and add gradually to sugar and oil, beating well after each addition.

Sift plain flour (place wholewheat flour into bowl containing sugar and oil if this is used), bicarbonate of soda, baking powder, cinnamon, nutmeg and salt together and beat into egg mixture. Stir in carrots.

Chop walnuts, if used, and stir into cake mixture with raisins, if used.

Place mixture into cake tin and bake in centre of oven for 50 minutes to 1 hour. Test by pressing with fingers. If cooked, cake should spring back and have begun to shrink from sides of tin. Turn out and cool on a wire rack.

Cream Cheese Frosting: place cream cheese, margarine and vanilla essence in a bowl. Mix together with a wooden spoon and beat until smooth. Sift icing sugar and beat into cream cheese mixture until smooth. Spread icing over top of cake. Serve cake cut into 2″ squares and decorate each square with a piece of walnut, if used.

Flapjacks

4 oz brown sugar
4 oz butter or margarine
1 rounded dessertspoon golden syrup
6 oz whole oats
¾ teaspoon ground ginger

First put the sugar, fat and syrup in a saucepan and heat gently until the fat has melted, giving it a stir now and then. Take this off the heat and stir in the oats and ginger, mixing thoroughly. Now pour the mixture into a prepared 8″ square baking tin and press it out evenly using a spoon or the back of your hand. Bake in the oven 300°F (Reg 2) for 40-45 minutes. Allow the mixture to cool in the tin for 10 minutes before cutting into oblong bars. Leave in the tin until quite cold before removing.

If you like sultanas and nuts, these can be added to the mixture before putting into the tin.

Gingerbread Cake

4 oz margarine
9 oz treacle or golden syrup
4 oz brown sugar
10 oz flour
1 level teaspoon bicarb of soda
2 level teaspoons salt
1 teaspoon ground ginger
1 teaspoon cinnamon
1 egg
about ¼ pt milk

Melt the fat with the treacle or syrup and sugar over gentle heat. Sift the flour, bicarb, salt and spices into a bowl. Hollow out the centre and add the beaten egg and milk. Then pour in the syrup mixture. Beat until smooth and pour into a lined loaf tin, say 9″ x 5″, and bake in slow oven 325°F (Reg 3) for about 1½ hours until springy to the touch.

Can be eaten plain or spread with butter.

Gingerbread Man

Run, run as fast as you can
You can't catch me I'm the Gingerbread Man!

Once upon a time there was an old couple who were sad because they had no children. One day the old woman said 'Husband, I will make a gingerbread man.'

So she made some dough and rolled it out and cut a little gingerbread boy which she placed on a tray. She put currants for his eyes and buttons and melted some chocolate for his hair, his hands and his feet and then she put him in the oven.

The old man said 'That does smell good' and when it was ready the old woman opened the oven door and out jumped the Gingerbread Man who ran out through the door laughing, whilst the old couple shouted at him to stop.

'Run, run as fast as you can,
Your can't catch me I'm the Gingerbread Man!'
Down the street he ran with the old couple running after him. Eventually, he met a cat who meowed

'Stop, little Gingerbread Man, you look good enough to eat'. But the Gingerbread Man just laughed and ran away singing:

'Run, run as fast as you can
You can't catch me I'm the Gingerbread Man!'
Then he met a dog who woofed at him and said 'Stop, little Gingerbread Man, you look good enough to eat'. 'Oh no!' said the Gingerbread Man and he ran on down the street.

'Run, run as fast as you can
You can't catch me I'm the Gingerbread Man!'
So off he ran with the old couple, the cat and dog following behind him. Next he met a cow who mooed 'Stop, little Gingerbread Man, you look good enough to eat'. 'Oh no!' said the Gingerbread Man and he ran on down the road laughing.

'Run, run as fast as you can,
You can't catch me I'm the Gingerbread Man!'
Then he met a horse who whinnied to him 'Stop, little Gingerbread Man, you look good enough to eat.' 'Oh no!' cried the little Gingerbread Man and he ran off down the road with the old couple, the cat, the dog, the cow and the horse all following behind him.

Eventually he came to a river which he couldn't get across, and by the side lay a Sly Old Fox. 'Do you want to get across the river, little Gingerbread Man, because I'll carry you if you like?'

'No, No,' said the Gingerbread Man 'I don't trust you, you'll eat me up.'

'No, I don't eat Gingerbread Men – climb on my back.'

So the Gingerbread Man climbed onto the back of the fox, and the fox swam across the river.

'Help, help,' cried the Gingerbread Man, 'My feet are getting soggy and wet.'

'Climb onto my head little Gingerbread Man.' So he climbed onto the fox's head.

As they got deeper and deeper into the river the Gingerbread Man began to get wet again.

'Climb onto my nose, to keep dry little Gingerbread Man.'

So the silly Gingerbread Man climbed onto the fox's nose, and with a sniffle, a snaffle and a snap the fox swallowed the Gingerbread Man and that .... was ......the end of the Gingerbread Man ....

'Very tasty', said the fox, 'Very tasty indeed'.

Damp Gingerbread

12 oz golden syrup
4½ oz margarine
9 oz plain flour
½ teaspoon salt
1¾ teaspoons bicarb of soda
2 teaspoons ground ginger
½ teaspoon mixed spice
1 large egg
½ pt milk

Prepare a tin approx 7" x 11" and line the base with greased greaseproof paper. Melt the margarine and syrup together gently. Meanwhile put the dry ingredients into a bowl and pour on the syrup mixture, mixing thoroughly. Then beat the egg and milk together in a separate bowl and add that little by little to the other ingredients. Pour this into the cake tin and bake in centre of oven, 350°F (Reg 4) for 50 minutes or until the centre is springy. Cool in the tin for 5 minutes before turning out onto a wire tray. Sprinkle with sieved icing sugar.

Gingerbread Men and House

1½ lb plain flour
1 tablespoon bicarb of soda
½ teaspoon salt
1 dessertspoon ground ginger
½ teaspoon each ground cinnamon, nutmeg and cloves
¼ teaspoon ground cardamom
4 oz butter
8 oz soft brown sugar
1 teacup black treacle (or golden syrup)
2 tablespoons evaporated milk
a little juice and rind of orange and lemon

Sift the flour with the soda, salt, juice, rind and spices into a mixing bowl. Place the butter, sugar and treacle in a saucepan and stir over gentle heat until dissolved. Allow this to cool a little, then mix it into the flour with enough evaporated milk to give a very firm dough. Chill the mixture for 30 minutes before rolling out and shaping as required.

For decoration:
currants, glace cherries, soft Royal Icing (see May Day cake).

The above dough, makes 3-4 dozen gingerbread men about 3½" high. Set oven at 325°F (Reg 3). Grease several baking sheets. Roll out the mixture a good ¼″ thick. Cut out a cardboard gingerbread man or use a cutter for making the men and women. Lift them up carefully and place them on the prepared baking sheets. Press currants in to make the eyes and waistcoat buttons and a small piece of glacé cherry for the mouth. Bake in a pre-set oven for 10-15 minutes: cool slightly and then carefully remove them from the baking sheet. With a little icing and a writing tube you can decorate the details of the men putting in their noses, belts, cuffs, etc. If you know which children are coming to the Guy Fawkes party you can put the initial of each child at the bottom. Melted chocolate can be put on with a brush to make hair, hands and feet.

Gingerbread House

Use the same amount of dough as in the original recipe, a little sugar syrup (dissolve 1 lb granulated sugar in ½ pt water and boil steadily without stirring until sugar is about 280°F (use sugar thermometer). Allow syrup to cool, then store by pouring it into a large, clean, dry screwtop jar). You will also need some soft royal icing.

Set oven at 325°F (Reg 3). Grease several baking sheets. Cut out a paper guide as follows: for long walls, 1 rectangle 5″ x 10″: for roof, 1 rectangle 4″ x 10″: for side walls, 1 piece, basically 5″ square rising to a gable with 4″ sides.

Roll out gingerbread to about one-eighth inch thick. Use paper guide to cut 4 walls, 2 roof pieces. Place sections carefully on baking sheets and bake in pre-set oven for 10-15 minutes. When cold, use the forcing bag and writing tube and decorate with royal icing, marking the windows and doors and the tiles of the roof. Join the pieces together by dipping the edges in sugar syrup boiled to 280°F. Then cover the joins with icing, and decorate with silver balls, smarties etc. You can finish it off with your own touches – it is quite a treat to put something special

in the middle for them to find when the cake is dismantled.

You can, for example, use silver foil for the windows and doors or for a pond outside.

Brandy snaps make good chimneys and the fencing could be slivers of chocolate flake.

The ridge tiles on top could be little jelly sweets and there could be climbing roses made out of angelica and crystallised rose petals or fruits.

One secret is that the gingerbread needs to be fairly hard when it comes out of the oven. Tap it and make sure it sounds hollow to the touch. Sometimes people cheat and leave the cardboard cut outs inside!

Cheese Straws

6 oz plain flour
salt, pepper, pinch of cayenne
4 oz butter
1 egg yolk
4 oz finely grated cheese (cheddar or cheshire)
1 tablespoon water

Preheat the oven to 375°F (Reg 5). Sift the flour with the seasoning into a mixing bowl, drop in the butter and cut it into the flour. Rub it in lightly and quickly with your fingertips until the mixture looks like breadcrumbs. Add the cheese and stir it in with a knife. Mix the egg yolk and water, add to the dry ingredients and mix quickly to a firm dough. Knead lightly until smooth and chill for ½ hour before rolling out to about ¼″ thick. Cut into narrow strips about 2″ long or into rounds with a fluted cutter. Children can happily work this dough using their own star and animal cutters. Bake on a lightly greased baking sheet until cooked, 15-20 minutes; it makes them look very attractive if you decorate the tops with a small amount of celery salt, or paprika.

Apple Pigs

Take a large red, rosy apple and put it on its side. Place 4 cocktail sticks underneath for legs and you will have the stalk as a tail. Cut a small apple in half and attach one half to the body and the opposite end to the tail using another cocktail stick. The cut side of the apple forms the face. You can make eyes by inserting silver balls or currants and use little leaves or angelica for ears. To stop the face from turning brown dip it in a little lemon or vinegar.

Toffee Apples

Choose good apples without bruises

Melt 1 tablespoon of butter with 2 large tablespoons golden syrup
Add 1 large tablespoon of sugar
Juice of half a lemon

Allow the ingredients to boil to a deep toffee brown and then dip the apples into the mixture, having inserted a lollypop stick, small length of bamboo or thin dowling, in one end. Dip into cold water to set and lay out on greaseproof paper.

OR

8 apples
1 lb. demerara sugar   3 oz. butter
8 oz. treacle or golden syrup   ¼ pt. water

Bring ingredients to the boil and test whether it is ready by dropping a small amount into cold water – if it separates into a hard nodule but not brittle it means it is ready. Let it stand off the heat a little while before dipping apples in it.

5. Bonfire Songs

The Animals –
to the tune of 'When Johnny Comes Marching Home'

The animals went in two by two, hurrah, hurrah (repeat once)
The animals went in two by two, the elephant crashed with the kangaroo,
And they all went into the ark, all to get out of the rain.

The animals went in three by three, hurrah, hurrah, (repeat)
The animals went in three by three, the wolf was stung by the bumblebee,
And they all went into the ark, all to get out of the rain.

The animals went in four by four, hurrah, hurrah, (repeat)
The animals went in four by four, the great hippopotamus stuck in the door,
And they all went into the ark, all to get out of the rain.

The animals went in five by five, hurrah, hurrah, (repeat)
The animals went in five by five, the snail ran in to stay alive,
And they all went into the ark, all to get out of the rain.

The animals went in six by six, hurrah, hurrah, (repeat)
The animals went in six by six, on the back of the turtle the monkey did tricks,
And they all went into the ark, all to get out of the rain.

The animals went in seven by seven, hurrah, hurrah, (repeat)
The animals went in seven by seven, the little pig thought he was going to heaven
And they all went into the ark, all to get out of the rain.

The animals went in eight by eight, hurrah, hurrah,
(repeat)
The animals went in eight by eight, the snake rode
the zebra 'cause he was late,
And they all went into the ark, all to get out of the
rain.

The animals went in nine by nine, hurrah, hurrah,
(Repeat)
The animals went in nine by nine, the frog jumped
in at the end of the line,
And they all went into the ark, all to get out of the
rain.

The Goose Round

Why doesn't my goose speak as well as thy goose
When I paid for my goose twice as much as thine.

Why doesn't my goose fly as well as thy goose
When I paid for my goose twice as much as thine.

Why doesn't my goose lay as well as thy goose
When I paid for my goose twice as much as thine.

Why doesn't my goose sing as well as thy goose
When I paid for my goose twice as much as thine.

The animals went in ten by ten, hurrah, hurrah,
(Repeat)
The animals went in ten by ten, hurrah, hurrah,
(Repeat)
The animals went in ten by ten, if you want any
more you must sing it again,
And they all went into the ark, all to get out of the
rain.

Old John Braddle-um

Number one, number one,
Now my song has just begun,
With a rum tum taddle-um
Old John Braddle-um
Oh what country folks we be.

Number two, number two,
Some likes boots but I likes shoes,
With a rum tum taddle-um
Old John Braddle-um
Oh what country folks we be.

Number three, number three,
Some likes coffee but I likes tea,
With a rum tum taddle-um
Old John Braddle-um
Oh what country folks we be.

Continue right up to twelve and let the children fill in
their own rhymes.

101

There was an Old Woman

There was an old woman who swallowed a fly.
I wonder why she swallowed a fly.
Perhaps she'll die.

There was an old woman who swallowed a spider,
That wriggled and jiggled and tickled inside her.
She swallowed the spider to catch the fly.
I don't know why she swallowed a fly.
Perhaps she'll die.

There was an old woman who swallowed a bird.
How absurd, she swallowed a bird.
She swallowed the bird to catch the spider,
That wriggled and jiggled and tickled inside her.
She swallowed the spider to catch the fly.
I don't know why she swallowed a fly.
Perhaps she'll die.

There was an old woman who swallowed a cat.
Fancy that! she swallowed a cat.
She swallowed the cat to catch the bird.
She swallowed the bird to catch the spider,
That wriggled and jiggled and tickled inside her.
She swallowed the spider to catch the fly.
I don't know why she swallowed the fly.
Perhaps she'll die.

There was an old woman who swallowed a dog.
She went the whole hog and swallowed a dog.
She swallowed the dog to catch the cat,
She swallowed the cat to catch the bird.
She swallowed the bird to catch the spider,
That wriggled and jiggled and tickled inside her.
She swallowed the spider to catch the fly.
I don't know why she swallowed a fly.
Perhaps she'll die.

There was an old woman who swallowed a cow.
I wonder how she swallowed a cow.
She swallowed the cow to catch the dog.
She swallowed the dog to catch the cat.
She swallowed the cat to catch the bird.
She swallowed the bird to catch the spider,
That wriggled and jiggled and tickled inside her.
She swallowed the spider to catch the fly,
I don't know why she swallowed a fly.
Perhaps she'll die.

There was an old woman who swallowed a horse.
She died, of course!

102

When I first came to this land.

When I first came to this land
I was not a wealthy man,
So I got myself a farm
And I did what I could.

So I called my farm - muscle in the arm
And the land was sweet and good
And I did what I could.

When I first came to this land
I was not a wealthy man,
So I got myself a shack
And I did what I could.

So I called my shack - break my back
And I called my farm - muscle in the arm
And the land was sweet and good
And I did what I could.

When I first came to this land
I was not a wealthy man.
So I got myself a wife
And I did what I could.

So I called my wife - run, for your life
And I called my farm - muscle in the arm
And I called my shack - break my back
And the land was sweet and good
And I did what I could.

When I first came to this land
I was not a wealthy man,
So I got myself a daughter
And I did what I could.

So I called my daughter - didn't ought'er
And I called my wife - etc.

When I first came to this land
I was not a wealthy man,
So I got myself a cow
And I did what I could.

So I called my cow - no milk now,
And I called my daughter - etc.

When I first came to this land
I was not a wealthy man,
So I got myself a hen
And I did what I could.

So I called my hen - now and then
And I called my cow - etc.

When I first came to this land
I was not a wealthy man,
So I got myself a duck
And I did what I could.

So I called my duck - out of luck
And I called my hen - etc.

When I first came to this land
I was not a wealthy man,
So I got myself a horse
And I did what I could.

So I called my horse - lame of course,
And I called my duck - etc

When I first came to this land
I was not a wealthy man,
So I got myself a donkey
And I did what I could.

So I called my donkey - horse gone wonkey,
And I called my horse - etc.

When I first came to this land
I was not a wealthy man,
So I got myself a pig
And I did what I could.

So I called my pig - dance a jig,
And I called my donkey - etc.

When I first came to this land
I was not a wealthy man,
So I got myself a son
And I did what I could.

So I called my son - my work's done
And I called my pig - dance a jig,
And I called my donkey - horse gone wonkey,
And I called my horse - lame of course,
And I called my duck - out of luck,
And I called my cow - no milk now,
And I called my daughter - didn't ought'er,
And I called my wife - run for your life,
And I called my farm - muscle in the arm,
And I called my shack - break my back,
And the land was sweet and good
And I did what I could.

London's Burning - Round   ## A Round

London's Burning, London's Burning,
Fetch the engine, fetch the engine,
Fire, Fire!   Fire, Fire!
Pour on water, pour on water.

Kookaburra sits on the old gum tree,
Merry, merry king of the bush is he,
Laugh Kookaburra, laugh Kookaburra,
Gay your life must be.

John Barleycorn

There came three men from out the West,
Their victory to try,
And they had sworn a solemn oath
John Barleycorn should die –

CHORUS:
Sing Right-fol-lol,
The diddle-ah-the-dee,
Right fol-lee-ro-dee.

They took a plough, and ploughed him in,
Laid clods upon his head,
And they had sworn a solemn oath,
John Barleycorn is dead –

So then he lay for three long weeks,
Till the dew from heaven did fall,
John Barleycorn sprang up again,
And that surprised them all –

There he remained till midsummer,
And looked both pale and wan,
For all he had a spiky beard,
To show he was a man –

But soon came men with their sharp scythes,
And chopped him to the knee,
They rolled and tied him by the waist,
And served him barbrously –

We'll tip white wine into a glass,
And scarlet into a can
John Barleycorn and his brown bowl
Shall prove the better man –

Head, Shoulders, Knees and Toes

Head, shoulders, knees and toes,
Knees and toes,
Head, shoulders, knees and toes,
Knees and toes,
Eyes and ears and mouth and nose,
Head, shoulders, knees and toes,
Knees and toes.

To the tune of 'There is a Tavern in the Town'

6. Martinmas – November 11.

From France comes the legend of St. Martin, who as a young man passed under an archway in the city of Amiens and discovered a poor beggar huddled there. The man was nearly naked, shivering with cold, and had received no alms to assist him. On seeing him, the young Martin took his own cape from his shoulders, tore the garment in half and covered the poor man to warm him. The following night Martin had a dream in which he saw Christ wearing this same piece of his cape. The experience confirmed in him his devotion to all mankind regardless of their station in life, as expressed so beautifully in the Gaelic Rune of Hospitality.

'I saw a stranger yesterday.
I put food in the eating place –
Drink in the drinking place –
And in the blessed name of the Triune,
He blessed myself and my house,
My cattle and my dear ones,
And the lark said in her song:
'Often, often, often goes the Christ in the stranger's guise.' '

Martin went on to become patron saint of beggars, drunkards and outcasts. He was known for his gentleness, his unassuming nature and his ability to bring warmth and light to those who were previously in darkness.

On the evening of Martinmas he is remembered in many French households with a festival of lanterns, carrying light throughout the darkened home, singing songs, and sharing a simple cake, perhaps decorated with the symbol of the sun.

Lanterns

Children in many countries identify with lanterns at this time of year, and are keen to see the dark evenings brightened. They carefully make their own lanterns of construction paper. Have firm paper or card long enough to bend in a round fashion; say, enough for a circumference of 15-16" or more. Lay the paper flat and cut simple window shapes or picture themes out, then cover with tissue paper pieces over the openings. Glue the two ends so that your round shape will stand, then draw around it for a correctly fitting base. Add two inches diameter, cut and fold in the extra so that it will glue inside to form your lantern shape. Now make a fairly tall handle (heat rises) and staple or glue this on. Fasten a safety candle or 'night light' on the bottom; as these have their own guard container and will extinguish themselves if tipped over.

Lantern Songs

The sunlight fast is dwindling,
My little lamp needs kindling,
Its beam shines far in darkest night
Dear Lantern guard me with your light.

The Sunlight fast is Dwindling

The sunlight fast is dwindling, my little lamp needs kindling, the beam shines far in

darkest night, dear lantern guard me with your light.

Glimmer, Latern, glimmer,	Glimmer, Lantern, glimmer,
Little stars a-shimmer,	*Little stars a-shimmer,*
Over meadow moor and dale,	*Over rock and stock and stone,*
Flitter flutter elfin veil,	*Wander tripping little gnome,*
Pee-witt, pee-witt, tick-a-tick-atick,	*Pee-witt, pee-witt, tick-a-tick-atick,*
Rou-cou, rou-cou.	*Rou-cou, rou-cou.*

Glimmer Lantern Glimmer

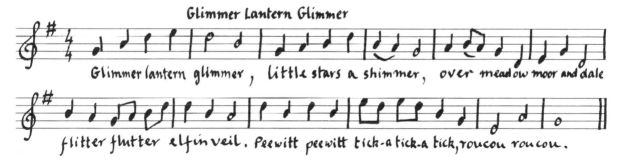

Glimmer lantern glimmer, little stars a shimmer, over meadow moor and dale

flitter flutter elfin veil. Peewitt peewitt tick-a tick-a tick, roucou roucou.

Father sky, Father sky,
Widely loving blue and high,
Widely loving blue and high.
Mother Earth, your warming glow
Makes the seeds and apples grow,
Makes the seeds and apples grow.

Father Sky

Father sky, father sky, widely loving blue and high, widely loving blue and high.

Mother earth your warming glow, makes the seeds and apples grow, makes the seeds and apples grow.

7. What to do with all the apples!

Here's to thee, good apple tree,
Stand fast at root,
Bear well at top,
Every little twig
Bear an apple big.
Every little bough
Bear apples now,
Hats full! Caps full!
Three score sacks full!
Hurrah, boys! Hurrah!

Old Roger is Dead – Ring Game

'Old Roger is dead, and he lies in his grave,
Lies in his grave, lies in his grave,
Old Roger is dead and he lies in his grave,
Heigh ho, lies in his grave.'

Other Verses:
They planted an apple tree over his head, etc.
The apples grew ripe and they all tumbled down, etc
There came an old woman a picking them up, etc.
Old Roger got up and he gave her a poke, etc.
This made the old woman go hippety-hop, etc.

Actions:
One child lies in the centre of the ring of children who walk round as they sing. For apple trees they raise their arms above their heads. For apples tumbling they drop their fingers with a wriggling movement. One child then pretends to pick up apples and puts them into her apron. Roger gets up and pokes her. And the old woman hops all round the ring.

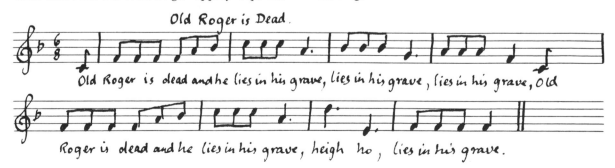

Old Roger is Dead.

Old Roger is dead and he lies in his grave, lies in his grave, lies in his grave, Old Roger is dead and he lies in his grave, heigh ho, lies in his grave.

My nice red rosy Apple

My nice red rosy apple
Has a secret unseen,
You'd see if you could slip inside,
Five rooms so neat and clean.

In each room there are living
Two pips so black and bright,
Asleep they are and dreaming
Of lovely warm sunlight.

And sometimes they are dreaming
Of many things to be,
How soon they will be hanging
Upon the Christmas Tree.

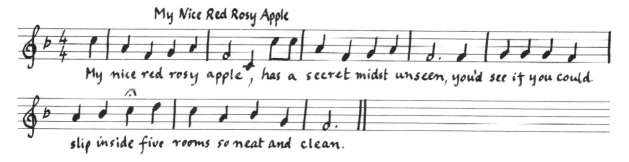

It is very beautiful to take an apple and cut it across the middle because throughout the centre you find the shape of a star. We cut the apple into very thin slices this way and give them to the children and they eat round the centre star.

Another trick children love is to cut the apple into a flower by cutting into it this way right to the centre:

When you have gone right around, the apple will come away in two pieces and it is fun to give it to the child with the two pieces in the wrong notches and they have to make the apple whole again.

109

Clove Apple Cake

8 oz self-raising flour
pinch of salt
½ level teaspoon ground cloves
3 oz butter or margarine·
3 oz soft brown sugar
1 oz sultanas
8 oz cooking apples, peeled, cored and chopped
1 egg
4 tablespoons skimmed milk

Preheat a cool oven, 300°F (Reg 2). Grease and line the base of a 2lb loaf tin with greaseproof paper.

Sift flour, salt and cloves into a mixing bowl. Rub in the fat until mixture resembles fine breadcrumbs. Stir in the sugar sultanas and chopped apples.

Lightly beat the egg with the milk and add to the mixture. Beat until smooth, about 1 minute. Spoon into the loaf tin and level top.

Bake in the oven for about 1½ hours until the cake is browned and firm to the touch.

Turn onto a wire rack and cool. Serve warm or cold.

Apfelstrudel

2½ cups flour
1 teaspoon salt
2 tablespoons margarine
2 eggs, slightly beaten
½ cup warm water
5 cups sliced apples
1 cup brown sugar
½ cup seedless raisins   ½ teaspoon cinnamon
½ cup chopped nuts   Grated rind of 1 lemon
3 tablespoons melted butter

Sift the flour and salt together. Cut in the 2 tablespoons margarine and add the eggs and water. Knead well, then throw or beat dough against board until it blisters. Stand it in a warm place under a cloth for 20 minutes. Cover the kitchen table with a small white cloth and flour it. Put dough on it. Pull out with hands very carefully to thickness of tissue paper. Spread with mixture made of the sliced apples, melted butter, raisins, nuts, brown sugar, cinnamon and grated lemon rind. Fold in outer edges and roll about 4 inches wide. Bake in a very hot oven 450°F (Reg 8) for 10 minutes, reduce the heat to moderately hot oven 400°F (Reg 6) and continue to bake about 20 minutes. Let cool. Cut in slices about 2 inches wide.

Apple Tart

1 lb finely chopped Bramley apples, peeled and cored
A handful of currants
½ teaspoon each ground cinnamon and nutmeg
brown sugar to taste
1 dessertspoon flour
small carton of cream

For a delicious apple tart – make your pastry base and cook blind in a moderate oven for 20 minutes. Then pile it high with a mixture of finely chopped Bramley apples, currants, cinnamon and nutmeg, sugar to taste, a dessertspoon of flour and a carton of cream. Cook in a moderate oven for 40 minutes until apples are tender and serve with cream.

Apple Cake

Make a basic sponge mix with:
6 oz self-raising flour
6 oz margarine
6 oz sugar
pinch of bicarb of soda
1 teaspoon of baking powder
3 tablespoons cold water   3 eggs

Grease and flour a cake tin and put half the mixture in the bottom, then add some peeled and thinly sliced cooking apples (or puréed apple). Put some brown sugar, cinnamon and nutmeg over the apple and a few currants if you like. Now add a carton of sour cream (or thick cream with a little lemon juice) and put the rest of the sponge mix on top.

Cook at 375°F (Reg 5) for 20 minutes and then put some greaseproof paper on top to avoid burning and continue cooking at a lower temperature for a further 30 minutes or so – until the whole cake is firm and the apple mixture cooked. It is difficult to do the knife test on the cake as the apple and cream in the middle do not give a clean look to the knife when you pull it out. Allow to cool in the tin and serve with whipped cream (or yoghurt) or by itself.

Dorset Apple Cake

½ lb self-raising flour
pinch of cinnamon
¼ lb butter, softened
¼ lb soft brown sugar
½ lb dessert apples, coarsely grated or chopped, (skinned)
2 beaten eggs
2 tablespoons soft brown sugar
pinch of nutmeg
pinch of cinnamon

Mix the flour and cinnamon into a bowl and rub in the butter. Add the sugar, apples and eggs then stir the mixture into a fairly stiff dough. Spread it into the prepared 9″ cake tin, mix the sugar and spices together and sprinkle this over the top of the cake.

Bake at 350°F (Reg 4) for 30 minutes, cover with greaseproof paper and continue baking for a further 30 minutes, so that the cake has risen and cooked through.

Dutch Apple Cake

Shortcrust pastry:
8 oz plain flour
2 oz margarine
2 oz butter
1 oz sugar
8 tablespoons cold water
1-2 lbs cooking apples
2 oz butter
3 oz brown sugar
Cinnamon/nutmeg

Line a swiss roll tin with the pastry and prick and bake blind for 10 minutes at 375°F (Reg 5). Meanwhile peel and slice the apples and arrange them attractively on top of the pastry. Gently warm together 2 oz butter, 3 oz brown sugar, some cinnamon and nutmeg, and pour over the apples. Bake in a moderately hot oven, 375°F (Reg 5) for about half an hour, check that the apples are cooked. Delicious served with cream.

Apple and Nut Cake

3 oz butter or margarine
4 oz sugar
4 oz flour
½ teaspoon salt
1 teaspoon bicarb of soda
½ teaspoon nutmeg
¼ cup chopped nuts
½ teaspoon cinnamon
2 cups diced apple
1 teaspoon vanilla essence
1 egg, well beaten

Cream butter and sugar, add egg and mix well. Sift together dry ingredients and add to creamed mixture. Stir in apples, nuts and vanilla. Pour into a greased pan (8″ x 8″ x 2″) and bake at 350°F (Reg 4) for 45/50 minutes. Serve hot or cold as preferred.

Spiced Apple Teabread

2 oz butter
¾ lb self-raising flour
pinch of salt
pinch of allspice
pinch of ground nutmeg
1 teaspoon mixed spice
3 oz soft brown sugar
2 large eggs
6 tablespoons single cream
10 oz bramley apples, grated
3 oz dates, stoned and chopped
½ oz walnuts, chopped

Melt the butter in a pan, mix the flour, salt and spices into a mixing bowl and add the brown sugar. Beat the eggs into a basin, blend in the melted butter and cream and stir this liquid into the dry ingredients. Add the apples, dates and walnuts, mixing well. Turn the mixture into the prepared loaf tin and bake at 325°F (Reg 3) for 1½ hours until it is golden brown. Cool on a wire rack and serve sliced and spread with butter.

Apple Harvest

O down in the orchard
'Tis harvesting time,
And up the tall ladders
The fruit pickers climb.

Just ripe for the picking,
All juicy and sweet!
So pretty to look at
And lovely to eat!

Among the green branches
That sway overhead
The apples are hanging
All rosy and red.

Helen Leuty

111

8. Things to make with Autumn Nuts, Berries, Grasses and Leaves

Among the Nuts

A wee little nut lay deep in its nest
Of satin and down, the softest and best;
And slept and grew, while its cradle rocked,
As it hung in the boughs that interlocked.

Now the house was small where the cradle lay,
As it swung in the wind by night and day;
For a thicket of underbush fenced it round,
This little long cot by the great sun browned.

The little nut grew, and ere long it found
There was work outside on the soft green ground;
It must do its part so the world might know
It had tried one little seed to sow.

And soon the house that had kept it warm
Was tossed about by the winter's storm;
The stem was cracked, the old house fell
And the chestnut burr was an empty shell.

But the little seed, as it waiting lay,
Dreamed a wonderful dream from day to day,
Of how it should break its coat of brown,
And live as a tree to grow up and down.

In Autumn when you go walking in the parks and woods, pick up pretty leaves that have fallen. When you get home you can either put the small leaves into the flower press for use later or use the leaves to make pictures. For example, place a chosen leaf under some paper with the underside of the leaf turned upwards so that the skeleton is more visible, and let the children gently draw over the paper with crayons and the shapes and patterns of the leaves will show up beautifully.

Make *conker men* which you stick together with cocktail sticks. You can make similar rosehip men.

Conker necklaces which you first skewer (an adult should do this) then let the children thread.

Make *little gnomes* made from a fir cone with a conker for a head attached with glue or Blutac and then you can make a coat out of felt or other material or crepe paper, and a red hat and white beard made from sheeps wool or cotton wool.

112

Sheepswool is a beautiful material to use with children as it is soft and can be shaped to things with ease. It is now much easier to get hold of from craft shops but if you are lucky enough to have sheep near you, it is often possible to pick it off the barbed wire fencing around the fields. When it is washed and dried, it is soft and fluffy, and can be used for stuffing, hair and beards and the insides of nests etc.

A simple gnome

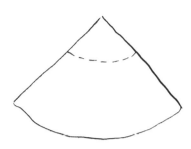

Sew through with wool or cotton where indicated and pull together. Stuff with wool to make face and body.

Autumn Fairies

To hang later on the Christmas tree or to have as a centrepiece to the table in Autumn or hanging from a few twigs or dried cow parsley.

Collect some beechnut shells with open sides, or acorn cups and make a little fairy out of coloured tissue paper very simply with a little cotton around the head and arms – just twisted into shape – you can stick little wings of paper on.

Put this into the beechnut shell with a little glue. Now they are ready to hang up.

Mobiles

Very simple mobiles can be made with the use of feathers, pine cones, ivy and beech nut cups. For example: stick some Blutac or plasticine into the cup of the beech nut and press in some feathers to make the wings and tail feathers. They can be hung from a lampshade or the ceiling with a little cotton, or made into a mobile by placing several on a piece of wire or cane.

113

Other kinds of birds can be made by using pine cones as the body and fixing little feathers for wings and tails.

If you make a circle of wire or cane and bind it round with ivy or other greenery you can hang these little birds from it or make little angels out of tissue paper (or butterflies) to hang beneath. Use pretty ribbon to attach the circular wire to the ceiling.

Make little fairies with sycamore wings or hazelnuts.

Honesty seeds and a little wool can all make pretty angels or fairies.

Make a very simple *weaving board* with four sticks and with string strung between, and allow the children to weave grasses, heathers and ferns through; thus forming a kind of woven autumn mat.

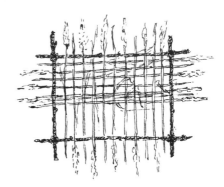

Cut out some cardboard hedgehog shapes and get the children to colour them in. Then they can glue on pine needles to make the hedgehog's spikes.

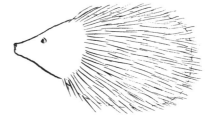

Little conker table and chairs (using pins and cotton) for the dolls' house:

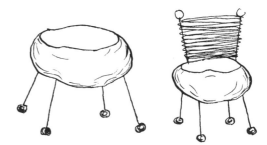

This looks very attractive on the table in autumn. Take some ferns and leaves (which have been pressed in the flower press for a short while) and make a four-sided cardboard frame. Cut out the centre of each side to form a window and then stick into that the ferns and leaves stuck with glue between two pieces of tissue paper. When you place a candle in the middle the ferns and leaves show up beautifully through the tissue paper.

Winter is nearly upon us ....

Pudding Charms

Our Christmas pudding was made in November,
All they put in it, I quite well remember:
Currants and raisins, and sugar and spice,
Orange peel, lemon peel – everything nice
Mixed up together, and put in a pan.
'When you've stirred it,' said Mother, 'as much as
you can,
We'll cover it over, that nothing may spoil it,
And then, in the copper, tomorrow we'll boil it'.
That night, when we children were all fast asleep,
A real fairy godmother came crip-a-creep!
She wore a red cloak, and a tall steeple hat
(Though nobody saw her but Tinker, the cat!)
And out of her pocket a thimble she drew,
A button of silver, a silver horse-shoe,
And, whisp'ring a charm, in the pudding pan popped
them,

Then flew up the chimney directly she dropped them;
And even old Tinker pretended he slept
(With Tinker a secret is sure to be kept!),
So nobody knew, until Christmas came round,
And there, in the pudding, these treasures we found.

Charlotte Druitt Cole.

Logs

Oak logs will warm you well
If they're old and dry.
Larch logs of pinewood smell
But the sparks will fly.
Beech logs for Christmas time,
Yew logs heat well.
Scotch logs it is a crime
For anyone to sell.
Birch logs burn too fast,
Chestnut scarce at all.
Hawthorn logs are good to last
If you cut them in the fall.
Holly logs will burn like wax,
You should burn them green.
Elm logs like smouldering flax,
No flame to be seen.
Pear logs and apple logs,
They will scent your room.
Cherry logs across the dogs
Smell like flowers in bloom.
But ash logs, all smooth and gray,
Burn them green or old;
Buy up all that come your way,
They're worth their weight in gold.

If you are lucky enough to have an open fire, throw bunches of bay leaves into it to sweeten the smell of the room and remove odours.

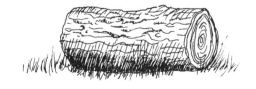

115

Spindle Wood

Spindle wood, spindle wood, will you lend me pray, a little flaming lantern to light me on my way? The

fairy folk have vanished from the meadow and the glen, and I would fain go seeking till I find them once a-

gain. O lend me now a lantern that I may bear a light to show the hidden pathway in the darkness of the night.

V. Winter Days

Winter Morning

Winter is the king of showmen,
Turning tree stumps into snow men
And houses into birthday cakes
And spreading sugar over the lakes.
Smooth and clean and frost white
The world looks good enough to bite.
That's the season to be young,
Catching snowflakes on your tongue.

Snow is snowy when it's snowing
I'm sorry it's slushy when it's going.

Ogden Nash

Elfin Skates

They wheeled me up the snow-cleared way,
And left me where the dazzling heaps were thrown;
And as I mused on winter sports once known,
Up came a tiny man to where I lay.

He was six inches high; his beard was grey;
As silver frost; his coat and cap were brown,
Of mouse's fur; while two wee skates hung down
From his wee belt, and gleamed in winter's ray.

He clambered up my couch, and eyed me long.
'Show me thy skates', said I; 'for once, alas
I too could skate. What pixie mayest thou be?'

'I am the king', he answered, 'of the throng
Called Winter Elves. We live in roots, and pass
The summer months asleep. Frost sets us free'.

'We find by moonlight little pools of ice,
Just one yard wide, 'the imp of winter said;
'And skate all night, while mortals are in bed,
In tiny circles of our elf device;'

'And when it snows we harness forest mice
To wee bark sleighs, with lightest fibrous thread,
And scour the woods; or play all night instead
With snow balls large as peas, well patted thrice.'

'But is it true, as I have heard them say,
That thou canst share in winter games no more,
But liest motionless year in, year out?'

'That must be hard. Today I cannot stay,
But I'll return each year, when all is hoar,
And tell thee when the skaters are about.'

Written by Eugene Lee-Hamilton when an invalid.

'Cider with Rosie'

'Well, don't catch cold. And remember to get some wood'.

First we found some old cocoa-tins, punched them with holes, then packed them with smouldering rags. If held in the hand and blown occasionally they would keep hot for several hours. They were warmer than gloves, and smelt better too. In any case, we never wore gloves. So armed with these, and full of hot breakfast, we stepped out into the winter world.

It was a world of glass, sparkling and motionless. Vapours had frozen all over the trees and transformed them into confections of sugar. Everything was rigid, locked-up and sealed, and when we breathed the air it smelt like needles and stabbed our nostrils and made us sneeze.

Having sucked a few icicles, and kicked the water-butt – to hear its solid sound – and breathed

118

through the frost on the window-pane, we ran up into the road. We hung around, waiting for something to happen. A dog trotted past like a ghost in a cloud, panting his aura around him. The distant fields in the low weak sun were crumpled like oyster shells.

Presently some more boys came to join us, wrapped like Russians, with multi-coloured noses. We stood round in a group and just gasped at each other, waiting to get an idea.

Laurie Lee

Winter Snow

O where do you come from
You little flakes of snow
Falling, falling, softly falling
On the earth below?

On the trees and on the bushes
On the mountains afar
Tell me snow flakes do you come from
Where the angels are?

Snow Song

Oh where do you come from, you little flakes of snow? Falling
falling softly falling, on the earth below

Mulberry Bush Ring Game

CHORUS:
Here we go round the mulberry bush,
The mulberry bush, the mulberry bush,
Here we go round the mulberry bush,
All on a frosty morning.

This is the way we clap our hands,
Clap our hands, clap our hands,
This is the way we clap our hands,
All on a frosty morning,

This is the way we wash our clothes,
Wash our clothes, wash our clothes,
This is the way we wash our clothes,
All on a frosty morning.

You can then add your own verses, such as:-
'This is the way we scrub the floors..'

The chorus is sung as the children hold hands and dance round in a circle. The other verses are sung in a circle but with the hands free to do the actions; or moving round in the circle with hands free as in the case of 'This is the way we walk to school...'

As winter draws on the children enjoy the daily ritual of feeding the birds and possibly putting out some water when it is freezing.

Even quite young children can manage to thread peanuts in shells onto a string with a large needle, under supervision, and these can be hung up for the bluetits. Sometimes our children make a sort of bird pudding, which is made from stale bits of bread, some currants, seeds and perhaps some bacon rind, all mixed with some water and put out for the birds on special days such as Christmas, either as it is or put into coconut shell. A small hole drilled into half a coconut will enable you to hang it up and it can swing freely as the birds land. If you remove all the coarse 'hair' from the coconut and carefully cut the coconut in the shape of a cradle, the children can use it for small dollies once the birds have finished eating all the coconut inside. Our children love eating strips of coconut so it doesn't all go to the birds by any means!

At the end of winter, as spring approaches and the nesting season begins, the children can hang up nesting materials for the birds. For example, pieces of coloured wool, feathers, straw and string.

Apart from being fun to watch the birds taking these things and learning the names of the different birds, you may be lucky enough to discover later a nest with some of the coloured wool you put out!

Spiced Tea

For cold winter evenings.

6 cups water
1 teaspoon whole cloves
1 inch stick cinnamon
2 tablespoons black tea
¾ cup orange juice
2 tablespoons lemon juice
½ cup sugar

Combine water, cloves, and cinnamon. Heat to boiling. Add tea; cover and let brew 5 minutes, then strain. Heat orange juice, lemon juice and sugar to boiling; stir and add to hot tea. Makes six to eight servings. For children, this can be made with apple juice instead of tea.

1. Advent

Advent, from the Latin 'to come', is the period including the four Sundays just before Christmas. In the tradition of the Christian Churches one candle was lit each Sunday until the light of four candles heralded the birth of Christ. Yet Advent and even the Feast Day we now celebrate as Christmas have a far wider traditional context. Throughout Europe, in northern Asia and in ancient Egypt this holiday has had festival connotations of light and the sun; of the time when winter draws to its close and spring begins. Indeed, the Jewish festival of Lights – Hanukkah – falls very near to Christmas on the calendar.

If we bring an awareness of Advent to the home it still brings light and warmth to winter days. A wreath, or simply the attractive arrangement of four candles on the table with red ribbon, a bit of evergreen, or pine cones, is a symbolic centre piece. Children enjoy an Advent Calendar – either the paper picture one with opening 'windows', one to be opened each day, or a string of tiny presents – one for each day up to Christmas. The latter need involve only tiny things – nuts, a marble, bell, biscuits, sweets, shell, small picture, etc. It's the sheer anticipation that children enjoy.

Advent is a time of preparation. Children can busy themselves making cards and gifts. A crib or small 'stable' may be made at home of wood, cloth, bits of attractive bark, or an adapted box. Then figures may be introduced gradually to it – the ox, the donkey, a shepherd boy, an angel, Mary and Joseph and finally – on Christmas morning – the Baby Jesus. If you haven't a crib, do try making one. You may model the figures from coloured beeswax or clay, make cloth ones with felt and scraps of fabric, or try papier mâché. (See Rainy Day ideas for papier mâché recipe.)

In Scandinavian, Dutch, and German-speaking families an assortment of decorative biscuits are special to the Advent season. They are made in large variety and quantity to be offered during Advent gatherings of friends and family when carols are sung and good company enjoyed. This can become a tea-time tradition during Advent for the children of the family with the Advent candles lit and the Advent biscuits to share. Carols may be selected with a gradual build-up to Christmas Day; 'People Look East' - being particularly appropriate to Advent. 'We Three Kings', for example can be saved till after Christmas itself as tradition held that the Wise Men came later at Epiphany on January 6th.

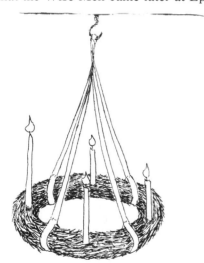 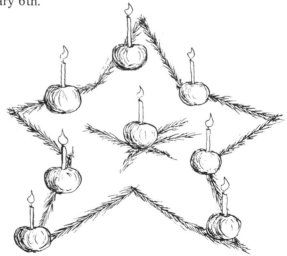

Just as the custom of having a Christmas Tree only became widespread in Britain in the late nineteenth century, advent wreaths are now becoming popular. These are made with fir branches, weaving them into a circle one to two feet across and using wire to clasp the branches firmly. Red ribbon can be wrapped around the wreath.

Some people hang advent wreaths by the front door. Others place it on the dining table, or suspended from a hook in the ceiling, or in a special place. Four large red advent candles can be put in home-made wire holders on the wreath. We light one candle for the first Sunday in Advent, a second one a week later, and so on. Often, we light the candle(s) at mealtimes and at story times.

121

There are some very lovely Advent Calendars now available in the shops but one year, if you have time, try making your own. You will be able to bring your own ideas to this but here is one suggestion:

Place two sheets of card paper on a flat surface and cut out the overall shape that you want i.e. oval, heart, oblong, etc. Using a sharp pencil, make the shapes of the 24 windows on the top sheet, so that the shapes leave an outline on the sheet of paper beneath. When you have done this, remove the top sheet and make sure all 24 windows are shown beneath. Lightly draw into the windows the symbols of Christmas, for example a robin, Christmas tree, piece of holly, a pine cone, a star, a turkey, pudding or present, perhaps ending up on Christmas Eve with the baby Jesus in a crib or the Christmas Tree.

Place this sheet on a board and with a stanley knife or razor carefully cut out the shapes you have drawn in. Select appropriate coloured tissue paper and on the underside glue on the tissue paper to cover well the shapes. When you hold the card up to the light the tissue paper shapes shine through.

Now comes the difficult part: Take the top piece of card paper and very carefully go round the window shapes but make sure you leave threads of paper attached, otherwise the window will fall out before the appointed day. Alternatively, arrange the window so that it can be turned back, like a door, instead of being taken off. Stick on a little bead as a door-handle for each day. Now you have to stick the two pieces of card together with glue, being careful not to stick the top card where the windows are. Use Blutak to stick to the window so that the tissue pictures can shine through and decorate or write on the front as you like. Silver glitter is very effective.

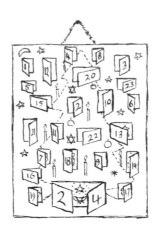

Chocolate Pretzels

4 oz unsalted butter
2 oz sugar
1 oz unsweetened cocoa
2½ tablespoons hot water
½ lb plain flour
1 egg lightly beaten
½ teaspoon vanilla essence
Glaze:
A little milk
5 oz sugar
2 oz sweet chocolate
2 oz cocoa
6 oz golden syrup
1 teaspoon butter

Cream the butter and sugar together in a large mixing bowl until light and fluffy. Dissolve cocoa in hot water, let it cool to room temperature and beat it into the butter mix. Then beat in the flour, 4 oz at a time, and when it has all been absorbed, add the egg and vanilla. Pat and shape the dough into a cylinder 7″ x 2″. Wrap in greaseproof and refrigerate for 30 mins. until firm. Preheat oven 350°F (Reg 4). Slice dough into little ⅜″ rounds from the roll and into thin rope-like strips with your hands. Shape them into pretzel shapes and arrange on ungreased baking trays and bake for 10 mins. until firm. Cool on cake rack.

To make the glaze: put milk, sugar, sweet chocolate, cocoa, and golden syrup into small saucepan in double saucepan of water. Cook over low heat until sugar and chocolate dissolved, stirring all the time. Add a knob of butter, remove the pan from the heat and cool to lukewarm. Dip pretzels into glaze one at a time. Dry on cake rack for 15 mins.

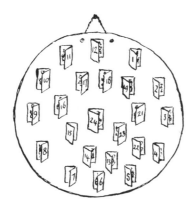

From Heaven's Arch so High - Song -

*From heaven's arch so high, a little light draws nigh,
Stops to hear, stands quite near, wonder what is
happ'ning here.*

*And shining ever clearer, the light draws softly
nearer
In the night, shine so bright, that the child may take
delight.*

*The mother with her baby, calls the light in gaily
Come in here, come in here, light us with your
radiance clear.*

*Then all the light divine, they bring their golden
shine
And they bow, deep and low, bringing him their
heavenly glow.*

Directions:

2 to 4 children sit on stools in the centre of the circle, while the same number, each holding a candle in a holder, walks outside the circle, anti-clockwise.

Verse 2: the circle and lights have stopped. The circle and mothers do rocking movements and then make a beckoning gesture with the whole arm.

Verse 3: The circle join hands again raising the arms. The lights enter the circle and hand the candles to the mothers, bow down and step back into the circle.

Verse 4: The circle cup hands gently in front, as if holding a light, contract to the centre and act the rest as beautifully as possible.

Haselnussmakronen

¼ oz butter
2 egg whites
6 oz sugar
7½ oz shelled hazelnuts, blanched, ground in blender
1½ oz unsweetened cocoa
2 teaspoons finely grated lemon rind
pinch salt
½ teaspoon vanilla essence

Coat baking sheet with ¼ oz soft butter with pastry brush. Beat the egg whites in a large bowl with a whisk until they foam and thicken. Sprinkle the sugar over them and continue beating until they form stiff peaks. Put ground hazelnuts, cocoa, lemon rind, salt and vanilla into a bowl and fold the mixture into the whites with a spatula, using a gentle folding motion. Drop the dough by the tablespoonful onto prepared baking sheet about 1″ apart. Let them rest for 1 hour at room temperature before baking.

Preheat oven 300°F (Reg 2). Bake the biscuits in the centre of oven for 30 mins until firm. Carefully transfer to cake rack to cool. Can be stored for several weeks in tightly sealed tins. (Can cook on rice paper.)

123

Christmas Aniseed Biscuits – 'Springerle'

1 oz butter
3 oz aniseeds
2 eggs
10 oz sugar
1 teaspoon finely grated lemon rind
Drop of vanilla essence
¾ lb plain flour

Grease the baking sheets well, using melted butter and a pastry brush. Sprinkle the trays with aniseeds and set aside.

Beat the eggs with a whisk in a large bowl until they are thick and lemon coloured. Add the sugar slowly and continue beating until the mixture is thick enough to fall back on itself in a slowly dissolving ribbon when the whisk is lifted from the bowl. Beat in the lemon rind and vanilla and then the flour, 4 oz at a time. Shape the dough into a ball and place it on a floured board.

Knead the dough with lightly floured hands for 10 minutes until smooth and pliable and not sticky.

Sprinkle the board with flour, roll out half the dough to ¼″ thick. The Germans have special moulds which you sprinkle with flour (woodcuts) to press patterns on the dough. If you have one you press the mould down firmly on the dough to print the pattern as deeply and clearly as possible. Alternatively, cut with different shaped cutters. (See recipe for Speculatius opposite.) Cut the biscuits into shapes and put on prepared aniseed trays pressing gently down on the aniseeds. Now use the rest of the dough in the same way: work quickly because the dough dries rapidly. Set the biscuits aside uncovered at room temperature for 24 hours.

Preheat oven 250°F (Reg ½) and bake for 20-30 mins until firm but not brown. Put on rack to cool. Leave them uncovered for a few days to soften. They can be stored for several weeks in sealed jars.

Pinwheels

A favourite with children of all ages.

6 oz sugar
4 oz soft butter or marg
1 beaten egg
1 teaspoon vanilla extract
6 oz flour – self raising, sifted with a pinch of salt
1 oz plain chocolate

For the basic dough, add sugar to creamed butter, blending in until light. Mix in beaten egg and vanilla, then add flour.

Now divide the dough in half. Add to one half of it 1 oz melted chocolate. If the dough seems soft, chill for a while until it can be easily rolled. Then roll the plain and chocolate doughs separately into oblongs, the thickness of ⅛ inch. Place the chocolate dough on top of the plain one, then carefully roll the layers up like a swiss roll. Cut your biscuits off the resulting roll end, place on greased baking sheet, bake at 400°F (Reg 6) for 8 to 10 minutes. Allow to cool on cake racks.

Speculatius

This is a rich cookie of Danish origin, which was pressed into carved wooden moulds for Santas and Christmas symbols. You'll want to work the dough as for pastry, with a rough crumb texture.

About 5 oz butter or margarine
4 oz flour
1 egg
4 oz brown sugar
pinch of cloves, cardamom
1 teaspoon cinnamon

Mix the flour into the butter until crumbly. Cream egg with sugar, and add to flour mixture. Mix slowly and well. Spread the dough out flat on a baking sheet - about 14″ by 17″ or similar. Let it rest to chill for 12 hours.

Preheat oven to 350°F (Reg. 4). Then stamp figures with floured moulds if you have them, otherwise draw your own little shapes using a spoon handle, knife edge or brush end. Trees (Christmas ones), stars, flowers, birds, etc. are possible motifs.

Bake 10 minutes or until a reasonable golden brown and cool on cake racks.

S-shaped butter biscuits

½ lb unsalted butter
½ lb sugar
7 egg yolks
1 teaspoon finely grated lemon rind
1 lb plain flour
1 egg white
coarsely crushed cube sugar for decorating

Cream butter and sugar in a bowl until light and fluffy. Beat in the egg yolks, one at a time, add lemon rind and continue beating until smooth. Sift the flour into the mixture a little at a time, beating well.

Pat and shape the dough into a long roll about 2″ in diameter, wrap in greaseproof paper and refrigerate for 30 mins. Preheat oven 400°F (Reg 6). Lightly coat baking sheets with melted butter using a brush. Slice dough into rounds about ½″ thick. Shape each biscuit by rolling a slice of dough between your hands to form a rope ½″ thick and 5″ long. Gently press the rope flat on a pastry board to make a strip ¾″ wide and ¼″ thick. Form the strip into an 'S' shape. Arrange biscuits one inch apart on baking sheets and refrigerate for 10 mins.

Beat the egg white in a large bowl until frothy, Brush thetop of each biscuit lightly with the white and srinkle it with a little of the decorating sugar. Bake in centre of oven for ten minutes, until firm. Cool on cake racks. They can be stored for several weeks in sealed tins.

German Spice Biscuits

1 lb plain flour
1 teaspoon baking powder
1 teaspoon ground cloves
½ teaspoon ground allspice
½ teaspoon ground cinnamon
9 oz honey
¾ lb golden syrup
6 oz sugar
1 oz butter
½ oz lard

Heat the oven 400°F (Reg 6). Coat two baking sheets with melted butter using a brush. Put the flour, baking powder, cloves, allspice and cinnamon into a bowl and set aside. Bring the honey, golden syrup and sugar to boil in large saucepan over moderate heat, stirring until sugar is dissolved. Reduce heat to low and simmer, uncovered for 5 mins. Remove the pan from the heat, add the butter and lard, stir until melted. Beat in the flour, 4 oz at a time. When the batter is smooth, drop it by teaspoon-fuls onto baking sheets, leaving an inch or so between biscuits. Bake in centre of oven for 15 mins until the biscuits are firm to the touch. Cool on cake rack.

You can glaze these with:
4½ oz icing sugar   ½ teaspoon almond essence
1 teaspoon lemon juice   5 teaspoons cold water

Stir all the ingredients together without the water, then add the water stirring constantly, until glaze is smooth and thin enough to spread easily.

Lizzies

6 oz raisins
¼ cup orange juice
1 oz butter or margarine
2 oz brown sugar
1 egg
3 oz flour
¾ teaspoon each cinnamon and baking soda
½ teaspoon each nutmeg and cloves
8 oz broken walnuts
4 oz candied peel
8 oz glace cherries

Stir together the raisins and the orange juice; let stand one hour. Cream butter until fluffy, beat in brown sugar and then beat in egg. Mix flour, soda and spices; add to creamed mixture and stir well. Add raisins, nuts, and fruits; mix well. Drop by the teaspoon about one inch apart on greased baking sheets, bake about 15 minutes in a 325°F (Reg 3) oven. Remove at once to cool on racks. If you wish, they may be sprinkled with icing sugar before serving. Store airtight in a cool, dry place and they will last for ages.

These improve with a few weeks ageing in a tightly closed tin.

Best Oatmeal Cookies

3 oz rolled oats
3 oz flour
3 oz brown sugar
4 oz margarine or butter
1 egg
¼ teaspoon salt
½ teaspoon baking soda
½ teaspoon vanilla essence
Optional: nuts or raisins or chocolate drops to add.

In a large bowl beat the above ingredients well until mixed to a thick creamy texture. Add nuts or extras if desired, then drop batter by teaspoon onto baking sheet. Bake in 375°F (Reg 5) oven about 12 minutes until slightly brown. Remove immediately to wire racks for cooling.

Roll Cookies

A dough that can be cut out into seasonal shapes – bells, Christmas trees, stars, wreaths, etc. If possible use a pastry cloth and flour the rolling pin before rolling out.

3 oz sugar
4 oz butter
2 eggs
10 oz flour
2 teaspoons baking powder
1 teaspoon vanilla essence

Cream sugar and butter, then beat in other ingredients. Chill dough three or four hours before rolling, for best results. Bake in 375°F (Reg 5) oven for 7-12 minutes or until just golden. These can be glazed with a mixture of icing sugar and a little milk and decorated as desired.

Sand Tarts

7 oz caster or fine sugar
6 oz soft butter
1 whole egg
1 egg yolk (save the white for later)
1 teaspoon vanilla
1 teaspoon grated lemon rind
12 oz flour, sifted before measuring
pinch of salt

Beat butter until soft and add sugar very slowly so as to blend until soft and creamy. Beat in egg, egg yolk, vanilla and lemon rind. Stir flour gradually into mixture – the last of it may have to be kneaded by hand. Chill the dough several hours and preheat a hot oven 400°F (Reg 6). Roll the dough until fairly thin, cut into rounds, and brush their tops with the egg white you saved. Sprinkle with sugar and garnish with blanched almonds. Bake on greased sheets for about 8 minutes.

Said to have their origin in Normandy.

2. St. Nicholas

The feast of St. Nicholas falls on December 6, the day when many European children receive their gifts.

In Holland the festival of St. Nicholas is celebrated on St. Nicholas' Eve, the evening of 5th December. The Dutch legend is that St. Nicholas arrives on his white horse and accompanied by several 'Black Peters', by steamship from Spain, where he normally resides. He brings sweets and presents to the good, but for those who have been bad, there may be a (light) smack on the bottom with a bunch of twigs, or worse still one might end up in one of his sacks to be taken back to Spain. The Saint carries his big, old book in which from year to year good and bad behaviour is recorded, whilst his Black Peters carry the bunch of twigs, the sack full of presents and the empty sack for the naughty children. About 10 days before the 5th, St. Nicholas arrives in this way in several parts of the country and St. Nicholas' songs ring through the air. Now he will appear in schools, his Black Peters disturbing lessons by throwing handfuls of sweets and small spicey biscuits, called 'pepernoten' (peppernuts) into classrooms, so everyone dives onto the floor and grabs what he can. Also now children will leave their shoe filled with some hay, a carrot and a piece of bread for the horse by the fireplace, hoping that maybe St. Nicholas will pass by in the night and exchange the horse's food for a small present or some sweets. The atmosphere around the house becomes increasingly mysterious as each member of the family prepares his or her suprises. There are locked doors and notices saying 'Don't come in'. Scissors, string, glue, sellotape are in continual use and gladly lent or borrowed as long as one doesn't look at what the other is doing. In families with young children, the parents and the older ones (7/8 years upwards) do all the work; the mystery of St. Nicholas is very real for the little ones.

The custom is to have presents for everyone and often disguise them in elaborate parcels with completely different shape or in clever models which have some significance in the life of the person who the present is for. This is also usually accompanied by one or more poems or riddles relating to the person's life, making fun of him, etc. All the presents and poems are signed by St. Nicholas so one is never quite sure who gave what, specially with presents coming from outside the family.

When all is ready, the things are put in a large sack or basket put ready for the purpose, each member of the family adding their contributions without the others seeing. When all the things have been contributed this sack or basket mysteriously disappears. Then suddenly in the evening of the 5th there is a loud lengthy ring on the bell and a knocking on the door and there on the doorstep is the basket – but no-one there who could have delivered it. The magic of this moment always seems to work for older and younger ones alike.

Then the basket is brought in and the feast can begin. Family and relatives gather in a circle, the presents are handed out one at a time, the poems and riddles are read out loud – hot chocolate or 'bishops wine' is drunk and sweets and sweet pastries are passed round. Among the presents there is always at least one of each person's initials made out of chocolate and often too the sweet pastry is made in the shape of the initial of the family name. It is usually puff pastry roll filled with almond paste and covered with cherries, angelica, flaked almonds etc.

All through the long exciting evening the bell will ring long and loud at times and everyone (the younger ones especially) rushes to the door to catch the bringer but always in vain: there is a little or big present on the doorstep, with a poem – but no-one to be seen.

So St. Nicolas is a very exciting event in Holland – a long evening of fun and surprises and of delivering presents to friends' houses without being seen. It is the main event in the year, apart from Christmas and Easter.

Cornelie Morris

The St. Nicholas Story

Once upon a time there lived far away in the East a pious man, the Bishop Nicholas. One day he heard that far in the West was a big town. In this town all the people had to suffer hunger, the children also. Then Bishop Nicholas called his servants who loved him and said to them 'Bring me the fruits of your gardens and the fruits of your fields that we can still the hunger of the children in that town'. The servants brought baskets full of apples and nuts, and on top lay honey cakes which the women had baked. And the men brought sacks of wheat. Bishop Nicholas had all these things taken onto a ship. It was a beautiful ship, quite white and the sails of the ship were as blue as the sky and as blue as the mantle of the Bishop Nicholas. The wind blew into the sails and sped the ship along. And when the wind grew tired the servants took to the oars and rowed the ship westward. They had to sail for a long time; for seven days and seven nights.

When they arrived in front of the big town it was evening. The roads were empty, but in the houses there burnt lights. Bishop Nicholas knocked at a window. The mother in the house thought a late wanderer had come and she asked her child to open the door. Nobody was outside. The child ran to the window. There was nobody outside the window either. But instead, there stood a basket filled with apples and nuts, red and yellow, and a honey cake lay on top. By the basket stood a sack which was bursting with golden wheat grains. All the people ate the gifts and once again became healthy and happy.

Today St. Nicholas is in the heavens. Every year on his birthday he starts on his journey down to the earth. He asks for his white horse and journeys from star to star. There he meets Mother Mary, who gathers silver and golden threads for the shift of the Christ Child. Mother Mary says to him:'Dear St. Nicholas, please go again to the children and bring them your gifts: Tell them; 'Christmas is nigh and soon the Christ Child will come'.

The earth is wide and great. There, where St. Nicholas cannot go himself, he asks a good and pious person to go to the children and take them apples and nuts and tell the children of the coming of the Christ Child.

M. Meyerkort.

German Honey Cake

3 oz blanched slivered almonds
Almond Glaze:
4½ oz icing sugar
½ teaspoon almond essence
1 teaspoon fresh lemon juice
5 teaspoons cold water

Cake:
½ oz softened butter
1¼ lb plus 1½ tablespoons plain flour
1½ teaspoons baking powder
3 oz ground almonds
2½ tablespoons finely chopped candied lemon peel (optional)
2½ tablespoons unsweetened cocoa
1 flat teaspoon ground cloves
1 flat teaspoon ground cinnamon
1½ teaspoons ground cardamom
1 teaspoon finely grated lemon rind
½ teaspoon almond essence
¾ lb honey
½ lb sugar
6 tablespoons cold water

Preheat the oven 350°F (Reg 4). If the cake is to be topped with nuts spread the slivered almonds on a baking sheet and toast them in oven, stirring frequently for 10 mins until light brown. Watch for burning and set aside.

If the cake is to be glazed, prepare glaze by stirring the icing sugar, almond essence and lemon juice together in a bowl. Stirring constantly, add about 5 teaspoons cold water, 1 teaspoon at a time, until the glaze is smooth and thin enough to be spread easily.

Coat the inside of an 11″ x 17″ Swiss roll tin with ½ oz butter using pastry brush. Sprinkle 1½ tablespoons of flour over the butter and tip the tin from side to side to spread evenly. Remove excess flour.

Stir together 1¼ lb flour, baking powder, ground almonds, chopped peel, cocoa, cloves, cinnamon, cardamom, lemon rind and almond essence in a large bowl. Bring the honey, sugar and water to boil over moderate heat stirring until sugar dissolves. Reduce heat to low and simmer, uncovered for 5 mins. Pour the hot honey mixture over flour mixture and beat them together with wooden spoon until a smooth dough. Pat and spread the dough evenly into tin using your fingers. Bake in centre of oven for 20 mins until top firm to touch. Remove tin from oven and if you are using almonds sprinkle them over the cake immediately pressing them gently into surface. Let the cake rest for 5 mins. then cut into rectangles and transfer to wire rack. If glazing the cake, brush the top with almond glaze before it is cut. It should be wrapped well and allowed to mellow for several days.

128

Bischopswyn (Bishops Wine)

1 bottle red wine
1 orange filled with cloves
1 teaspoon cinnamon or a cinnamon stick
Peel of lemon
sugar to taste.

Simmer wine with above ingredients for about ½ hour and serve hot. It is a good idea to put the orange with cloves in the wine the day before heating it up.

Peppernuts and Speculaas Biscuits

½ lb flour
4-6 oz butter or margarine
6 oz dark brown sugar
1 teaspoon baking powder
2 good teaspoons mixed spice
2 good teaspoons cinnamon
1 dessertspoon milk
grated rind of a lemon
touch of salt

Mix butter with sugar, salt and lemon rind finely grated. Add flour mixed with spices and baking powder. Add milk and mix to a stiff dough. For peppernuts: just roll little balls of the dough about the size of a marble or a little bigger – put them on a greased baking tray and bake until firm about 15 mins. 350°F (Reg 4). Eat them by the handfull!

For speculaas biscuits: (one really needs special moulds, available in Holland: these are made out of wood and have a variety of figures, windmills, etc.) Roll out dough to a variety of thicknesses, the biscuits can be anything from ¼" downwards and cut out shapes. One can decorate with flaked almonds but be careful not to burn them whilst cooking!

THESE RECIPES SHOULD BE MADE IN ADVANCE OF CHRISTMAS

Stollen

Stollen is a Christmas cake exchanged throughout Germany as a holiday gift. It is a fruit bread which improves with keeping. It is also available at Easter time on the continent.

Dresdner Stollen   To make 2 loaves
2½ oz seedless raisins
2½ oz currants
5 oz mixed candied citrus peel
1½ oz angelica diced
2½ oz glace cherries cut in half
6 tablespoons rum
3 tablespoons lukewarm water
1½ oz fresh yeast
1 lb 6 oz plus 1½ tablespoons plain flour
⅜ pint milk
½ teaspoon salt
¼ teaspoon almond essence
½ teaspoon finely grated fresh lemon rind
6 oz unsalted butter in small pieces
4 oz melted unsalted butter
3 oz blanched slivered almonds
1 oz icing sugar   2 eggs   6 oz sugar

Put the raisins, currants, candied peel, angelica and cherries into a bowl. Pour the rum over them, and soak for 1 hour.

Pour the lukewarm water into small bowl and sprinkle with the yeast and a pinch of sugar. Let the mixture stand for 2-3 mins, then stir to dissolve the yeast completely. Set bowl in a warm, draught free place for 5 mins, to double in volume.

Meanwhile drain the fruit, reserving the rum, and pat it completely dry with kitchen paper. Put the fruit into a bowl, sprinkle it with 1½ tablespoons flour, and set aside.

Put milk, 4 oz sugar and salt in a heavy saucepan. Heat to lukewarm, stirring constantly until sugar dissolved. Stir in reserved rum, almond essence and fresh lemon rind **off** the heat and finally yeast mixture.

Put 1¼ lb flour in large bowl and with a fork stir in yeast mixture ¼ pt at a time. Beat the eggs until frothy and stir them into the dough, then beat in 6 oz pats of softened butter. Gather dough into a ball and place on board sprinkled with the rest of the flour. Knead the dough for 15 mins until all the flour is incorporated and dough is smooth and elastic: flour hands lightly from time to time. Now press the fruit and almonds into the dough, 4 tablespoons or so at a time but do not handle the dough too much. Coat a deep bowl with 1 teaspoon melted butter and drop in the dough. Brush top of the dough with 1½ teaspoons melted butter and set in warm place for 2 hours until double in size, with a towel on top.

Punch the dough down and divide into two pieces. Shape into a plait, circular ring or loaf and brush with melted butter and sprinkle with remaining sugar. Grease and flour swiss roll tins. Place loaves on tins. Set aside to rise again for 1 hour in warm place and put in oven 375°F (Reg 5) for 45 mins until golden brown and crusty. Transfer to wire rack to cool and put sifted icing sugar over the loaves. Delicious served on its own or with butter!

129

'Belsnickel' Christmas Cakes

6 oz sugar
4 oz melted butter
2 eggs
6 oz flour
½ teaspoon bicarb. of soda
pinch salt

Beat the butter and sugar until smooth and creamy. Add eggs one at a time into the mixture, beating well. Sift the dry ingredients and add to cake.

Stand dough out in a cold place to chill for one hour, roll out to about ¼ inch thick, cut into shapes, bake at 400°F (Reg 6) for ten minutes.

Carla's Christmas Cake

12 oz ground wholemeal flour, or equivalent
1 teaspoon salt
2 teaspoons ground allspice
8 oz brown sugar
large tablespoon treacle or golden syrup
12 oz mixed fruit
1 pkt pressed dates
4 oz cherries
handful of chopped walnuts
grated rind and juice of lemon
6 oz butter
1½ teaspoons baking powder
1½ teaspoons bicarb. of soda
¼ pt milk
3 beaten eggs

Mix the butter and sugar and add the beaten eggs. Gradually work in everything else making sure that the fruit and nuts are chopped up well. Greaseproof and grease and flour a large cake tin and cook cake for at least 2 hours on 325°F (Reg 3). It is a good idea to check after 2 hours and leave it in until it feels nice and springy – possibly putting a piece of greaseproof or buttered paper on the top until it is properly cooked. Allow to cool in the tin for some time and then place on a wire rack. This cake should be prepared well in advance of Christmas and then a week later, make holes all over the top and pour a spoonful or two of brandy into the cake. Wrap well and keep in a cake tin. Nearer Christmas it can be coated with marzipan: first spread the surface of the cake with a little melted apricot jam or jelly and then roll out the marzipan and mould onto the cake. It is possible to buy good marzipan or you can make you own. (recipe) Some people prefer the traditional

Royal icing, alternatively, if you add a little glycerine you will achieve a softer icing and the addition of lemon juice to the marzipan and icing takes away some of the sweetness.

Mincemeat

1 lb currants
1 lb sultanas
1 lb raisins
½ lb dates stoned
½ lb mixed peel
2 oz glace cherries
1 lb cooking apples, grated
½ lb shredded suet
¼ lb blanched chopped almonds
1 teaspoon ground nutmeg
1 teaspoon cinnamon
pinch of mixed spice
juice and grated rind of 1 lemon
¼ pt brandy

Finely chop or mince the dried fruit, peel and cherries and place them in a large mixing bowl together with the apples, suet, almonds and spices. Add the lemon rind and juice, stirring the mixture thoroughly. Pour in the brandy, cover and leave to stand for 2 days in a cool place. Stir the mincemeat again and pack it into jars. Cover and store in a cool place and leave for at least 2 weeks before use.

Alternatively you can put all the ingredients through a mincer, adding the brandy and spices afterwards. It is traditional for everyone in the family to stir the mincemeat with the right hand in a clockwise direction and wish. It is also traditional for the younger members of the family to pinch the ingredients!

Christmas Plum Pudding

¼ lb plain flour
1 teaspoon salt
1 teaspoon mixed spice
1 teaspoon ground ginger
1 teaspoon ground cinnamon
a pinch of nutmeg, freshly grated
¼ lb fresh breadcrumbs
½ lb shredded suet
¼ lb soft brown sugar
¼ lb dried apricots, chopped
¼ lb prunes, chopped and stoned
¼ lb dates, chopped and stoned

¼ lb currants
¼ lb sultanas
2 cooking apples, peeled, cored and chopped
1 oz cut mixed peel
2 oz shredded almonds
juice and grated rind of orange and lemon
¼ lb black treacle
4 large eggs
2 tablespoons brandy

You will need three 1 pint pudding basins or a large 3 pint one, well greased. Sift the flour, salt and spices into a large mixing bowl and stir in the breadcrumbs, suet and sugar. Add the chopped dried fruits, currants, sultanas, apples, peel, almonds and grated orange and lemon rind. Beat the lemon and orange juice, treacle and eggs together and add to the other ingredients with the brandy. Mix together to form a soft consistency. Turn the mixture into the pudding basins, cover with greaseproof paper and aluminium foil and secure with string.

Steam for 5 hours for the large pudding or 3½-4

hours for the smaller ones. The pudding needs to be steamed for a further 2 hours before serving.

Home-made Candied Peel

Peel of 4 oranges or lemons and grapefruits
½ oz bicarb. of soda
water
granulated sugar

Wash the fruit. Remove peel in quarters, remove as much loose pith as possible. Soak the peel in bicarb. and 2 pints water for 30 mins, then strain away water, cover peel with fresh water and simmer until tender for 30 mins. Now make a sugar syrup: 8 oz sugar and ½ pt water in which peel was boiled, add the drained peel and simmer for 30 mins until transparent and syrup thickens. Remove peel onto wire rack to drain overnight. Boil up the syrup again and drop peel into it. Leave to dry on rack. Roll peel in granulated sugar and store in cool place in tin. Keeps 3-4 months.

3. Christmas-tide Decorations

St. Thomas's Day is past and gone,
And Christmas almost come.
Maidens arise,
And make you pies,
And save young Bobby some.

DECORATIONS

Christmas Stars
Variations of the star symbol may be created simply in the home for use as decorations or gifts. If you have straw pieces, cane or even drinking straws on hand, try the following, tying at joins with bright red or gold cotton.

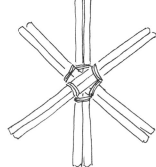

There are two fairly classic paper folded stars, best made from strong gold or silver craft paper. Each involves scoring lines and folding.

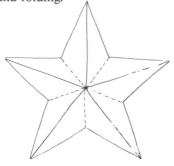

Score solid lines on front of paper, broken ones on back. Fold towards you on solid lines, and backwards for broken lines.

Fold along scores so that centre sticks out

Bells, Stockings and Snowflakes

A double bell shape of card or coloured paper may be cut with patterns cut through. Insert a small bit of bright tissue paper, and hang in the window against the light.

If you have bits of brightly coloured felt, the small child likes to sew a little stocking for his or her teddy or dolly. In bright red these are effective additions to the Christmas tree as decorations, too.

Snowflake forms for the window or wall may be made from folded serviettes, or white squares of paper. Fold from the centre – experiment with newspaper if you like – and cut as intricate or basic a form as you like. Remember – no two real snowflakes are alike!

a

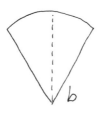

b

c

Cut paper into circle
Fold circle in half.
Fold again along dotted
lines (a)

Fold once more (b) Cut pattern
stage c.

A combination of any of the above, made to a fairly small scale, make a pleasing seasonal mobile. Simple twigs and cotton thread may be used for this; the key being, of course, in the balance.

Hanging Decorations

Even such a basic material as plasticine may form the base of an attractive round hanging decoration. Choose a suitable colour and model it into a sphere shape. Tie a ribbon around it for hanging, and decorate with either holly and mistletoe pieces, bits of evergreen, or everlasting flowers.

Small sprays of greenery tied to a soft rope (so as to cover it completely) makes a hanging garland.

For the Tree

One traditional American decoration has been strings of popcorn! Pop your own, then 'string' it using needle and long thread until you have lengths suitable for the tree's branches. This takes some patience, but in a warm surrounding with a friend or two and perhaps a few carols – it's fun and the result is very pleasing to the eye. The popcorn strings are draped from branch to branch around the tree. Later they can be put out for the birds. Rosy red apples may be hung for their brightness (and eventual enjoyment) as can little oranges or satsumas. Place the latter in a net bag, or tie a ribbon twice around for hanging.

For lanterns, take some gold or silver paper and cut oblong shapes so that when glued end to end (A to B) they form a suitably sized cylinder to hang on the tree.

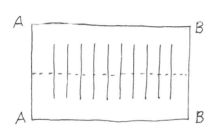 

Fold gently along the dotted line and use scissors to cut lines as shown in the diagram. When you glue ends A to B it forms a cylinder which, when the glue has dried, can be shaped into a pretty lantern and hung up with silver or gold thread. These are very effective and children can easily help with them.

Cut out the shape of a star using some coloured card paper. Then place the star on a board and with a razor or Stanley knife carefully cut round the star about a ¼" from the edge. Take the middle out of the star and cut a piece of tissue paper to stick into the middle. You can make these all different colours and vary the shape, for example, bells or moons. These look very effective when the light shine through them.

Gather some pine cones on autumn walks to hang on the tree: they look very effective with silver glitter or painted with gold and silver paint. If you can find some Scots pine or Corsican pine cones which are of a reasonable size and open up well when warm in the house, you can decorate them by gluing little polished stones or crystals on them and hang up with pretty ribbon.

If you can get hold of some sheepswool and wash it well, and brush out the matted pieces, you can make pretty little angels by shaping it and putting tiny gold crowns on the head and perhaps little gold wings. Use thread to make arm and neck shapes.

133

Use either gold or silver stiff paper and cut out a circle. Then carefully use the scissors to cut a spiral to the centre. Thread the centre and hang it on the tree and the spiral will hang down.

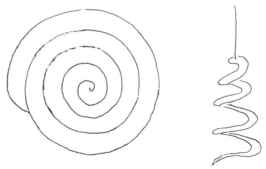

Walnut and Tangerine Father Christmas

Make a Father Christmas by attaching a walnut on top of a tangerine by using a cocktail stick (it goes into a walnut quite easily at the join of the shell at the bottom). Use the line of the shell of the walnut to form the face and nose of the Father Christmas. Now decorate it with a cloak of red crepe paper, using coloured wool to tie, and put whiskers and beard around the face using fluffy wool or cotton wool.

Christmas Candle Decorations

This is something the children can help to make as a gift for relatives or friends, or for the centre of the Christmas table.

Try and find some interesting pieces of bark or a log with interesting patterns on it and saw off a strip or flat piece. If it is a piece of log showing the grain of wood, get the children to sand it a little and put linseed oil into it.

Now drill a couple of holes into the wood for the candles and decorate the wood with fir cones, perhaps with silver or gold paint on, some holly or other greenery.

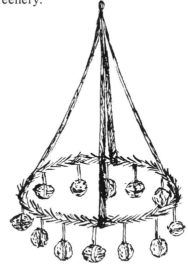

Walnuts

If you want to make a clean cut in order to have two halves of the walnut, we have found it best to put the walnut in a vice and use a fret saw and cut down the line of the shell. Take out the walnuts for use in the kitchen and here are some ideas for things to make with the shells:

Little cribs to put baby Jesus in; he can lie on some wool and be moulded out of beeswax or made from a little tissue paper or felt.

We sometimes put a little gift inside an empty walnut shell. For example, put a little piece of wool, cottonwool or tissue paper inside the empty shells and put a little charm, a shell or a few little sweets in the middle – you really have to stretch the imagination to think of tiny items to fit inside. Then glue the two pieces of shell together; it is a good idea to hold the two halves together with an elastic band until the glue has dried. Then you can either put them into a pretty dish of moss for the table to have after Christmas lunch, or you can paint them with gold or silver paint and hang them with some gold thread and put them on the tree.

These little walnut gifts make a good present for visiting children to take home or they can be put on a ring of greenery and each child in the family can take it in turn to have one during the 12 days of Christmas – this can help to alleviate the drop in mood which can take place after all the excitement and build-up before Christmas.

Heart shaped woven Baskets for Christmas Tree Decorations

This sounds difficult when you read it and a bit fiddley the first time you do it but becomes quick and easy and is well worth doing as it is a very effective decoration. The size can be modified and it is fun to experiment with different colours; gold and silver paper can also be used.

Take two pieces of different coloured card paper (art shops usually have a good colour range) and these should measure approx. 8″ top to bottom, 3″ wide and shape the ends.

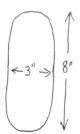

Fold the two pieces in half and with some scissors cut two lines in both pieces up to the point where the paper start to curve:

It is best to cut two pieces of paper together to ensure exact measurements.

Now you want to weave the two folded pieces together to form a heart.

The **A strip of Right** into the middle of the **Left A**, then put the **B** of the **Left** into the **A** of the **Right**. Then put the **A** of the **Right** into the middle of the **Left C**. Slide the **Right A** up to the top.
Now take the **B** of the **Right** and put it over the **Left A**, then into the **Left B** and over the **Left C** and slide up.
Finally, take the **Right C** and weave it into the **A** of the **Left**, over the **Left B** and into the **Left C**.
Now you have a heart shaped woven pocket which can be filled with nuts and currants or a little present to hang on the tree. Thread with gold string or wool.

This is a Christmas mobile which can be varied to suit your tastes. Start with a strip of cane which you can hang from the ceiling with thread: from these hang two very simple angels made with perhaps pink tissue paper. The fiddley bit comes when you try to hang between them half a walnut shell which acts as the crib for baby Jesus and is best done by gluing the gold thread underneath the walnut. Make a little baby out of tissue paper or modelling materials. When you have this hanging, it is very effective as the angels swing about freely.

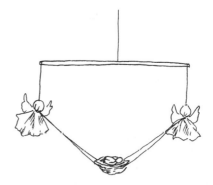

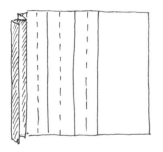  

Little red tissue balls can look very beautiful on the tree or larger ones can be hung from the ceiling. For the larger ones – take 6 or 8 sheets of tissue paper, lie them on top of each other, then fold into a fan, longways, tie in the middle with some thread and gently open out each sheet of tissue paper till you form a flower ball.

Christmas Tree Biscuits

This biscuit is very versatile and can be used in different shapes to hang on the Christmas Tree or at other times of the year as a Valentine biscuit, summer butterfly biscuit and at Easter time.

Makes about 30 biscuits.

1 lb. self-raising flour
½ teaspoon cinnamon
¼ teaspoon ginger
1 level teaspoon grated lemon rind (or orange rind)
6 oz. butter or marg.
7 level teaspoon clear honey

To decorate: glace icing or royal icing. Narrow ribbon.

Sieve together the dry ingredients and lemon rind and rub in the butter until mixture resembles fine breadcrumbs. Melt the honey over a very gentle heat and pour this into the mixture. Work this in using your hands until it forms a dough. Knead lightly on a floured board and roll out thinly. Cut out shapes such as hearts, stars, moons or even Kings and put them onto a greased baking tray. Use a knitting needle or skewer to make a small hole near the top of the biscuit and bake in the oven 300°F. (Reg.2) for about 20-25 minutes until golden coloured. Then cool on a wire tray and decorate when they are cool with glace icing or royal icing using whatever colour is suitable. Thread the ribbon through the hole and hang on the Christmas Tree.

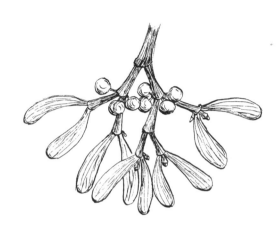

Evergreens

Since ancient times, evergreens have been used for winter decorations, symbolic as they are of life when all other plants appeared dead. The Romans, for example, used evergreens in honour of Saturn, god of plant life and agriculture. Mistletoe, holly and ivy were held in special regard because they bore berries in the winter.

The holly tree is known in Norway and Sweden as the 'Christ-thorn' and in Danish it is called 'Kristdorn'. Some say that the English term 'holly' may well be derived from 'holy', and that the prickly leaves remind us of the Crown of Thorns, and the red berries of drops of blood when the Crown was worn by Jesus.

We usually hang mistletoe up at Christmas and kiss under it but mistletoe once hung in the house throughout the year and was a sign that guests greeted under it were safe in that house. It was endowed with the qualities of power to ensure peace and friendship. This may be traced to an old Norse legend. Baldur, son of Odin, was the god of light and peace, and as such the other gods deemed that nothing should harm him. Water was not to drown him, by their order. Arrows, swords and poisons were not to touch him. But they forgot about the mistletoe, and the evil Loki sharpened a mistletoe branch, placed it in the hand of the blind Hodur and guided his hand such that it struck, pierced, and killed Baldur. The other gods brought Baldur back to life, making the mistletoe promise never to harm anyone again; but to stand protector instead.

Christmas Legend

Legend has it that at midnight on Christmas Eve the animals speak as they celebrate the birth of the Christ Child in a stable warmed by an ox, ass and sheep so many years ago. There are farmers who sing carols to the cows in their shed on Christmas Eve night, to pay them tribute. And in some families, children are encouraged to place a lit lantern or candle in their garden after dark on Christmas Eve, singing a carol or two to all the wild-life nearby who will share this special night.

136

'Some say that ever 'gainst that season comes
Wherein our Saviour's birth is celebrated,
The bird of dawning singeth all night long.
And then, they say, no spirit dare stir abroad,
The nights are wholesome, then no planets strike,
No fairy takes nor witch hath power to charm,
So hallowed and so gracious is the time.'

W. Shakespeare
from 'Hamlet'

4. Christmas Eve

Apart from the Scandinavian countries, where the Christmas Eve meal is a lavish and important one, in most European traditions the supper is a light one. This may be because of the custom of many people to go to communion at midnight, or quite simply a recognition of all the good things to come.

Here are a few ideas for cold dishes: the Italians serve several cold dishes which they call Antipasta:

Avocado cut in half and served with a vinaigrette dressing i.e.

1 tablespoon vinegar
3 tablespoons olive oil
a little salt, pepper and sugar
small amount of dried mustard,
garlic – optional
a little cream or sour cream
basil or oregano

A variation on this is to add some chopped up blue cheese – Stilton or Gorgonzola which goes very well with avocado. You can put the dressing into the shell or alternatively make a salad of chopped up avocado, celery, tomato and onion and use the dressing over it.

Artichoke hearts with vinaigrette dressing.

Melon, cheese and walnut salad. Dice the melon and the cheese and chop the walnuts into it.

Stuffed tomatoes with a mixture of cottage cheese, tuna fish, seasoning.

Cook courgettes and allow them to cool. Mix chopped celery, tomatoes and courgettes together and put vinaigrette dressing over them.

Make winter salad of mustard and cress, chicory and mint, or celery, beetroot, and watercress. Grated raw marrow, kohlrabi, celeriac, swede and leeks are delicious with a good dressing.

For Egg Dressing, whisk together 2 yolks, 1 tablespoon oil and 1 tablespoon lemon juice – add honey as desired.

For Almond Dressing, soften 1 dessertspoon honey, add 1 tablespoon water and 2 oz. ground almonds, then beat with 2 tablespoons lemon juice.

Tapioca for Tea

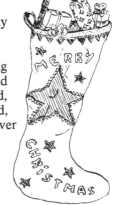

".... then we hung up our empty pillow-cases, and climbed into bed with little secret smiles of satisfaction, confident of finding them filled in the morning. I did not want the mystery explained, or the journey of that red-robed, white-bearded old gentleman ever ever to change its colourful conclusion.
    The distance from the icy caves of Greenland, where he kept his store of presents for

good girls and boys, to our remote village of Kent was covered in the space of a few hours, I considered. The reindeer were faster than horses and had magic in their hoofs, for they did not keep to the roads, but carried the sleigh over the rooftops, in a most delightful way. With bells tinkling merrily, and the sleigh piled with parcels, they raced through the night, while the snowflakes drifted down, softly and silently, like tiny balls of cotton wool, on to the red hood and white beard. He always chose the widest chimney in the house, and if you remembered to scamper downstairs quiickly, on Christmas morning, before Mother lit the fire in the front room you could see his footprints in the hearth.''

Sarah Shears.

It is difficult today when children are brought up from an early age to live in a world of facts, for us to help them to weave together fact and fantasy and allow them the space to develop their imaginative life when they are little. It is sad that teachers of young children speak of how they hear frequently "There's no such things as fairies, gnomes, dragons, Father Christmas, etc". Something has been lost for these children and their inner world of knights and castles and princesses.

It can create a one-sidedness in approach to life and as a result of being deprived of this outlet when little, they fall over into it in perhaps a far more unbalanced way when they are adolescent and are totally swept up in the pop-star scene, 'trips', etc. It should also be added that a child encouraged to be imaginative when little, finds no difficulty when older, in bringing in facts and finding their own imaginative way to link fact and fantasy, e.g. "Father Christmas did happen a long time ago but he needs helpers today to carry on the joy he brings."

In our household Father Christmas arrives in the usual manner. We always remember before we go to bed to put out a drink and mince pie for Father Christmas and a carrot or two for the reindeer, and possibly some hay in the fireplace. In the morning the food and drink are gone, only the tops of the carrots are left.

A Child's Christmas in Wales

...'They were just ordinary postmen, fond of walking and dogs and Christmas and the snow. They knocked on the doors with blue knuckles...'

'Ours has got a black knocker...'
'And then they stood on the white Welcome mat in the little, drifted porches and huffed and puffed, making ghosts with their breath, and jogged from foot to foot like small boys wanting to go out.'
'And then the Presents?'
'And then the Presents, after the Christmas box. And the cold postman, with a rose on his button-nose, tingled down the tea-tray-slithered run on the chilly glinting hill. He went in his ice-bound boots like a man on fishmonger's slabs. He wagged his bag like a frozen camel's hump, dizzily turned the corner on one foot, and, by God, he was gone.'
'Get back to the Presents.'
'There were the Useful Presents: engulfing mufflers of the old coach days, and mittens made for giant sloths; zebra scarfs of a substance like silky gum that could be tug-o'-warred down to the galoshes; blinding tam-o'-shanters like patchwork tea cosies and bunny-suited busbies and balaclavas for victims of head-shrinking tribes; from aunts who always wore wool next to the skin there were moustached and rasping vests that made you wonder why the aunts had any skin left at all; and once I had a little crocheted nose bag from an aunt now, alas, no longer whinnying with us. And pictureless books in which small boys, though warned with quotations not to, would skate on Farmer Giles' pond and did and drowned; and books that told me everything about the wasp, except why.'

Dylan Thomas

Christmas Eve Songs

Christmas is coming, the geese are getting fat,
Please put a penny in the old man's hat.
If you haven't got a penny a ha'ppeny will do,
If you haven't got a ha'penny,
God bless you.

We wish you a merry Christmas
We wish you a merry Christmas
We wish you a merry Christmas
And a happy New Year.

We all want some figgy pudding
We all want some figgy pudding
We all want some figgy pudding
So bring some out here.

138

We won't go until we get some
We won't go until we get some
We won't go until we get some
So bring some out here.

Dame get up and bake your pies
Bake your pies, bake your pies
Dame get up and bake your pies
On Christmas day in the morning.

Good tidings we bring to you and your kin
We wish you a Merry Christmas and a Happy New
Year.

Dame get up and bake your pies, bake your pies, bake your pies.

Dame get up and bake your pies on Christmas day in the morning.

Bells at Midnight

O tell how the trees are grim and bare
And sharp the frost on dale and mountain;
While sheep turn their backs against the wind.
That shakes the brown and scanty grazing.
And men pull their hats about their ears
And hard at their heels stalk winter fears:
'O when shall we ever see the sun?
And when will these hard times be done?'
But care with the bells at midnight flees away
And joy comes in on Christmas morning.

And in her icy furrow sits the hare,
The stormy blast about her beating.
She fears not the frozen fields so bare,
For courage will find her winter feeding.
So why should we fear the winter's cold
When under the furrow sleeps the gold?
The earth bears the seed of future sun
And out of the dark new life will come,
And care with the bells at midnight flees away
And joy comes in on Christmas morning.

So sweep the hearth clean and lay the fire
And welcome each friend and stranger passing.
And spread a fine cloth upon the board
With nuts and fruit for Christmas feasting;
And forget not the steaming cup to share
And songs to delight the heart and ear.
Every soul a candle now shall light
To welcome the child that's born tonight,
When care with the bells at midnight flees away
And joy comes in on Christmas morning.

Sylvia Mehta, Folk singer.

Bells at Midnight

O tell how the trees are grim and bare, and sharp the frost on dale e mountain, while sheep turn their backs against the wind, that shakes the brown and scanty grazing. And men pull their hats about their ears, and hard at their heels stalk winter fears, O when shall we ever see the sun, and when will these hard times be done, but care with the bells at midnight flees away, and joy comes in on Christmas morning.

5. Christmas Day

At a Swedish breakfast table on Christmas Day, each family member is likely to have a 'julhög' or yule pile. You may be quite imaginative in using what you have for such a breakfast treat; it is the thought and the appearance which make it special:

Here pictured is an example:

A slice of rye bread on the bottom, next a wheat roll sprinkled with nuts and sugar, then a raisin bun, a heart or star-shaped biscuit, and a big red apple.

An important part of German Christmas is a brightly coloured dish laden with apples, nuts, raisins and all the biscuits baked over the past weeks. Symbolically the apple stands for the Tree of Knowledge in Paradise, nuts and almonds with their hard shells and sweet kernels stand for the mysteries and difficulties of life as expressed in the proverb 'God gives the nuts, but man must crack them'. Apples go on the Christmas tree, and so do the nuts, gilded and silvered. Nuts and almonds go into the cakes and marzipan that are the heart and soul of German Christmas.

Star Mother's Youngest Child

A story about how the star child visits earth and breaks through the loneliness and bitterness of an old woman and warms her Christmas day. This is a story our children insist on hearing throughout the Christmas period.

Once upon a Christmas an old woman sat drowsing and grumping before a low fire ..."Just once, I'd like to have a real Christmas, with a Christmas tree, and presents, and candles lit, and music, and a feast-".

Now there was another old woman who was troubled on that winter night. Up in the sky, the Star Mother was in great agitation. She was sweeping and smoothing the clouds, scrubbing the faces of the smaller stars, and cleaning the windows of Heaven so all of their brightest light could shine through. Worst, of all, she was constantly bothered by the peevish whining of her youngest child. The Star Mother's Youngest Child – so new he had not yet been given a name – was dawdling and diddling around the sky, banging into constellations and scuffing up the clouds his mother had smoothed out so carefully. He fussed and he pestered, and nothing would please him.

Finally, in a rage, Star Mother seized a comet by the tail and waved it over her head. "Now, Youngest Child, unless you stop this chittering and chattering, this clittering and clattering, I'm going to thrash you!".

Youngest Child howled and hopped around, and sobbed.

"What's the matter?" cried Star Mother. "Here it is Christmas Eve, and of all nights of the year, the sky must be its most beautiful! And with all this work I have to do – cleaning and polishing and dusting and sweeping – I have to be bothered by a cranky Youngest Child!"

Youngest Child howled even louder. "Mother!" he wailed, "just once I want to celebrate Christmas like they do down there –." He leaned out of the window and pointed to the earth, floating like an iridescent green Christmas bauble far below.

Star Mother put down her comet and stopped to listen, as all good mothers do, her hands on her hips and her hair all spangled with dust of stars. "Well," she said thoughtfully, "if that's all that's troubling you, I suppose it could be arranged – but only this once! Would it really make you happy, Youngest Child?"

"Oh, yes! mother," cried Youngest Child. "After all, by next year I'll have grown so big I'll have to take my place in one of the constellations, like all your children, but this year – this Christmas – I would so love to celebrate with a Christmas tree, and candles, and presents, and music. Is that too much to ask?"

"Suppose not," grumbled Star Mother, smiling to herself. "Now, run along, and I'll think of a plan..."

(The Star Child Comes to Earth)

...But then there was a sound that did wake the old woman. Bang! Bang! Bang! "Hello, the house! Wake up!".

Grumbling and wheezing the Old Woman roused herself, threw back her blankets. Fumbling for her

141

slippers, she drew a quilt around her shoulders and stumbled across the floor. "Who's there?"

The Old Woman opened the door.

There upon the doorstep stood the raggedest, ugliest, most unattractive child she had ever seen. He had patched up clothes of some uncertain style, a wrinkled brown face, and spiky, yellow hair that stood up like dry grass all over his head. Worst of all, he looked both cold and hungry.

"Well? Well?" shouted the Old Woman, who was a little deaf, and like all deaf people thought it was others who could not hear.

"Who are you? What do you want?"

The Ugly Child stood blinking and shuffling on the doorstep. He seemed as nonplussed upon seeing the Old Woman as she was upon seeing him.

"Did you want to see me?"

"Not very bad," admitted the Ugly Child.

"Well?" shouted the Old Woman again. "What is it you want? We'll both freeze to death with the door open while you stand there tongue-tied."

"I was looking," said the Ugly Child at last, "for Christmas."

With a howl the Old Woman threw up her hands, "Mercy! Mercy!" she cried. "To be wakened on a freezing day like this by a vagabond whose wits have evidently frozen too! Looking for Christmas! I'll be bound – and where did you expect to find Christmas? Here??"....

(*Later*)

"What are you going to do?" asked the Ugly Child.

"Chores," snapped the Old Woman. "What else?"

She took a couple of buckets from the bench and went out. The Ugly Child followed her.

The sun had risen into a dazzling blue sky but seemed not to have warmed the air at all. As they walked toward the cow shed their breath hung in front of them in a white mist and their noses pinched together.

The Ugly Child followed at the Old Woman's heels, while Uproar (the dog) floundered beside them through the drifted snow. All the roofs were capped with heavy snow and the fir trees hung heavy with icicles that gleamed in the sun like festoons of diamonds.

"Hey!" cried the Ugly Child. "I see one! I see one!"

"What? What? Where?" cried the Old Woman, expecting a wolf at the very least.

"A Christmas tree!" cried the Ugly Child. He had left the path and gone a bit toward the woods, and he stood there pointing. His strange little face glowed and his spiky hair stood up as if the wind were blowing through it. Before him was a small green fir so plump and pretty it would have made a model for any Christmas tree in the world. Its feathery branches moved and the icicles danced and tinkled.

The Old Woman stared. Well, it did look a little like a Christmas tree...

"What do we do?" cried the Ugly Child. "Now that we've found our Christmas tree?" He was dancing round in the snow and yanking on the fringes of her shawl. "Is there something more we should do?"

"Well, I should think so," growled the Old Woman. "We have to cut it and take it inside the house. You certainly don't think a body can have a proper Christmas tree out here beside the cow-shed, do you?"

In a moment the Old Woman fetched her axe from the lean-to, cut the tree, and carried it into the house.

"There, you dolt!" she cried in some irritation, "that's what a Christmas tree looks like!" She stuck the end of the trunk of the tree in an old leaky bucket and made it tight with rocks. And so it sat beside the fireplace, green and wonderful. "Well," said the Old Woman, pinching her lip between her fingers, "it lacks a few things yet..." And so she went about the house, opening boxes and drawers and fumbling on shelves and under the bed. At last she had assembled a little pile of things; bright yarn, an old thimble, a little bell, some broken beads. In a few moments her nimble fingers had attached them to the tree. The tree fairly glowed. "Now, that's what a proper Christmas tree should look like," said the Old Woman.

The Ugly Child sighed. "It's beautiful," he said, and his odd brown eyes twinkled deep in his crumply face. "Now, it must be time for the feast". "Feast!" screamed the Old Woman. "Well, I never!"....
But Later

"Come and eat," she said as she lighted a candle and set it out in the middle of the table. "Tut!" she cried then as the Ugly Child grabbed his spoon – "not till after I've asked the blessing: – For what we are about to receive, dear Lord, we thank Thee. Now –"

The spoons clinked and clanked against the bowls and the bread crunched as they bit into it. The candle spluttered and the fire sparkled and the feast, if that's what it was, was merry. The Old Woman told a few jokes and the Ugly Child laughed, and the sound of his laughter was so great it must have echoed clear up to the stars, for it filled the house to overflowing.

"Now, it's time for you to open your gift," said the Old Woman at last. "Of course, it's not much..." she handed him the little package – almost, no-, not at all reluctantly.

The Ugly Child took the gift and turned it silently over and over in his hands. He seemed to be absorbing the whole weight and feel of it – the crackle of the paper, and silky feel of the string. At last he opened it.

And the smile that spread across his ugly face so transformed it that the last bit of resentment left the Old Woman for ever. "A buckle!" he shouted, "A silver buckle! Of all things in the world, the one I most wanted!" And he threw his arms around the Old Woman and hugged and kissed her till she was quite worn out with all that love.   ......

*(Later when the Ugly Child had left to return up the long slope of the great black night sky...)*The Old Woman sat on by the fire, rocking and grumping. She was aching tired but happy, in the strangest way. "Uproar," she said, nudging the old dog at her feet, "what a day it's been, what a day it's been, what a day it's been. What a Christmas –"

Louise Moeri

Robin Redbreast

The night after Jesus was born in the stable, it was very cold. Joseph went out to search for wood because the fire he had kindled for Mary and the Babe was in danger of going out. He was away longer than he intended because he could not find much wood. Mary became anxious that the fire might go out before his return – she was worried about the Babe because she knew he must be cold. Suddenly some small brown birds which had been roosting outside the stable, flew in and made a circle round the dying fire. They began to fan it with their wings and as the sparks appeared, the remaining twigs and straws caught fire and burnt away. Mary threw a last handful of straw onto the glowing embers and the little brown birds hopped closer and beat the air with their wings even more vigorously. In this way they kept the fire alight until Joseph returned with sticks and logs. But Mary saw that the birds had scorched their breasts with their efforts to save the fire, so she said to them: "Because of the love you have shown my Child, from henceforth you little brown birds shall always have fiery red breasts in memory of your deed of keeping the fire alight. People will always love you and will call you Robin Redbreast. And that is how the Robins got their red breasts.

The Christmas Rose

Robber Mother, who lived in Robbers' Cave up in Göinge Forest, went down to the village one day on a begging tour. Robber Father, who was an outlawed man, did not dare to leave the forest. She took with her five youngsters, and each youngster bore a sack on his back as long as himself. When Robber Mother stepped inside the door of a cabin, no one dared refuse to give her whatever she demanded; for she was not above coming back the following night and setting fire to the house if she had not been well received. Robber Mother and her brood were worse than a pack of wolves, and many a man felt like running a spear through them; but it was never done, because they all knew that the man stayed up in the forest, and he would have known how to wreak vengeance if anything had happened to the children or the old woman.

Now that Robber Mother went from house to house and begged, she came to Övid, which at that time was a cloister. She rang the bell of the cloister gate and asked for food. The watchman let down a small wicket in the gate and handed her six round bread cakes – one for herself and one for each of the five children.

While the mother was standing quietly at the gate, her youngsters were running about. And now one of them came and pulled at her skirt, as a signal that he had discovered something which she ought to come and see, and Robber Mother followed him promptly.

143

The entire cloister was surrounded by a high and strong wall but the youngster had managed to find a little back gate which stood ajar. When Robber Mother got there, she pushed the gate open and walked inside without asking leave, as it was her custom to do.

Övid Cloister was managed at that time by Abbot Hans, who knew all about herbs. Just within the cloister wall he had planned a little herb garden, and it was into this that the old woman had forced her way.

At first glance Robber Mother was so astonished that she paused at the gate. It was high summer-tide, and Abbot Hans' garden was so full of flowers that the eyes were fairly dazzled by the blues, reds, and yellows as one looked into it. But presently an indulgent smile spread over her features, and she started to walk up a narrow path that lay between many flower-beds.

In the garden a lay brother walked about, pulling up weeds. It was he who had left the door in the wall open, that he might throw the weeds and tares on the rubbish-heap outside.

When he saw Robber Mother coming in, with all five youngsters in tow, he ran towards her at once and ordered them away. But the beggar woman walked right on as before. The lay brother knew of no other remedy than to run into the cloister and call for help.

He returned with two stalwart monks, and Robber Mother saw that now it meant business! She let out a perfect volley of shrieks, and, throwing herself upon the monks, clawed and bit at them; so did all the youngsters. The men soon learned that she could overpower them, and all they could do was to go back into the cloister for reinforcements.

As they ran through the passage-way which led to the cloister, they met Abbot Hans, who came rushing out to learn what all this noise was about.

He upbraided them for using force and forbade their calling for help. He sent both monks back to their work, and although he was and old and fragile man, he took with him only the lay brother.

He came up to the woman and asked in a mild tone if the garden pleased her.

Robber Mother turned defiantly towards Abbot Hans, for she expected only to be trapped and overpowered. But when she noticed his white hair and bent form, she answered peaceably: "First, when I saw this, I thought I had never seen a prettier garden; but now I see that it can't be compared with one I know of. If you could see the garden of which I am thinking you would uproot all the flowers planted there and cast them away like weeds."

The Abbot's assistant was hardly less proud of the flowers than the Abbot himself, and after hearing her remarks he laughed derisively.

Robber Mother grew crimson with rage to think that her word was doubted, and she cried out: "You monks, who are holy men, certainly must know that on every Christmas Eve the great Göinge Forest is transformed into a beautiful garden, to commemorate the hour of Our Lord's birth. We who live in the forest have seen this happen every year. And in that garden I have seen flowers so lovely that I dared not lift my hand to pluck them."

Ever since his childhood, Abbot Hans had heard it said that on every Christmas Eve the forest was dressed in holiday glory. He had often longed to see it, but he had never had the good fortune. Eagerly he begged and implored Robber Mother that he might come up to the Robbers' Cave on Christmas Eve. If she would only send one of her children to show him the way, he could ride up there alone, and he would never betray them – on the contrary, he would reward them in so far as it lay in his power.

Robber Mother said no at first, for she was thinking of Robber Father and of the peril which might befall him should she permit Abbot Hans to ride up to their cave. At the same time the desire to prove to the monk that the garden which she knew was more beautiful than his got the better of her, and she gave in.

"But more than one follower you cannot take with you," said she, "and you are not to waylay us or trap us, as sure as you are a holy man."

This Abbot Hans promised, and then Robber Mother went her way.

It happened that Archbishop Absalon from Lund came to Övid and remained through the night. The lay brother heard Abbot Hans telling the Bishop about Robber Father and asking him for a letter of ransom for the man, that he might lead an honest life among respectable folk.

But the Archbishop replied that he did not care to let the robber loose among honest folk in the villages. It would be best for all that he remained in the forest.

Then Abbot Hans grew zealous and told the Bishop all about Göinge Forest, which, every year at Yuletide, clothed itself in summer bloom around the Robbers' Cave. "If these bandits are not so bad but that God's Glories can be made manifest to them, surely we cannot be too wicked to experience the same blessing."

The Archbishop knew how to answer Abbot Hans. "This much I will promise you, Abbot Hans," he said, smiling, "that any day you send me

144

a blossom from the garden of Göinge Forest I will give you letters of ransom for all the outlaws you may choose to plead for."

The following Christmas Eve Abbot Hans was on his way to the forest. One of Robber Mother's wild youngsters ran ahead of him, and close behind him was the lay brother.

It turned out to be a long and hazardous ride. They climbed steep and slippery side paths, crawled over swamp and marsh, and pushed through windfall and bramble. Just as daylight was waning, the robber boy guided them across a forest meadow, skirted by tall, naked leaf trees and green fir trees. Behind the meadow loomed a mountain wall, and in this wall they saw a door of thick boards. Now Abbot Hans understood that they had arrived, and dismounted. The child opened the heavy door for him, and he looked into a poor mountain grotto, with bare stone walls. Robber Mother was seated before a log fire that burned in the middle of the floor. Alongside the walls were beds of virgin pine and moss, and on one of these beds lay Robber Father asleep.

"Come in, you out there!" shouted Robber Mother, without rising, "and fetch the horses in with you, so they won't be destroyed by the night cold."

Abbot Hans walked boldly into the cave, and the lay brother followed. Here were wretchedness and poverty, and nothing was done to celebrate Christmas.

Robber Mother spoke in a tone as haughty and dictatorial as any well-to-do peasant woman. "Sit down by the fire and warm yourself, Abbot Hans," said she; 'and if you have food with you, eat, for the food which we in the forest prepare you wouldn't care to taste. And if you are tired after the long journey, you can lie down on one of these beds to sleep. You needn't be afraid of oversleeping, for I'm sitting here by the fire keeping watch. I shall awaken you in time to see what you have come up here to see."

Abbot Hans obeyed Robber Mother and brought forth his food-sack; but he was so fatigued after the journey he was hardly able to eat, and as soon as he could stretch himself on the bed, he fell asleep.

The lay brother was also assigned a bed to rest and he dropped into a doze.

When he woke up, he saw that Abbot Hans had left his bed and was sitting by the fire talking with Robber Mother. The outlawed robber sat also by the fire. He was a tall, raw-boned man with a dull, sluggish appearance. His back was turned to Abbot Hans, as though he would have it appear that he was not listening to the conversation.

Abbot Hans was telling Robber Mother all about the Christmas preparations he had seen on the journey, reminding her of Christmas feasts and games which she must have known in her youth, when she lived at peace with mankind.

At first Robber Mother answered in short, gruff sentences, but by degrees she became more subdued and listened more intently. Suddenly Robber Father turned towards Abbot Hans and shook his clenched fist in his face. "You miserable monk! did you come here to coax from me my wife and children? Don't you know that I am an outlaw and may not leave the forest?"

Abbot Hans looked him fearlessly in the eyes. "It is my purpose to get a letter of ransom for you from Archbishop Absalon," said he. He had hardly finished speaking when the robber and his wife burst out laughing. They knew well enough the kind of mercy a forest robber could expect from Bishop Absalon!

"Oh, if I get a letter of ransom from Absalon!" said Robber Father, "then I'll promise you that never again will I steal so much as a goose."

Suddenly Robber Mother rose. "You sit here and talk, Abbot Hans," she said, "so that we are forgetting to look at the forest. Now I can hear, even in this cave how the Christmas bells are ringing."

The words were barely uttered when they all sprang up and rushed out. But in the forest it was still dark night and bleak winter. The only thing they marked was a distant clank borne on a light south wind.

When the bells had been ringing a few moments, a sudden illumination penetrated the forest; the next moment it was dark again, and then light came back. It pushed its way forward between the stark trees, like a shimmering mist. The darkness merged into a faint daybreak. Then Abbot Hans saw that the snow had vanished from the ground, as if someone had removed a carpet, and the earth began to take on a green covering. The moss-tufts thickened and raised themselves, and the spring blossoms shot upwards their swelling buds, which already had a touch of colour.

Again it grew hazy; but almost immediately there came a new wave of light. Then the leaves of the trees burst into bloom, crossbeaks hopped from branch to branch, and the woodpeckers hammered on the limbs until the splinters fairly flew around them. A flock of starlings from up-country lighted in a fir to rest.

When the next warm wind came along, the blueberries ripened and the baby squirrels began playing on the branches of the trees.

The next light wave that came rushing in brought with it the scent of newly ploughed acres. Pine and spruce trees were so thickly clothed with red cones that they shone like crimson mantles and forest flowers covered the ground till it was all red, blue, and yellow.

Abbot Hans bent down to the earth and broke off a wild strawberry blossom, and, as he straightened up, the berry ripened in his hand.

The mother fox came out of her lair with a big litter of black-legged young. She went up to Robber Mother and scratched at her skirt, and Robber Mother bent down to her and praised her young.

Robber Mother's youngsters let out perfect shrieks of delight. They stuffed themselves with wild strawberries that hung on the bushes. One of them played with a litter of young hares; another ran a race with some young crows, which had hopped from their nest before they were really ready.

Robber Father was standing out on a marsh eating raspberries. When he glanced up, a big black bear stood beside him. Robber Father broke off a twig and struck the bear on the nose. "Keep to your own ground, you!" he said; "this is my turf." The huge bear turned around and lumbered off in another direction.

Then all the flowers whose seeds have been brought from foreign lands began to blossom. The loveliest roses climbed up the mountain wall in a race with the blackberry vines, and from the forest meadow sprang flowers as large as human faces.

Abbot Hans thought of the flower he was to pluck for Bishop Absalon; but each new flower that appeared was more beautiful than the others, and he wanted to choose the most beautiful of all.

Then Abbot Hans marked how all grew still; the birds hushed their songs, the flowers ceased growing, and the young foxes played no more. From far in the distance faint harp tones were heard, and celestial song, like a soft murmur, reached him.

He clasped his hands and dropped to his knees. His face was radiant with bliss.

But beside Abbot Hans stood the lay brother who had accompanied him. In his mind there were dark thoughts. "This cannot be a true miracle," he thought, "since it is revealed to malefactors. This does not come from God, but is sent hither by Satan. It is the Evil One's power that is tempting us and compelling us to see that which has no real existence."

The angel throng was so near now that Abbot Hans saw their bright forms through the forest branches. The lay brother saw them, too; but behind all this wondrous beauty he saw only some dread evil.

All the while the birds had been circling around the head of Abbot Hans, and they let him take them in his hands. But all the animals were afraid of the lay brother; no bird perched on his shoulder, no snake played at his feet. Then there came a little forest dove. When she marked that the angels were nearing, she plucked up courage and flew down on the lay brother's shoulder and laid her head against his cheek.

Then it appeared to him as if sorcery were come right upon him, to tempt and corrupt him. He struck with his hand at the forest dove and cried in such a loud voice that it rang throughout the forest: "Go thou back to hell, whence thou art come!"

Just then the angels were so near that Abbot Hans felt the feathery touch of their great wings and he bowed down to earth in reverent greeting.

But when the lay brother's words sounded, their song was hushed and the holy guests turned in flight. At the same time the light and the mild warmth vanished in unspeakable terror for the darkness and cold in a human heart. Darkness sank over the earth like a coverlet; frost came, all the growths shrivelled up; the animals and birds hastened away; the leaves dropped from the trees, rustling like rain.

Abbot Hans felt how his heart, which had but lately swelled with bliss, was now contracting with insufferable agony. "I can never outlive this," thought he, "that the angels from heaven had been so close to me and were driven away; that they wanted to sing Christmas carols for me and were driven to flight."

Then he remembered the flower he had promised Bishop Absalon, and at the last moment he fumbled among the leaves and moss to try and find a blossom. But he sensed how the ground under his fingers froze and how the white snow came gliding over the ground. Then his heart caused him even greater anguish. He could not rise, but fell prostrate on the ground and lay there.

When the robber folk and the lay brother had groped their way back to the cave, they missed Abbot Hans. They found him dead upon the coverlet of snow.

When Abbot Hans had been carried down to Övid, those who took charge of the dead saw that he held his right hand locked tight around something which he must have grasped at the moment of death. When they finally got his hand open, they found that the thing which he had held in such an iron grip was a pair of white root bulbs, which he had torn from among the moss and leaves.

When the lay brother who had accompanied Abbot Hans saw the bulbs, he took them and planted them in Abbot Hans' herb garden.

He guarded them the whole year to see if any flower would spring from them. But in vain he waited through the spring, the summer, and the autumn. Finally, when winter had set in and all the leaves and the flowers were dead, he ceased caring for them.

But when Christmas Eve came again, he was so strongly reminded of Abbot Hans that he wandered out into the garden to think of him. And look! as he came to the spot where he had planted the bare root bulbs, he saw that from them had sprung flourishing green stalks, which bore beautiful flowers with silver leaves.

He called out all the monks at Övid, and when they saw that this plant bloomed on Christmas Eve, when all the other growths were as if dead, they understood that this flower had in truth been plucked by Abbot Hans from the Christmas garden in Göinge Forest. Then the lay brother asked the monks if he might take a few blossoms to Bishop Absalon.

When Bishop Absalon beheld the flowers, which had sprung from the earth in darkest winter, he turned as pale as if he had met a ghost. He sat in silence a moment; thereupon he said: "Abbot Hans has faithfully kept his word and I shall also keep mine."

He handed the letter of ransom to the lay brother, who departed at once for the Robbers' Cave. When he stepped in there on Christmas Day, the robber came towards him with an axe uplifted. "I'd like to hack you monks into bits, as many as you are!" said he. "It must be your fault that Göinge Forest did not last night dress itself in Christmas bloom."

"The fault is mine alone," said the lay brother, "and I will gladly die for it; but first I must deliver a message from Abbot Hans." And he drew forth the Bishop's letter and told the man that he was free.

Robber Father stood there pale and speechless, but Robber Mother said in his name: "Abbot Hans has indeed kept his word, and Robber Father will keep his."

When the Robber and his wife left the cave, the lay brother moved in and lived all alone in the forest, in constant meditation and prayer that his hard-heartedness might be forgiven him.

But Göinge Forest never again celebrated the hour of our Saviour's birth; and of all its glory, there lives today only the plant which Abbot Hans had plucked. It has been named CHRISTMAS ROSE. And each year at Christmastide she sends forth from the earth her green stalks and white blossoms, as if she never could forget that she had once grown in the great Christmas garden at Göinge Forest.

Selma Lagerlöf.

A Large Christmas Cracker

In our family the children have an aunt who makes a special gift for them at Christmas. She brings a large cracker which is laid out on the Christmas table in the evening after tea. It is always arranged with great ceremony. When the children and adults pull from both ends there is a bang as the two balloons inside are pricked with a pin and out scatter a number of little presents carefully wrapped up and there are always two for everyone!

You will need two stiff pieces of card paper available from craft or art shops. Make these into cylinders so that one end can fit into the other and either use sellotape, a large stapler or glue to make the cylinders. This forms the body of the cracker. Use pretty decorative paper to cover the cylinders and attach crepe paper at both ends to form the pulling areas. Sometimes it is a good idea to put some stiff paper inside the ends to retain the shape and because you want to put an inflated balloon into each end ready to make the bang. Use sellotape to join the crepe paper at each end and then tie with ribbon to keep presents within the cylinder. Cover all the joins with decorative sellotape or pretty paper.

When you come to pull the cracker, one adult at each end must surreptitiously use a pin to pop the balloons, or if you don't want to bother with balloons inside have someone standing aside ready to pop a balloon at the right moment.

Home-made Crackers

Crackers can be very expensive to buy and can be more individual and to the family's taste if done at home.

Collect the inside cardboard cylinders from rolls of toilet paper and put a little gift in the middle, perhaps a few nuts or sweets, and also a cracker bang which you can usually get from Joke Shops.

Now take another roll and cut it in half and place at either end of the main one

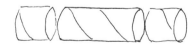

Roll the whole thing into some crepe paper. Fix an elastic band at one end and then at the other, and decorate the ends of the cracker by making jagged edges. At the centre fix securely by sticking on a pretty picture which you can now buy in sheets of gummed stickers, or wrap some silver paper round the middle.

Italian Torrone – a Christmas sweetmeat.

12 oz honey (clear)
2 egg whites
14 oz sugar
14 oz almonds
rice paper
4 oz cocoa powder

Melt the honey in a saucepan but don't allow it to boil. Gently mix in the egg whites previously beaten to a dry firm snow. Melt the sugar together with the cocoa in a little honey and when it has dissolved add the honey and egg white mixture and stir in well. Now add the almonds, which should have been blanched and slightly toasted for a better flavour. Line an oblong mould with rice paper. Pour in the mixture, smooth it, and cover with more rice paper. Put a weight on top and leave to set for 24 hours. For plain torrone omit the cocoa.

Brandy Snaps

4 oz soft unsalted butter
1¾ oz caster sugar
1½ oz golden syrup
2 oz plain flour
½ teaspoon ground ginger
3 tablespoons brandy
1½ teaspoons finely grated lemon rind.

Set oven 350°F (Reg. 4). Grease a large baking sheet and coat the handle of a long wooden spoon with butter. Set aside.

Bring 2 oz butter, the sugar and syrup to the boil over moderate heat in a heavy pan, stirring until melted. Remove pan from heat. Beat in the flour, ginger, brandy and lemon rind, using a large wooden spoon. Beat until smooth. Drop batter by the teaspoon onto a baking sheet about 4″ apart. Bake in centre of oven for 8-10 mins until spread to 3″ or 4″ rounds and golden brown. Turn off heat and open oven door and leave biscuits in oven to keep warm. If they cool too much they will harden and become difficult to shape.

Work quickly and remove one brandy snap at a time with a palette knife and curl round butter-coated handle of spoon. Slide off handle onto cake rack and repeat process. Keep spoon handle well coated with melted butter. When cool you can keep them in tightly covered tin. Fill with whipped cream when you come to use them.

Christmas Chestnut Refrigerator Cake

17 oz sweetened puree of chestnuts (available in tins)
4 oz butter
28-30 sponge fingers
5 fl oz strong hot coffee
1½ tablespoons brandy
4 oz plain chocolate

Melt the chocolate in a double saucepan and cream the butter, chocolate and chestnut puree together. Dip the sponge fingers into the coffee/brandy liquid and place on a dish and join together in the shape desired*. Cover each layer with creamed chestnut mix and build up layers. Cover the whole thing with a layer of the chestnut mix and finish off decorating with whipped cream and roasted almonds. Leave in the refrigerator overnight and serve cold.

* for example, build an oblong shape.

Christmas Chocolate Log

1 oz plain flour
1 dessertspoon cocoa
pinch salt
3 separated eggs
large pinch cream of tartar
4 oz caster sugar
2-3 drops vanilla essence
icing sugar

Grease and flour a swissroll tin, 8″ x 12″. Sift the flour well with the cocoa and salt. Separate the eggs and whisk the whites with the cream of tartar until stiff, then gradually beat in half the sugar. Continue whisking until the mixture looks shiny and will stand in peaks.

Cream the egg yolks until thick then beat in remaining sugar and add the vanilla essence. Stir the flour into the yolks and pour this mixture over the whites. Using a metal spoon cut and fold carefully until thoroughly blended.

Turn the mixture into the prepared tin and bake at 325°F (Reg. 3), for 20-25 mins. Turn at once onto a sugared tea towel and roll it up with the towel inside the cake. When it is cool unroll the cake carefully and fill with either a chocolate butter cream or chantilly cream. Roll it up.

Chantilly cream: Whip ¼ pt double cream until thickening and then add 1 teaspoon caster sugar and 2 drops vanilla essence. Continue beating until good and thick.

Using some marzipan you can make little knots on the bark and ends for the log – add a little coffee to the marzipan to make it brownish. Cover the cake in chocolate butter icing and make little green ivy leaves and stalks with green marzipan. You can dust the whole thing with icing sugar to look like snow and make a few little meringue mushrooms (see p. 165.) to add to the scene.

Christmas Apples

8-10 Apples

Remove the cores from the apples and put them in a casserole dish with a lid. Mix the grated rind and juice of a lemon with some mincemeat and moisten with a little cider and fill the centre of each apple. Boil ¼ pt water with 3 tablespoons granulated sugar until it makes a light syrup and pour around the apples. Cover apples with buttered paper and put the lid on and cook at 350°F (Reg. 4) until tender, about 20-25 mins. Allow the apples to cool a little. Then pile them on to a shallow dish. Soak 8 lumps of sugar well with 3 tablespoons brandy and place them on the apples in various places. Reduce any syrup left in the casserole dish and pour around the apples. Take the dish to the table with the brandy-soaked sugar lumps set ablaze. This makes a nice accompaniment to Christmas Pudding.

Cranberry and Apple Flan

(The combination of hazelnuts and cranberries gives this flan a rich, sharp taste)

Serves 4 – 6

PASTRY	FILLING
1 oz shelled hazelnuts	1 lb cooking apples
8 oz plain flour	1 oz butter
4 oz soft margarine	2 level tablespoons sugar
1 oz caster sugar	Cranberry sauce
1 egg	1 red-skinned eating apple
	2 tablespoons lemon juice
	milk to glaze
	caster sugar

Prepare a moderately hot oven (400°F, Reg. 6).

Roast hazelnuts on a baking sheet on top shelf of oven. Finely chop. Place in a mixing bowl with flour, margarine, caster sugar and egg. Mix together with a fork to form a firm dough. Turn out on to a lightly floured surface; knead lightly. Chill 30 minutes.

Peel, core and slice cooking apples. Place in a saucepan with butter and 3 tablespoons water. Cover and cook gently until apples are pulpy. Add 2 level tablespoons sugar and 2 rounded tablespoons cranberry sauce, mix well. Leave to cool.

Roll out three quarters of pastry and line a 7½" flan ring placed on a baking sheet. Gently ease pastry on to base and up sides of flan tin. Roll off surplus pastry with a rolling pin across top of tin. Line flan case with a large circle of greaseproof paper; cover base with baking beans or rice. Bake 15 minutes; remove flan from oven and take out paper with beans or rice.

Spread filling in flan. Roll out remaining pastry and cut into rounds with 1½" fluted cutter. Quarter, core and thinly slice red eating apple; toss in lemon juice. Arrange overlapping slices of apple on pie, radiating from centre. Overlap pastry rounds around edge.

Brush pastry with milk and sprinkle pastry and apple with caster sugar. Return to oven for about 15 minutes until pastry rounds are golden brown. Place a teaspoon of cranberry sauce in centre of flan. Serve warm or cold.

Ambrosia – from the American South

If you don't always feel like a hot Christmas Pudding, this makes a very exotic fruit salad:

Very finely sliced oranges with the pips and pith removed, sprinkled with sugar and grated fresh coconut. To this you can add other fruits available such as pineapple, bananas and so on. Add whipped cream and nuts to taste.

Grandpa's Up Jenkins

This is an old game that Grandpa Joe has handed on to us and is traditionally done at Christmas time, along with the charades, card games and other pastimes.

Have equal numbers sitting on either side of the table to form two teams. Use a tiny coin, it used to be the old sixpence but can now be the halfpenny or even a ball-bearing for tiny hands. You can toss to see which team begins: they then have the coin and decide with hands under table which one amongst them will hide the coin in their hand – usually it is put between the thumb and the forefinger in the fold of the skin so that it is difficult to see when you put the palm upwards.

When all is ready the other team shout UP JENKINS and the team with the coin have to put their hands up in the air, palms facing their opponents and keep their fingers and thumbs tightly together so that hopefully the coin cannot be seen. The other team ask them to perform various actions and the team with the coin can do these with a certain amount of theatrical action, pretending that each has the coin hidden. The other team has to guess who has the coin at the end.

Actions:

1. When ready to begin at the shout UP JENKINS up go the hands in the air.
2. Windows: hands held upwards with fingers together and palms facing the other team and waved or fluttered from side to side.
3. Crabs: hands on the table and crawling a few paces backwards and forwards.
4. 'Wibbly Wobbly': clenched hands must be turned over and back on the table.
5. Grand Slam: hands slammed face downwards onto table (if the coin hasn't been noticed before a tinkle will often reveal it at this point).

You can make your own variations to the game and the cunning part is how well the team with the coin use themselves as decoys for the one who really has it. At the end, the other team has a turn.

150

6. New Year

God be here, God be there,
We wish you all a happy year,
God without, God within,
Let the Old Year out and the New Year in.

New Year's Eve

The word January comes from the name of a Roman god, Janus, which derives from the Latin word JANUS – gate or opening. All the gates of ancient Rome were held to be under the care of Janus and because through gates there is a great deal of coming and going, the god had two faces, one looking forward and the other looking back. Perhaps this is what we do on New Year's Eve when we look back at the year gone by and make New Year resolutions for the coming year.

Because we characteristically look both behind and ahead, predictions also play a role on this holiday, and playful ones may be made when gathering with friends. For a mixed group of adults and children, floating walnut boats is one method of doing this. For adults only, there is the age-old custom of 'throwing lead'.

Walnut Boats

You will want a 'fortune' written out on a small piece paper, one for each person present. These may be elaborate or simple depending on your enthusiasm for prose. Keep it fairly light.
'When come the Ides of March you'll find
A new Idea comes to Mind
And some three friends will you take
A fine new journey for to make'
might also be 'You will go on a journey with three friends in March'! Finding treasure is a favourite and suitably vague theme!

Each paper fortune should be rolled and tied in the middle with string. The ends of the string are placed in a wide basin of water, such that the paper fortunes dangle all around the outside rim of the basin. Now take a walnut half for each person and prepare boats by placing a drop of wax or plasticine in the centre to hold a little paper sail. If you like you may initial each sail with the first letter of each friend's name.

Gather around the basin and take turns seeing which fortune your boat selects. One way, if the gathering is not too big, is to have each person choose a seasonal song as they push or blow their own boat into action. Sing the song as a group, and when you've finished, choose the string nearest which your boat is resting. Happy New Year!

Throwing Lead

This is for the grown-ups and should be done with utmost care. You will need a smallish lump or piece of lead, an old saucepan (which is no longer used for cooking), and a basin (enamel ones are good) of cold water.

Melt the lead carefully, on the cooker or at the grate of the fire or even on a primus stove. The idea is for each person to pour from the saucepan a tiny amount – about a tablespoon or so – of lead into the cold water. It will instantly harden into a shape, and the shape may be lifted from the water and placed on paper or table for examination. The shapes are tremendously varied, and it is from them that you and the group must decide what is in store for you in the coming New Year! One year the group thought my little lead figure resembled a dragon with a tiny dragon at its side. A year later I gave birth to one of our children! No comment on the dragon please!

Observe fire precautions and do wash hands after handling the lead! Some people keep the lead forms as little sculptures for the year, to be melted down again in future.

'The Merry Year is born like the Bright Berry from the Naked Thorn'

On New Year's Eve family and friends gathered together with a bowl of spiced ale and the head of the family would drink first, saying WAES-HAIL ('Be thou whole') then the bowl would be passed round so that everyone might drink. As they did so they would say DRINK-HAIL.

The first person to cross the threshold after midnight was the 'lucky-bird' or 'First-foot': in some areas he had to be fair, in others dark. Traditionally the fortunes of the household for the coming year were determined by the first person to enter after midnight and he would bring with him bread, salt and coal – the symbols of life, hospitality and warmth. Sometimes tradition demanded a sweep should enter the house through the front door, shake hands with everyone, wish them a Happy New Year, and then he would go out through the back door with a shilling in his pocket.

Gloucestershire Wassail sung at Christmas and New Year

Wassail, wassail, all over the town!
Our toast it is white, and our ale it is brown,
Our bowl it is made of the white maple tree;
With the wassailing bowl we'll drink to thee.

So here is to Cherry and to his right cheek,
Pray God send our master a good piece of beef,
And a good piece of beef that may we all see;
With the wassailing bowl we'll drink to thee.

And here is to Dobbin and to his right eye,
Pray God send our master a good Christmas pie,
And a good Christmas pie that may we all see;
With our wassailing bowl we'll drink to thee.

So here is to Broad May and to her broad horn,
May God send our master a good crop of corn,
And a good crop of corn that may we all see;
With the wassailing bowl we'll drink to thee.

And here is to Fillpail and to her left ear,
Pray God send our master a Happy New Year,
And a happy New Year as e'er he did see;
With our wassailing bowl we'll drink to thee.

And here is to Colly and to her long tail,
Pray God send our master he never may fail
A bowl of strong beer; I pray you draw near,
And our jolly wassail it's then you shall hear.

Come, butler, come fill us a bowl of the best,
Then we hope that your soul in heaven may rest;
But if you do draw us a bowl of the small,
Then down shall go butler, bowl and all.

Then here's to the maid in the lily white smock,
Who tripped to the door and slipped back the lock!
Who tripped to the door and pulled back the pin,
For to let these jolly wassailers in.

Cherry and Dobbin are horses
Broad May, Fillpail and Colly are cows.

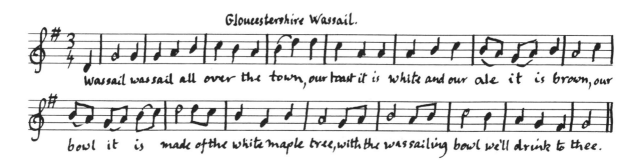

152

Here We come a Wassailing

Here we come a wassailing among the leaves so
green,
Here we come a wandering, so fair to be seen:
Love and joy come to you, and to you your wassail
too,
And God bless you, and send you a happy New Year,
And God send you a Happy New Year.

We are not daily beggars that beg from door to door,
But we are neighbours' children, whom you have
seen before,
Love and joy come to you, and to you your wassail
too,
And God bless you, and send you a Happy New Year,
And God send you a Happy New Year.

God bless the master of this house, likewise the
mistress too,
And all the little children that round the table go;
Love and joy come to you, and to you your wassail
too,
And God bless you, and send you a Happy New
Year,
And God bless you, and send you a Happy New Year,
And God send you a Happy New Year.

And God bless you, and send you a Happy New Year,
And God send you a Happy New Year.

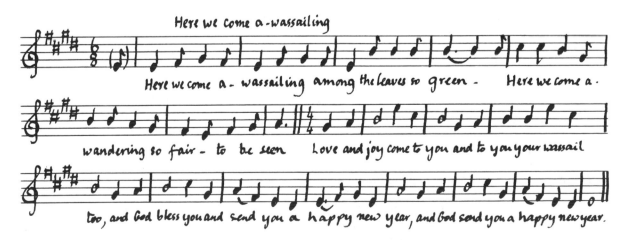

7. Twelfth Night - Epiphany

On the 12th night after the birth of Jesus, the Three Kings led by a star came to Bethlehem with gifts for the Baby Jesus of gold, frankincense and myrrh. It is the end of the Christmas festive period and the time when we take down the decorations and burn the Christmas Tree.

There is a special cake to have on this evening - the French call it a Galette des Rois and given below you will find a simple version. One tradition is that hidden treasure is put inside it - the one who finds the treasure is king for the night. Treasure could be a new coin or a little charm or trinket.

Another custom is to bake the cake with a bean and a pea (dried) in the mix. The one who finds the bean is king and the one who finds the pea is queen for the night. They rule over the party, perhaps wear crowns and lead the games. (See below)

8 oz butter
grated rind of lemon
5 oz sifted icing sugar
3 oz self-raising flour
3 oz ground rice
6 egg yolks
3 egg whites
extra sifted icing sugar

Cream the butter and grated lemon rind and then beat in the icing sugar. Sift the flour and ground rice together and add one third of it to the creamed mixture. Add two of the egg yolks and repeat with the remaining flour and yolks. Fold in the stiffly whisked whites and turn into a prepared tin (possibly a ring shape) and bake in oven 350°F (Reg 4) for about an hour. Then test to see if springy and cooked. Decorate with a lemon butter icing or just sifted icing sugar and decorate with little figures of the three kings or with crowns or stars.

Twelfth Night

Here's to thee, old apple tree,
Whence thou may'st bud
And whence thou may'st blow,
And whence thou may'st bear apples enow;
Hats full and caps full,
Bushels full and sacks full,
And our pockets full too.

In the West Country, the tradition of blessing the apple trees took place at this time. Villagers would gather in the orchards at dusk, firing guns through the branches to drive away evil spirits and pour cider on the apple tree roots. The orchards were then toasted with mugs of hot cider and the above song was sung.

Twelfth Night

Now, now the mirth comes
With the cake full of plums
Where Beane's the King of the sport here,
Beside we must knowe
The pea also
Must revell as Queene for the night here.

Which knowne, let us make
Joy-sops with the cake
And let not a man then be seen here,
Who inurged will not drinke
To the base from the brink
A health to the King and the Queene here.

Next crowne the bowle full
With gentle lamb's wooll;*
And sugar, nutmeg and ginger,
With store of ale too;
And this you must doe
To make the wassaille a stinger.

Give then to the King,
And the Queene wassailing:
And though with ale ye be whet here;
Yet part ye from hence,
As free from offence,
As when ye innocent met here.

Robert Herrick

Lamb's Wooll = spiced ale.

154

Lamb's Wool

6 cooking apples
2 pints ale
3-6 tablespoons caster sugar
½ teaspoon ground ginger
½ teaspoon grated nutmeg

Place apples in dish with a little water and bake in low oven until moist and soft. Cut up the apples and put them in a large mixing bowl. Heat the ale gently in a saucepan and pour hot all over apples. Add the sugar to taste and the spices. Leave in a warm place for ½ hour. Strain through a sieve back into saucepan and gently reheat. When you pour the warm punch into glasses put a spoon in the glass to prevent cracking, although the punch should not be very hot.
OR
3 quarts brown ale
1½ pints sweet white wine
½ grated nutmeg
1 teaspoon ground ginger
1 stick cinnamon
4 baked apples
brown sugar

Heat ale, wine and spices in pan. Skin apples, mash to pulp. Pour over liquid, having removed cinnamon. Mix well, then run through strainer. Add sugar to taste and reheat.

The Legend of Russia

Eastern Orthodox Christmas is celebrated in early January. In Russia the children talk at Christmas time of Mama Baboushka and wonder what gift she will bring them. Russian boys and girls place their shoes beside the fireplace, hoping that Baboushka will pile them high with toys and good things. They tell a story about Baboushka that shows why she loves to be kind to children, and this is the story.

The Story of Baboushka

Long ago, so the story tellers say, on the night when the Lord of all the earth was born in Bethlehem, Baboushka held a great feast. As she sat waiting for her friends in her great hall, the outer door suddenly opened. Baboushka turned to welcome her guest, but the figure that stood in the doorway was of a man she did not know. She looked wonderingly at him as he stood outlined against the snow and the frosty night. His appearance was strange yet he had the look of a great man: one whom Baboushka would delight to receive. She saw that he was old and stately. Was that a coronet on his brow?

"Will you not come in? You are welcome", she said.

The stranger bent his head. "I may not come in", he replied. "I have come to invite you to a pilgrimage. I have seen the star of a king and go to worship Him. Will you also come?"

Baboushka was very troubled. He was most certainly a king that stood in the doorway. How gladly she would have received him in her house! There was something about his noble face that made her long to obey his call, and yet the gay voices of her approaching guests called even more loudly. "The night is cold, good sir", she faltered, "and see, here come my guests. How can I leave them now? Another day I will come with you to find the King whose star shines in the East. But not tonight."

In that moment the old king had gone and Baboushka stood in wonder at the open door. But even as she peered into the darkness there stood before her another. He, too, wore a king's crown and the clothes of one from a far country. His face was lit with an inward light, and his eyes shone as though

155

into them had crept the glory of the star of the new-born King. He waved a golden censer before her from which there floated a thin-sweet-smelling cloud.

"I go to carry incense to a great king," smiled the stranger. "I have seen his star in the East and go to worship Him. Come with me and wave incense of adoration before Him".

The sweet-scented cloud wrapped Baboushka around, and she felt a great longing. Should she leave all and travel to find the King? Through the cloud of incense she saw the radiance of her candlelit room, warm and glowing. "I cannot come" she said: "but on another night I will travel on this pilgrimage. For I too, some day, would worship the King".

Then the incense-bearing king passed, and there stood yet another in his place. Very gentle and young, and yet still a king, he bore in his lifted hands a golden casket. His face was alight with youthful joy and his voice was like a carol, so full was it of melody and song. Baboushka greatly loved his looks and cried out at once, "Do not go further. Come within and rest and feast with my friends. Then tomorrow you may go on your pilgrimage for I see that you also are travelling to see a King".

But, with a smile, the third king shook his dark head. "How can one stay when one carries gifts to a King? I have seen his star in the East and would worship Him. He, but a child, new born it is said."

"I will go with you to worship Him also", Baboushka pleaded with the young king. But not tonight. Let us go tomorrow."

The joy in the young king's face died out. He looked within the candlelit room and saw the gifts, the fruit and the feast spread for the guests. "Ah come!" he said. "You have many things here that you could offer to the Child King for his worship and praise. Will you not bring them?" Then he too moved from the door and passed over the trodden snow, leaving Baboushka alone. As she gazed out over the track he had taken it seemed to her that there was nothing in all the world to see save the glorious star that shone low in the eastern sky. Then she went in to her guests and the feasting in the candlelit room.

That winter, with its feasting and its gay festivals, passed away. The snow and ice melted and summer came to the land. Whilst the feasting was with her, Baboushka was happy enough, but when the summer came to the land, she remembered more and more the coming of those three strange kings and of their pilgrimage. As winter drew near she wondered if she would see them again and promised herself that this time she would go with them. By the time that the night of the three kings came round again Baboushka was quite determined to make the pilgrimage. But where did the young king dwell whose star had appeared in the East? She was annoyed that she had not discovered that before the three kings had disappeared. Could they have been going to visit the baby boy born at the great castle two or three miles away? Was he the one heralded by a star? Baboushka gathered some of her treasures together, gold and sweet perfumes and fine clothing and when the night had come she, with a lady in waiting, carried them to the castle. The child's mother received the gifts, but seemed a little amused and somewhat surprised at such an offering. She showed Baboushka her baby, peevish and spoilt and whining. Baboushka went home very quietly and sad, for in all that dark night sky there was not a star to be seen, and the King she had been so willing to worship had not been found.

All through the long winter and the summer that followed and until winter began again Baboushka hoped and waited for the night of the Star and the three kings to return. "Perhaps I may find Him this year". With that thought in her mind she set aside gifts for the Kingly Child, all that remained of her gold and precious goods. But on that night when, with her treasures in her arms, she went out in the cold to find the King, she found only a starving family and no Kingly Babe at all. To the family she gave the gifts she had set apart for Him, and returned home with a sore and aching heart.

So it came to pass that with every returning Christmas, Baboushka set out to find the Child as the three kings had done on the first Christmas night. But as the years went on Baboushka found that she had less and less to offer. Her gold and precious jewels had gone and with them the fine clothing and sweet spices. At first this troubled her: she longed for a jewelled casket and golden vessel to carry to His feet.

One Christmas came and she had nothing in the world to give except for a few toys she had made out of soft wool and sweet cakes she had baked herself. When Baboushka looked at these poor gifts before setting out to find the Kingly Baby, she sighed, but afterwards she smiled.

"Of course", she reminded herself, "the baby is growing year by year. He is old enough now to play with the gifts I take him. I will carry a little tree to place these toys and sweets upon. It will make him laugh to see such a pretty tree.

And this she did: and it happened that although once again she searched in vain for the Kingly Child, she found other children who laughed with joy for the gift of the toy-laden tree. After that every

Christmas Baboushka carried a tree dressed with soft toys and gay ornaments and sweets. Although she grew poorer year by year, and never saw the Child and His star, every Christmas found her searching for him, and in her search bringing joy to boys and girls around her.

When Baboushka was quite old there came a Christmas-tide when she had nothing in the world to offer. She had almost given up hope of ever finding the young King, and on this night as she looked about her bare room she said to herself, "Even if tonight I found Him I should have only empty hands to offer". Yet, nevertheless, she meant to follow the quest although she had nothing worthy for the Child's hands to grasp. So after eating her supper of milk and bread she searched round to see if there was anything at all that a child might like.

In her wood shed Baboushka found a fir bough, fallen from its parent tree in the last storm. This would do for a tree if she were to put it carefully in one of her brown jars. But what had she to hang upon it? She found some precious candle-ends and a wooden toy and ball left over from the last Christmas tree. She lit the candles, held the tree in her hands to look at it. "Can there be any little child among my neighbours who would stretch out his hands in longing for this poor tree?" she wondered. The next moment she turned quickly to the door. "There is a child crying", she said. "Some child is out in this bitter cold. Who can it be?"

Baboushka ran quickly, not stopping to put down the tree, and opened the door. A little baby lay at her threshold. As she stood in astonishment she saw the baby stretch out his hands to the tiny lighted tree. He stopped crying and crowed with happiness at the bright ball hung upon it. Then Baboushka saw the ball was shining brightly, reflecting the light of the bright Star that shone in the sky. And she knew who the Child was.

In that instant, all about her was changed. She saw the Holy Family and the Shepherds. She knelt and knew that the three kings of long ago were kneeling with her. The place was thronged with children, and the faces of the children were the faces of the boys and girls who had shared her gifts and lovely trees. Even the child of the castle was there with all his peevishness vanished. It seemed to her that she heard the whispering of many trees, whose branches she had laden with gifts for the Holy Child. They had come to the Child's manger. Nothing, nothing, had been lost. Baboushka's heart was full of happiness. Her search was ended.

An Epiphany Story of the Tree

Once upon a time there was a little fir tree. He stood amongst many fir trees which were bigger than himself. He enjoyed standing there and growing and delighted in the grasses, flowers and creatures around him. But best of all he liked to look up to the sky. The sky was beautiful when it was a pure crystal blue but beautiful too when it bore the clouds which moved and changed, and it was beautiful again when the rain was pouring from the mysterious grey sky. But best of all the little fir tree had a real liking for the sky when it was full of stars. The little fir tree had a deep longing for the sky: he so wished to get up there. But although he grew into a fine, tall tree, there came the moment when he realised that trees do not grow into the sky and he became sad.

Then it happened one winter night that the skies opened. A light descended to the fir tree; the Christ Child himself pulled the fir out of the earth and flew away with him. The fir tree rejoiced: "Now I may go up into the heavens." But instead he was taken into the house of human beings and was decorated with gold, stars, flowers, fruits and lights. The fir tree received it all gratefully as a preparation for entering heaven in a dignified way. However, as the fir tree stood there in all his splendour the door opened and children came in, their eyes shining. And now the fir tree experienced something strange: from out of the eyes of the children there radiated so much love and purity that the fir forgot all about the Heavens; his wish to enter there changed into the wish to give the children delight and happiness.

So the fir tree shone and gave forth his scent throughout the twelve Christmas days. On the morning after the twelfth day the children came leaping and bounding into the room. Joyfully they started taking all the decorations off the tree. The tree gladly gave them up. Then came sorrow for the tree; his twigs sighed and groaned. A deep, black hole opened up before him and he was pushed and stuffed into it. A flame lit up and the pain of burning in the fire glowed in him.

But suddenly what happened? The fir tree's burnt twigs and branches gleamed from within, they grew light and golden. The darkness around the firtree lit up and his pain became soaring joy. He laid down his heavy, woody garment and instead grew wings of flaming light and rose and flew up into the heights.

Angels came to meet him and together they flew into the Heavens. So the wish of the little fir tree was fulfilled after all.

VI. BIRTHDAYS

Monday's child is fair of face
Tuesday's child is full of grace,
Wednesday's child knows how to sew
Thursday's child has far to go,
Friday's child is loving and giving
Saturday's child works hard for a living,
But the child that is born on the Sabbath day
Is bonnie and blithe and good and gay!

Ideas for Birthdays

We hope that you will find the themes of the different seasons and festivals something that you can incorporate into the celebration of your child's birthday – whenever it occurs in the calendar.

But here are some other ideas, games and recipes.

A verse for The Night before the Birthday

When I have said my evening prayer,
And my clothes are folded on the chair,
And mother switches off the light,
I'll still be .... years old tonight.
But, from the very break of day,
Before the children rise and play,
Before the darkness turns to gold
Tomorrow, I'll be ..... years old.
.... kisses when I wake,
.... candles on my cake!

My Happiest Birthday

I think that my birthday and Christmas Eve are the two happiest days in the whole year.

I woke early. I was still sleeping in Lars' and Pip's room, but when I woke Lars and Pip were fast asleep. My bed creaks so I began turning round and round in bed so that the creaking would awake the boys. I could not shout to them, for whoever has a birthday must always stay asleep until they are woken. But they went on sleeping instead of getting up and giving me my birthday tray.

However, I made my bed give a really loud creak, and at last Pip sat up and began to scratch his head. Then he woke Lars and they both crept out of the room and down the stairs. I heard Mother rattling the cups in the kitchen and I could hardly lie still, I was so excited.

At last I heard footsteps on the stairs, so I shut my eyes as tightly as I could. Then - bang - the door opened and there stood Father and Mother and Lars and Pip and Agda, our maid. Mother was carrying my tray and on it I saw a cup of chocolate, a vase of flowers and a big iced cake with "Lisa 7" on it in sugar icing.

"The Six Bullerby Children" by Astrid Lindgren

Every family has their own little rituals for birthdays; in our family we always try to make a special birthday card which is a closely guarded secret.

The card doesn't have to be expertly drawn, but the children are thrilled to get them because we try to put on the card all the most notable and important things about the child over the last year. For example, a favourite pet, an enthusiasm for trains or a particular toy; things they enjoy doing like swimming or a skill they have just achieved like riding a two-wheeler.

They tend to keep these over the years and it provides them with a special record of their childhood.

A similar idea would be to collect photographs of special events over the year to give on their birthdays.

A Birthday Place

Try to make the birthday child's place at the table special for the day by putting a candle or little bowl of flowers nearby.

For the party make a simple gold crown – perhaps incorporating something seasonal – like a little blossom or ivy – and make the birthday seat special by covering it in some material or by decorating white muslin with little gold stars and spreading this over the chair.

Party Activities

Take the children off for a walk and give them a bag each to collect any pretty stones, mosses, fir cones, small pieces of evergreen, berries or little flowers that they find, so that they can make a miniture garden when they return. You can do this on an old tin tray or table and cover with soil, sand and moss and a piece of mirror acts as a frozen lake. You can add a few tiny figures of animals or a few model buildings to finish off the scene.

Matchbox Game

Give each child a matchbox and ask them to go out in the garden, or indeed, you can do this indoors, with forethought, and find as many different small items as possible to fit into the boxes. The winner is the one with the most different objects: perhaps there could also be a prize for ingenuity.

Chinese Laundry

Hang different little bags of material on the washing line - each one containing a different smelling thing like coffee, tea, spices, herbs, moth balls, and get the children to write down as many as they can identify on a sheet of paper.

Beans are hot

A simple hiding game where one player is sent out of the room and the chosen article hidden.

The one outside is then called in with the chant:-
"Hot Beans and Melted butter,
Please, my lady, (or master) come to supper."

The search begins and when the finder is close, the players yell:-
"Hot Beans"
and when he is far away they call:-
"Cold Beans".

When the article is found the next one to go outside can be chosen by drawing straws.

Twirling the tin plate

All the players sit in a circle with a tin plate in the middle, and each player is given a number. No. 1 goes to the centre and spins the plate on the floor. He then darts back to his place and calls out a number. The person who has that number must dash forward and prevent the plate from stopping spinning and falling on the floor. If the plate does fall the player must pay a forfeit, and if it falls on the underside the loser must pay two forfeits!

The winner is the one with the least number of forfeits at the end. Forfeits could be shoes, socks, belts, pullovers, etc.

Hunt the Pairs

Collect a mass of small items before the party, for example, paperclips, nuts, macaroni, dried peas, nails, beads, cocktail sticks, rubber bands, conkers, leaves, etc.

Give each child a small bag containing, say, six different items.

Send them off on a hunt to find the right pairs which you have previously hidden around the house or garden.

The winner is the first to arrive back with all the pairs matched.

Fly away, Sparrow.
A quiet game!

All the players sit round a table with their right index finger on the table.

The host says "Fly away, Sparrow", or the name of any other flying creature, and each player raises his finger.

If anything that does not fly is mentioned, or if a creature's name is repeated, and any player raises his finger, that person suffers a forfeit or is out. Of course you are also out if you fail to raise your finger when you should have done!

Treasure Hunt

Give each child or team of children, a particular colour and start them off by giving them a clue each on appropriate coloured paper. Types of clues could include a cryptic message like - where visitors may sleep or where the garden tools hide. When they get there they will find another clue on the same coloured paper, which will send them off around the home and garden. 5-10 clues for each child or team really taxes the parents' imagination and ingenuity.

At the end, the children may find a clump of chocolate sovereigns or a little bag of home-made fudge to take home.

Ring Games.

Here we go Looby Loo,

Here we go Looby Loo,
Here we go Looby Light,
Here we go Looby Loo,
All on a Saturday night.

You put your right foot in,
You put your right foot out,
You shake it a little, a little,
And turn yourself about.

You put your left foot in, etc.

You put your right hand in, etc.

You put your left hand in, etc.

You put you whole self in, etc.

During the first verse the children skip round in a ring singing, then they let go hands and turn round in circles for "All on a Saturday night". In other verses they do the individual actions.

Cobbler Cobbler mend my Shoe

All the children except one sit on the floor in a circle. The one who is out is given a slipper. He hands this to any one of the children in the ring, saying as he does so:

Cobbler, cobbler, mend my shoe,
Get it done by half-past two,
If it can't be done by then,
Get it done by half-past ten.

The child to whom it is given then says:

Half-past ten is very late;
I'll get it done by half-past eight.

The child who originally had the shoe then turns his back for a moment and the shoe is rapidly passed behind the backs of the children in the circle and hidden by one of them. When the child comes back he asks any player in the ring, "Is my shoe ready?", and goes on until he comes to the one who has the shoe. He then changes places with this child and the game begins again.

161

One player is blindfolded and stands at the centre of a circle of players. The centre child holds a stick or ruler. Holding hands, the others skip and dance around singing:

"Have you seen the muffin man, the muffin man, the muffin man,
Have you seen the muffin man, who lives in Drury Lane?"

At the words "Drury Lane" they all stand still while the centre child points his ruler at one member of the circle. Whoever is in line with the pointer must step forward and grasp it. The blindfolded player may ask three questions now which require one-word answers. ("Are you having a nice time? Do you like cheese or peanut butter best? etc) The player pointed to must disguise his voice, and the Muffin Man (centre) is allowed three guesses as to their identity. If he guesses correctly, the other player takes the blindfold and becomes the Muffin Man. If the guesses are incorrect, the song and circle dance begins again to repeat.

Oranges and Lemons.

Oranges and lemons
Say the bells of St. Clement's.

You owe me five farthings,
Say the bells of St. Martin's.

When will you pay me?
Say the bells of Old Bailey.

When I grow rich,
Say the bells of Shoreditch.

When will that be?
Say the bells of Stepney.

I'm sure I don't know,
Says the great bell of Bow.

Here come a candle to light you to bed.
Here comes a chopper to chop off your head.

Two children form an arch and decide secretly which of them will be Oranges and the other Lemons. The words are sung and all the other children skip under the arch and round again. There is usually great excitement when it comes to the last verse when the hands making the arch drop down and catch one of the children in the middle. In a whisper they are asked whether they would like to be Oranges or Lemons and they then stand behind the one they choose. The game continues until all the children have been caught under the arch and chosen which team to be in. The game finishes with a tug-of-war between the two teams.

The Farmer in the Dell - Ring Game.

One child is the farmer. Others form a circle and walk around the farmer, singing:

The farmer in the dell.
The farmer in the dell.
Hi Ho the derrio
The farmer in the dell.

At this point the farmer chooses a 'wife', who joins him in the centre, while everyone sings:

The farmer takes a wife.
The farmer takes a wife.
Hi Ho the derrio
The farmer takes a wife.

The wife then takes a child, the child a nurse, the nurse a dog, the dog a bone. Then they all sing "We all pat the dog" and pat him or her, and the 'dog' may begin the next game as farmer if everyone wishes to repeat it.

From Mexico, the Pinata

The pinata is a large hanging papier mache ball or animal shape (in Mexico they are made into beautiful forms - donkeys, pigs, birds, etc.) filled with sweets and little toys. One child stands beneath the Pinata, surrounded by his friends (at a safe distance!). He is blindfolded and handed a large stick. His friends turn him round and round then tell him to try to hit the Pinata. After several swats the Pinata breaks and a cascade of toys and sweets are released for his delighted friends.
Note: make the Pinata at least a week in advance, or even a fortnight before the party to allow for plenty of 'drying-out' time.

A simple decoration to make, the Pinata can be decorated with lots of different coloured crepe papers.
You'll need:
Round balloon
A newspaper
½ cup of flour and water paste
crepe paper streamers
glue
white poster paint
scissors and long-nose pliers
small sweets and toys

To make:

The balloon is the base for the Pinata, so blow it up to the required size and hang it somewhere you can easily work on it. Tear the newspaper into 2½" strips, draw one through the paste, brush off excess paste and smooth it on to the balloon. Continue with each strip until you've covered the whole surface twice. Allow to dry. Repeat the process twice.

Burst the balloon and remove then cut a few inches off the top to make a larger hole and a more rounded shape. Paint with a couple of coats of the poster paint. Glue on paper streamers or decorate as you wish. Fill the Pinata with sweets, nuts, tiny toys and hang it up with string.

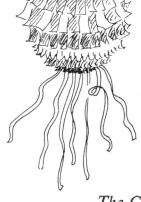

The Cake

Here are a few ideas for birthday cakes other than the obvious seasonal ones.

For most cakes where you want to make a special model, it is a good idea to start by making several sponge cakes (see p. 26 for recipe) on cake trays, so that you can cut these into the desired shapes.

Sailing boat
Make the hull of the boat out of two shaped pieces of sponge cake sandwiched together with butter icing. Cover with soft royal icing and make the sail out of rice paper with a knitting needle or stick to form the main mast. Perhaps make a rice paper flag at the top. Use liquorice strips for the various rubber tyres and ropes around the edges.

Steam engine
Build up the shape of the engine base and cab and use a swiss roll for the engine, large wagon-wheel biscuits for the wheels, liquorice for the bumpers, a small swiss roll or brandy snap for the funnel with whipped cream at the top for the smoke, and cover with icing and decorate. Chocolate fingers and liquorice make good tracks.

Fairy Castle suggestions
Sandwich together two large square pieces of sponge cake with butter icing (p.26) and make a courtyard in front with steps coming up and an arch over the gate. Use wafers for the front gates and upturned ice cream cones on top of small pieces of swiss roll for the turrets all covered in a layer of soft royal icing, (see p. 26) perhaps use wafer biscuits for the battlements. Decorate with silver balls, hundreds and thousands, and little sugared flowers.

Other ideas include making a hedgehog out of half a round sandwich cake on its side, covered in chocolate icing and with Matchstick chocolates to make the spikes.

A butterfly shape by using a swiss roll for the centre and shaped sponge cakes at the sides for the wings.

An angel — perhaps a side view — with wings at one side.

A star shape cut from a large round.

Young children particularly love to look at, and blow out, candles: an idea you could elaborate on is to place as many half walnut shell boats as the age of the child into a small bowl or dish of water. Now melt a little wax from a household candle into each empty shell and fix in a birthday candle.

These little walnut boats look very attractive bobbing in the water on the table and will delight the children.

Children so enjoy the candles that we give each child a little sponge cake with a little candle and holder in it, so that they can all blow out a candle after singing the Happy Birthday song.

Chocolate Leaves for Cake decoration

Take some small leaves, and some chocolate melted gently in the oven or over a pan of hot water. Wipe the leaves clean with a damp tissue and let them dry thoroughly before dipping them, upper side down, into the surface of the melted chocolate. Lay them chocolate side up on a plate and leave in a cool place to set. When they are set firm you will be able to peel the leaf off very gently and will find that the chocolate retains the shape of the leaf and is delicately imprinted with its veins.

Children love making these and they can be kept for a long time in an airtight tin and can be used on cakes, ices and trifles.

Sugared Rose Petals for Cake and Pudding decoration.

Take the petals from two red roses.

Beat the white of one egg and dip each petal in the egg white and then into some caster sugar.

Lay out on a non-greased tray and put in barely warm oven for 1-1½ hours, until they are dry and crisp. When they are cool, ease off the tray with a knife and keep in an airtight tin.

Frosted Grapes, or Cherries of small clusters of red or black currants

These are very sparkly and pretty. Beat the white of an egg to a slight froth and brush over the fruit. Dredge with caster sugar and chill until firm.

Together with all the sweet food for parties, it is advisable to have some savoury things as well.

Make sandwiches into attractive shapes and try having small open sandwiches on bread, rolls, or crackers:-

Mashed egg, grated cheese, cream cheese, marmite, peanut butter are a few ideas and decorate them with mustard and cress, little bits of tomato, celery, cucumber or lettuce.

Cheese straws (see p. 99) and little quiches in patty tins are also popular.

Fruit usually goes down well. Try hollowing out a large melon and fill with chunks of melon, pineapple and grapes mixed with a little sugar, and a few cherries on top.

This is delicious with ice cream.

Cut a swede in half and wrap in tin foil or use half a grapefruit or orange to make a base in which to stick cocktail sticks with pieces of pineapple and cheese, celery and cheese, melon and cheese, or sausages.

Cornflake Cakes

5 oz. brown sugar
1 tablespoon golden syrup
¾ oz. butter
½ cup milk
3 oz. cornflakes
3 oz. plain chocolate
few nuts and currants.

Cook the sugar, syrup, butter, milk and chocolate together over gentle heat. Make sure the cornflakes are crisp and fresh and if you feel they are a bit stale, toast them in the oven for a few minutes. Mix all the ingredients together and put into little buttered patty trays to set or into little paper cases.

You can mix in some currants and nuts if you like.

Meringue Mushrooms

2 egg whites
4 oz. caster sugar
1 oz. plain chocolate (finely grated)
little butter cream.

Beat the egg whites until they are stiff and whisk in 2 teaspoons of the measured sugar for 1 minute only. Fold in the remaining sugar quickly and lightly with a metal spoon, or electric whisk. Shape or pipe several small mushroom caps and stalks on an oiled and floured baking sheet. Dust the caps with grated chocolate and bake in an oven 275°F (Reg. 1) for 45 mins. Turn oven off, open door, and allow the meringues to cool in the oven. When the meringues are cool gently press a dent in the underside of each cap, pipe in a little butter cream and fix in the stalk.

You can also make little meringue mice by piping the body shape onto the floured baking sheet and putting a little tail of wool or string at one end of each mouse. When they are cooked and cold you can mark in the faces with painted-on melted chocolate.

Orange and Lemon Jelly

Grated rind of 3 or 4 oranges
Juice of 6-9 oranges and 1 lemon
(making about 1¼ pt juice)
2-3 tablespoons orange flower water
(from the chemist)
¾ pt water
4 oz sugar
1½-2 oz gelatine

Put the grated rind on one side. Squeeze the juice from the oranges and lemon and stir in the orange flower water to taste. Put through a sieve. Dissolve the sugar and gelatine in the water over a medium heat and mix well with the fruit juice and pour into individual dishes. Allow to set and decorate with chopped nuts, whipped cream and the grated rind.

Jelly Boats

Take some oranges and cut them in half: scoop out the inside being careful not to break the skin. Make up some jugs of different coloured jellies and fill the half orange peels with the jellies. Allow to set and then carefully cut each half in two pieces which then look like segments of different coloured fruit.

Children love these jelly boats and if you have some cocktail sticks you can make little masts with each child's name on a paper sail.

Alternatively, keep them in halves and make angelica handles and top the baskets with whipped cream and a sprinkling of nuts.

Wheaten Lattice Flan
– for the birthday table, delicious, very sweet –
a little bit goes a long way!

5 oz soft marg or butter
4 oz granulated or caster sugar
1 egg yolk
½ teaspoon almond essence
grated rind of one small lemon
juice of ½ a lemon
6 oz wholemeal flour
1 teaspoon ground cinnamon
2 oz ground almonds
4 rounded tablespoons apricot jam.

165

Prepare a cool oven, 325°F. (Reg 3). Place 8″ flan ring on a baking sheet (fluted ones are pretty if you have one) and grease ring and sheet. Now place in a mixing bowl the margarine, sugar, egg yolk, almond essence, lemon rind and juice, flour and ground almonds together with the cinnamon. Mix with a wooden spoon until the mixture begins to bind, then knead with your fingers to form a soft dough. Cover dough in a bowl, or wrap in foil and chill for one hour.

When chilled, roll ¾ of dough to place in flan ring and press out evenly over base and up to ¼″ of the top of the ring. Spread base with jam. Divide remaining dough into five pieces and roll each piece between the hands to a strip about 16″ long. Cut each strip in half and arrange in a lattice pattern over the jam, pressing ends onto its edge.

Bake in the centre of the oven 45-50 minutes until golden brown at edge, leave to cool and when almost cold remove flan ring.

Birthday Bread Horse

You will need a well-rounded loaf of bread, an oval bun or roll, five candy canes about 8″ long, raisins, almonds and a glace cherry.

Mount the loaf on four of the candy sticks as legs, then shorten the fifth for the neck and attach the head roll. Almonds may be stuck in for ears, raisins for eyes, and the cherry for a mouth. You may use the remaining candy bit for the tail, or be more imaginative! The horse may have a ribbon bridle, or a saddle of cheese – you'll be suprised what ideas come once you get going, and the children will doubtless appreciate him as much as anything sweet! If you are making your own bread for this, do a tiny plaited loaf for mane and tail.

Satsuma Animals

For winter birthdays Satsuma animals go down well. Little wooden cocktail sticks make legs and neck. Mould marzipan feet, use a date for the head, perhaps a sweet for the tail, whatever you have on hand.

VII.   Sweetmaking

Honeycomb

¼ pt cold water
1 tablespoon golden syrup
8 oz granulated sugar
¼ teaspoon cream of tartar
½ teaspoon bicarb. of soda
1 teaspoon warm water

Put the cold water in a heavy saucepan and add the golden syrup, sugar and cream of tartar. Put over a low heat and stir with a wooden spoon until the sugar has dissolved and all the ingredients are well blended. Raise the heat to bring the mixture to the boil without stirring. Continue to boil until it reaches 154°C (310°F) using sugar thermometer.

Grease 7″ square sandwich tin with butter. Remove saucepan from heat when mixture at appropriate temperature and stir in the bicarb. of soda and teaspoon of warm water – which have already been blended together.

Pour the mixture into the tin and leave to cool. Mark squares before it sets. Eat quickly as it soon softens and goes sticky!

Coconut Ice

2 lbs caster sugar
¼ pt milk
1 oz butter
8 oz desiccated coconut
pink colouring

Put the sugar, butter and milk in a heavy saucepan and bring slowly to the boil, stirring to dissolve the sugar. Boil for 4 mins. stirring all the time. Remove from heat, add the coconut, stir well and pour half the mixture into a greased tin, about 1″ deep. Allow to cool a little, then colour the other half pink and pour on top. Score when it is half set and cut when it is cool.

An added delight is to cover the top of the coconut ice – when it is cool – with melted plain chocolate.

Turkish Delight

1½ lb sugar
1 lemon
1 orange
¼ pt water plus a little extra
3 oz cornflour
1 oz gelatine
colouring if you wish
icing sugar

Put the sugar, the pared rind and juice of the orange and lemon and ¼ pt. water into a pan and bring to boil slowly, making sure the sugar is dissolved before boiling-point is reached. Boil to 230°F or the "long thread". 230°F - 238°F or 110 - 114°C (a little syrup in cold water will form a fine thread between finger and thumb if pressed on it and then pulled apart.)

Mix the cornflour with a little water and add to the syrup. Then add the gelatine which should previously have been softened in a little water and boil the syrup until clear, stirring occasionally. Colour if you wish. Strain into tins about 1″ deep and leave until the following day. Cut into squares and roll in icing sugar.

Chopped nuts can be added to the mixture before it is poured into the tins.

Chocolate Brazils

Melt some good plain chocolate in a double saucepan. Use two skewers to lift the nuts and dip them in the chocolate and then give a gentle tap at the side of the saucepan to remove the excess chocolate. Place them on a rack which you have first covered in waxed paper and allow them to cool for 30 minutes.

Noisette Chocolate

8 oz plain chocolate
2 fl oz double cream
½ oz butter
1 oz ground almonds
2 oz chopped hazelnuts
A little rum or brandy (optional)

Put the chocolate in a double saucepan and gently melt. Remove from heat and stir in the cream, butter, nuts, ground almonds, rum or brandy. Allow to cool until it is fairly firm and then put teaspoonsful into little sweet cases. You can decorate with half a hazelnut or a piece of cherry and cool for about two hours.

Peppermint Creams

1 lb icing sugar, well sifted
White of an egg
small quantity of thick cream
a few drops of peppermint essence

Mix the sugar and egg white and cream. Stir well into a firm paste and add the peppermint as you mix. Dust a board with icing sugar and roll out the paste and use a small cutter to make rounds. Put on a wire rack and leave to dry for about 12 hours.

You can add a minute quantity of green or pink colouring on the tip of a skewer if you like.

Use this recipe and make sugar mice – perhaps colouring some of the quantity to make pink or green mice. Put silver balls in for the eyes and a piece of string for the tail and whiskers.

Chocolate Fudge

2 lbs brown sugar
½ pt milk
¼ lb butter
3 tablespoons chocolate
a few drops of vanilla essence
grated rind and juice of an orange

Allow the sugar and milk to soak for 1 hour. Bring to the boil slowly with all the other ingredients except the vanilla. Allow it to boil fast for 10-15 minutes. It will rise in the saucepan: take it off the heat when it begins to sink and crystallise on the edge of the saucepan. It is important not to stir too often, just enough to stop it burning. Allow it to stand off the heat for 2 minutes then add the vanilla and beat with a wooden spoon to the consistency of thick cream. Pour quickly into a well-buttered tin and allow to cool. Score when half cold.

Butterscotch

1 lb granulated sugar
¼ pt hot water
¼ teaspoon cream of tartar
3 oz unsalted butter
¼ teaspoon vanilla essence

Put the sugar and water into a heavy saucepan and heat gently and stir carefully with a wooden spatula from time to time until all the sugar is dissolved. Add the cream of tartar and boil to 116°C (240°F). Remove the saucepan from the heat and add the butter in small pieces. Return to the heat and boil to 138°C (280°F).

Remove from heat and stir in the vanilla essence and pour the mixture into a well-oiled shallow swiss roll tin.

When it has nearly set, mark into little squares or rectangles and when cold break into pieces and wrap in cellophane or shiny metallic paper.

Honey Toffee

Boil 10 oz of butter and 4 oz of pure honey with ¼ pt water. Boil to 114-118°C (238-245°F) (when you place a little in cold water it will form a soft ball which can be squeezed flat.) Pour onto a greased tin, then cut the toffee into small squares before it sets. Later, wrap individually in greaseproof or cellophane paper. This is very good for colds.

Apricot Crunches

4 oz dried apricots
2 teaspoons honey
2½ oz finely chopped mixed nuts
½ teaspoon each of finely grated orange and lemon rind
2 teaspoons orange juice

Place apricots in a bowl, pour on boiling water to soak for five minutes. Drain and mince. Then mix all the ingredients together, knead very well and shape into small rounds.

Variations: these may be rolled in coconut or you can imprint each with a cashew nut or hazelnut.

Sesame Chews

6 tablespoons sesame seeds
2 tablespoons honey
flour to mix

Mix seeds and honey, add flour to stiffen. Pat onto rice paper in a pan and leave to chill and harden for a few days in a cold larder or the fridge. Then cut into squares.

Marrons Glacés

Split each nut with the point of a sharp knife and put in a pan with water to cover and boil until tender, 20 minutes. Shell the nuts, removing inner and outer skins: keep in hot water until you do each one. When shelled, drop into warm water with a little lemon juice.
   Make a plain syrup, using two parts sugar to one of water, boiling it until it coats the back of a spoon. Drain the nuts and dry. Put them in the syrup and boil until quite tender and unbroken. Drain on a wire rack. Boil syrup to crack stage i.e. a little syrup

dropped in cold water should set hard at once – remove pan from heat and dip chestnuts in one at a time on a skewer. Coat well and place on wire rack to dry off in a very cool oven for a few minutes. Put in waxed paper in a fancy box.

Marzipan Flowers

Form small balls of marzipan, then press into each centre a raisin or a chocolate drop. Put on a baking sheet about two inches apart and place briefly under the grill. The marzipan ball will brown slightly and spread into a flower-shape which is crisp and delicious when cooled.

Fruit and Nut Sticks

1 cup chopped nuts
½ cup chopped dates or prunes
1 egg
½ cup honey

Mix fruit and nuts with egg and honey and shape into sticks. Place on oiled baking sheet, bake 10-15 minutes at 375°F (Reg 5).

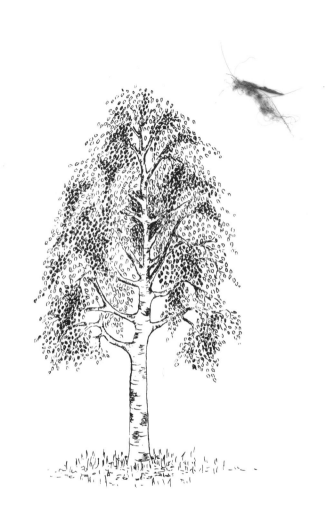

VIII.   Hungry Teatimes

You are going out to tea today,
So mind how you behave;
Let all accounts I have of you
Be pleasant ones, I crave.

Don't spill your tea, or gnaw your bread,
And don't tease one another;
And Tommy mustn't talk too much,
Or quarrel with his brother.

Say "If you please," and "Thank you, Nurse;"
Come home at eight o'clock;
And, Fanny, pray be careful that
You do not tear your frock.

Now, mind your manners, children five,
Attend to what I say;
And then, perhaps, I'll let you go
Again another day.

From Kate Greenaway's 'Under the Window'

Wholewheat Drop Scones

8 oz flour
¼ teaspoon salt
1 egg
1 oz sugar
½ pint milk
1 teaspoon cream of tartar
½ teaspoon bicarbonate of soda

Put the flour, salt, cream of tartar and bicarb. of soda into a bowl with the sugar. Mix thoroughly.

Make a well in the centre, beat the egg and stir into the flour, adding the milk gradually to make a smooth, thick batter, beat well.

Grease a griddle or frying-pan. When hot, drop tablespoons of the mixture on the griddle; cook until golden brown on one side, then turn and cook on the other side – serve immediately with butter.

Welsh Cakes

8 oz plain flour
pinch of bicarb. of soda
1 teaspoon baking powder
4 oz margarine or butter
3 oz mixed fruit or sultanas
3 oz caster sugar
1 egg
1 teaspoon mixed spice

Rub the margarine or butter with the dry ingredients as if you were making pastry. Then mix in the fruit and add the beaten egg – if the dough seems too dry add a little milk.

Roll out the dough onto a floured surface to about ¼″ thick and use a 2½″ cutter. Lightly grease a heavy pan or griddle and put over a medium heat and cook the cakes for about 3 minutes each side – don't let them brown too quickly. Serve warm with butter and jam.

Scotch Pancakes

2 oz butter
1 teaspoon golden syrup
5 oz plain flour
pinch of salt
1 level teaspoon bicarb. of soda
1 level teaspoon cream of tartar
1 teaspoon caster sugar
1 beaten egg
1 level teaspoon baking powder
small quantity of milk

Melt the butter and syrup together in a pan. Mix together the flour, salt, bicarb, cream of tartar into a mixing bowl, add the sugar and beat in the egg. Lastly stir in the baking powder and mix well together to form a thick batter, adding extra milk if necessary to give it the consistency of thick cream. Using a tablespoon drop the mixture onto a hot griddle or heavy-based frying pan, greased, and cook for 2-3 minutes, so that bubbles form and burst on the surface. Carefully turn each pancake and cook other side. Cool on a wire rack and serve spread with butter.

Gypsy Malt Loaf

½ lb plain flour
pinch of salt
1 teaspoon bicarb. of soda
2 oz golden syrup
1 oz soft brown sugar
2 tablespoons malt
2 oz raisins
2 oz sultanas
1 oz dates, chopped
¼ pt milk

Mix flour, salt and bicarb. into a mixing bowl. Gently melt the syrup, sugar and malt in a pan and pour it onto the dry ingredients. Mix well, add the dried fruit and mix to a stiff consistency with the milk.

Turn into a 1 lb prepared loaf tin and bake at 350°F (Reg 3) for 1-1½ hours until the loaf has risen and turned golden brown. Cool on a wire rack and keep in an airtight tin for at least two days before eating, then serve sliced with butter.

Crumpets

½ oz fresh yeast
5 teaspoons lukewarm water
4 oz plain flour
½ teaspoon sugar
¼ teaspoon salt
6 tablespoons milk or a drop more
1 egg
2½ oz butter
Round crumpet rings or 3″ metal biscuit cutters

Sprinkle the yeast over the 5 teaspoons of lukewarm water in a small bowl and stand for 2-3 mins. Then stir well to dissolve the yeast. Set the bowl in a warm, draught-free place with the sugar for a few minutes until the yeast bubbles up.

Put the flour and salt into a large mixing bowl and make a well in the centre. Pour in the yeast mixture and the milk and drop in the egg. Beat vigorously with a wooden spoon then add ½ oz of butter until smooth batter is formed. Set aside in warm place for 1 hour until batter doubled in size.

Clarify remaining 2 oz of butter in small pan: do not let it brown. Skim off the surface foam and spoon the clear butter into a bowl discarding the milky solids at the bottom of the pan. Grease griddle or large heavy frying pan and inside surfaces of crumpet rings with about half the clarified butter.

Arrange rings on griddle and put on moderate heat. For each crumpet drop about 1 tablespoon of batter into each ring. When it begins to bubble and the bottom becomes a light brown, remove the rings. Turn the crumpet over and cook for a minute or two the other side. With each batch you must grease the griddle and rings again.

American Muffins

Completely versatile, quickly mixed and baked, muffins make a warm contribution to any winter evening teatime.

The secret of nicely raised muffins is to keep mixing to an **absolute minimum.** The beaten liquid ingredients are added to the mixed dry ones in a few swift strokes – stir for a matter of 10 or 20 seconds only and ignore the lumps. The longer the beating, the tougher the muffin. Below is the basic recipe, but to it you may choose to add any one of the following ingredients:

a ¼ to a ½ a teacup of:
>nuts
>diced apricots
>figs, dates or prunes (or a combination)
>chopped apples and cinnamon
>grated cheese and caraway seeds
>crushed pineapple
>mashed ripe banana
>raisins and/or glace cherries

Preheat a hot oven, 400°F (Reg 6)

| Sift and mix: | 7 oz self-raising flour |
| | 2 oz sugar   pinch of salt |

In a separate bowl beat 2 eggs and into them mix 6 oz milk and two tablespoons melted butter (or one tablespoon of good vegetable oil). Mix well.

Form a hole in the middle of the dry ingredients, pour in liquid ones, mix as above, and fill well-oiled patty tins ⅔ full. Bake at once 20-25 minutes. If they remain in the tins for a few minutes after removing from oven, they will be easier to take out. Eat while warm; texture should be crumbly and moist.

Pita Bread
(Makes 12 Pita Breads)

Yeast Dough	Filling Suggestions
2 level teaspoons sugar	Lettuce
½ pint hand-hot water,	Tomatoes
plus one tablespoon	Cress
1 oz dried yeast	Coleslaw salad
1 lb strong flour	Grated cheese
1 level teaspoon salt	
2 tablespoons oil	

Dissolve sugar in water in a measuring jug. Sprinkle dried yeast on top; leave in a warm place until frothy, 5 to 10 minutes.

Place flour and salt in a bowl. Add yeast liquid and oil; mix to a soft, but not sticky dough.

Turn out dough onto a floured board and knead dough by folding towards you, then pushing away with the palm of the hand; give dough a quarter turn and repeat. Knead for about 5 minutes, until dough feels firm and elastic.

Place dough in a lightly greased bowl or saucepan, cover with tea cloth or a lid; leave to rise in a warm place until doubled in size, about 40 minutes. Prepare a very hot oven 450°F (Reg 8) and place rack to the lowest position.

Re-knead dough, as before, until smooth. Divide dough into 12 equal pieces. Flatten each piece of dough with the knuckles to disperse large air bubbles. Roll 2 pieces at a time to 5½" circles; leave remaining pieces covered. Place on a lightly greased baking sheet. Allow to rise in a warm place, uncovered, until barely doubled in thickness.

Bake 1 tray at a time for about 5 minutes, or until bread is puffed and just starting to brown. Roll out 2 more pieces of dough and place on a lightly greased baking sheet; continue until remaining dough is used. If they are to be eaten straight away, make a small hole in each one as they come out of the oven; cool slightly and slip into plastic bags to keep them moist and pliable.

To serve: serve warm, split and filled with shredded lettuce, sliced tomatoes, and a little coleslaw salad.

Oatie Ginger Biscuits

4 oz rolled oats
4 oz wholemeal flour
⅛ level teaspoon salt
1 level teaspoon baking powder
1 level teaspoon ground ginger
1½ oz butter or margarine
1½ oz soft brown sugar
1 egg
2 tablespoons skimmed milk
(Makes 14)

Preheat a moderately hot oven 375°F (Reg 5), shelf above centre. Grease two trays.

Put the oats in a mixing bowl and mix in the flour, salt, baking powder and ground ginger. Rub in the fat until the mixture resembles coarse breadcrumbs. Stir in the sugar. Beat the egg and milk together and stir into the dry ingredients. Mix to form a stiff dough.

Divide into 14 equal pieces and roll each into a ball. Place on the baking trays, allowing room for spreading and press out with the back of a fork.

Bake for 15-20 minutes until well browned and firm to the touch. Lift off onto a wire rack and cool. Store in an airtight container.

Carob Fingers

2 tablespoons raisins
4 oz margarine
2 oz soft brown sugar
2 tablespoons honey

2 tablespoons carob powder
4 tablespoons chopped nuts
1 teaspoon cinnamon
2 tablespoons coconut
2 tablespoons (approx.) wholemeal flour
2 tablespoons oats

Plump raisins in a little boiling water. Melt margarine, add sugar and honey. Stir together for 3-4 minutes. Pour into mixing bowl and cool slightly. Add carob powder, nuts, salt, cinnamon and drained raisins. Stir in coconut and oats and add enough flour to make a fairly stiff mixture.

Spread about ½″ thick in rectangular tin. Bake 350°F (Reg 4) for 25 minutes.

Coconut Jam Slice

6 oz self-raising flour
4 oz margarine
2 eggs
3 oz sugar
3 oz coconut
1 teaspoon vanilla essence
jam

Rub flour and margarine together. Bind with 1 beaten egg. Spread in a swiss roll tin approx. 7″ x 9″ and make level. Spread jam over. Mix coconut, sugar, essence and other beaten egg. Spread on top of jam. Cook 25 minutes 350°F (Reg 4). Cut when warm. Remove from tin when cold.

Wholewheat Scones

7 oz wholewheat plain flour
½ level teaspoons salt
3 rounded teaspoons baking powder
2 oz margarine
¼ pt liquid – milk and water mix
1 egg (optional)

Fruit Scones
Add: 1 oz brown sugar
2 oz dried fruit or sultanas

Sieve the flour, salt and baking powder into a bowl and mix well. Rub the fat into the flour with the finger tips. Make a well in the centre and add the liquid to make a soft dough.

Turn onto a floured board. Roll lightly until the dough is ½″ thick. Cut into rounds with a 2½″ pastry cutter. Brush with a little beaten egg and place on a greased baking tin and put into a hot oven 425°F (Reg 7) for 15 minutes.

Delicious served with homemade jams and on special occasions with whipped cream.

Savoury Scones

8 oz flour
2 oz butter or margarine
3-4 oz grated cheese
2 teaspoons baking powder
¼ pt milk or water
Salt and pepper and pinch dry mustard or marmite

Mix flour, baking powder and seasoning together and rub in the fat. Add the cheese and milk to make a soft dough. Roll out and use a 2½″ cutter to make ½″ thick. Place on greased baking sheets and put a little grated cheese on the top and bake for 10 minutes 425°F (Reg 7).

Eccles Cakes

½ oz butter, plus melted butter for baking tray
1 oz sugar
2½ oz currants
½ oz chopped mixed fruit peel
½ teaspoon ground allspice
½ teaspoon ground nutmeg

Short-crust pastry
3 oz butter, chilled
6 oz plain flour
little salt
2½ teaspoons caster sugar
2-3 tablespoons iced water

When made into dough, put in fridge for one hour before use, or you can use puff pastry (see Maids of Honour recipe p.177). Grease large baking sheet with softened butter. Put melted butter and sugar in small bowl and stir in currants, peel, allspice and nutmeg. Mix well.

Roll pastry into circle and use 3½″ cutters. Put tablespoon of fruit mixture in centre of each round. Bring up the outside edges of pastry and twist together to enclose the filling. Turn over and with rolling pin press gently but firmly into flat rounds. Make criss-cross slits in centre of each cake.

Place on baking sheet and bake for 15-20 minutes in centre of the oven 425°F (Reg 7). Transfer to rack and sprinkle with caster sugar.

Shortbread

5 oz plain flour	
1 oz rice flour	4 oz butter
2 oz caster sugar	caster sugar

Mix the flours and add the sugar and gradually work in the butter to form a firm dough. Knead well and press firmly into 7″ sandwich tin or into a shortbread mould. Refrigerate or chill for 30 mins. Carefully turn out the shortbread onto a prepared baking sheet, prick well and mark into cutting sections. Bake at 325°F (Reg 3) for 45 mins. until it is golden brown. Dredge with caster sugar, cut into sections and store in airtight tin.

Ragged Robins

2 egg whites
¼ teaspoon salt
8 oz sugar
1 teaspoon vanilla essence
3 oz chopped walnuts
3 oz chopped dates
3 oz crushed cornflakes

Beat the egg whites until light and gradually add the sugar, salt and vanilla then fold in the nuts, dates and cornflakes. Put a teaspoon as a time onto a buttered baking sheet and cook for about 30 minutes in a cool oven, 310°F (Reg 2).

Butter Leaves from Sweden

4 oz butter
2 oz sugar
1 egg
7 oz flour
1 oz chopped nuts (walnuts, hazelnuts or almonds)
2 extra tablespoons sugar

Cream the butter and sugar together until fluffy. Mix in the yolk of the egg and the flour. Chill. Roll out thinly and cut into shapes. Brush with the beaten egg white and sprinkle with the nuts and the extra sugar. Place on a buttered baking sheet and bake in a moderate oven, 355°F (Reg 4) for about 10 minutes.

175

New Zealand Biscuits

1 heaped tablespoon golden syrup
5 oz butter
4 oz caster sugar
3 oz rolled oats
2 oz desiccated coconut
4 oz plain flour
2 level teaspoons bicarb. of soda

Grease two baking trays and put the syrup, butter and sugar into a pan and leave to melt over a low heat. Remove the pan and stir in the dry ingredients. Dissolve the bicarb. in a bowl in 1 tablespoon hot water and mix in the other ingredients and leave to cool for a few minutes. Divide into 30 portions and roll into balls and place on the baking trays leaving **plenty** of room between each. Bake for 20 mins. until browned, 325°F (Reg 3) and allow to cool on tray for a few minutes before placing on wire trays.

Peanut butter cookies

2 oz crunchy peanut butter
2 oz butter or margarine
grated rind of ½ an orange
1½ oz brown sugar
2 oz caster sugar
1 egg
1½ oz sultanas
4 oz self-raising flour

Cream together the peanut butter and butter or margarine, orange rind and sugars. Beat in the egg; add the sultanas and stir in the sifted flour. Roll into balls the size of walnuts and place well apart on an ungreased baking sheet. Bake in a moderate over 355°F (Reg 4) for about 25 minutes.

Chocolate Shortbread

4 oz margarine
2 oz brown sugar
3½ oz plain flour
2½ oz desiccated coconut
2 tablespoons cocoa powder
2 oz plain chocolate

Cream together the margarine and sugar until well blended, then add flour, coconut and cocoa and mix well. Press mixture firmly into a greased swiss roll tin (a palette knife helps here) and bake in a moderate oven, 350°F (Reg 4) for 30 mins. Whilst shortbread is cooking, break chocolate into small pieces or grate coarsely. When shortbread is cooked, scatter chocolate over the top, and return shortbread to oven for a minute or two, until chocolate has melted. Remove from oven and spread chocolate evenly over the top. Cool in tin, then cut into slices.

Chocolate Orange Biscuits

2 oz margarine
3 oz butter
6 oz caster sugar
8 oz plain flour
2 teaspoons baking powder
3 oz plain chocolate, chopped
grated rind of 2 oranges
1 tablespoon orange juice

Beat the fats and sugar together until pale and fluffy, then sift the flour and baking powder straight onto the creamed mixture. Add the rest of the ingredients and work the mixture together until you get a fairly stiff dough. Now flour a working surface and roll the paste out to ¼-½" thick and then cut out the biscuits into different shapes and place on greased baking sheets. Sprinkle the biscuits with a little caster sugar and bake for 20 mins, until golden colour, 350°F (Reg 4). Leave to cool on baking sheets for 5 mins. and then cool on wire rack and store.

Shrewsbury Biscuits

¼ lb butter
¼ lb caster sugar
1 small egg, beaten
2 teaspoons grated lemon rind
½ lb plain flour
pinch of cinnamon

Cream the butter and sugar together until the mixture is light and fluffy, then beat in the egg and mix thoroughly. Stir in the lemon rind and gradually fold in the sifted flour and cinnamon. Knead the mixture lightly and place it on a floured pastry board.

Roll out thinly, prick well all over and cut into rounds; place on prepared baking sheets and bake at 350°F (Reg 4) for 15 mins. Cool on a wire rack and store in an airtight tin.

This is a wonderful way of using up all the odd bits of biscuits that get left at the bottom of the tin.

Granny's Cookies

½ lb plain biscuits
3 oz margarine or butter
1 tablespoon granulated sugar
1 tablespoon golden syrup
2 tablespoons cocoa
2 oz bar plain chocolate

To crumble the biscuits either mince, liquidise or place in polythene bag and crumble with rolling pin. Put margarine, sugar, syrup and cocoa into a saucepan and melt over low heat. Do not boil. Mix all together and press into a sandwich tin, allow to cool. Melt chocolate and spread over the top. Decorate with 100's and 1000's and cool in fridge.

Chocolate Brownies

4 oz flour
pinch of bicarb. of soda
1 teaspoon baking powder
¼ teaspoon salt
1½ oz cocoa
4 oz butter
8 oz soft brown sugar
2 beaten eggs
1 tablespoon milk

Icing: 1½ oz butter
         1 oz cocoa
         3 tablespoons evaporated milk
         4 oz icing sugar

Grease and flour an oblong tin about 11" x 7", 1" deep. Sieve together flour, salt and cocoa. In another bowl beat the butter and sugar until light and creamy. Add eggs a little at a time, beating well after each addition. Fold sieved ingredients into mixture with milk. Mix well and turn into prepared tin. Bake in a moderately hot oven 375°F (Reg 5), until the cake feels springy when lightly pressed (about 35 mins) and allow the cake to cool in the tin.

Melt the butter for the icing, add the cocoa and cook over a low heat for 1 minute. Remove from heat and add evaporated milk and icing sugar. Mix in thoroughly and spread over the cake in the tin and leave it to set. Then cut the cake into squares.

Maids of Honour

¼ lb cottage cheese or mixed with curd cheese
3 oz butter
2 egg yolks
3 oz caster sugar
2 tablespoons mashed potato
1½ oz ground almonds
Juice and grated rind of a lemon
Juice and grated rind of an orange
½ teaspoon almond essence
freshly grated nutmeg
½ lb puff pastry

Mix the cottage cheese with the butter, beat in the egg yolks and add the sugar; a blender or electric whisk are good for this. Mix the potato, ground almonds, rind and juice of the orange and lemon, almond essence and nutmeg one at a time and gradually add them to the cottage cheese mix.

Line about 36 patty tins with the puff pastry and put a dessertspoon of the mixture into each. Bake at 400°F (Reg 6) for 20-25 minutes until golden brown.

Puff Pastry

6 oz finest pastry flour
pinch of salt
6 oz not too soft butter
3-4 tablespoons ice cold water with a squeeze of lemon

Sift flour in bowl with salt. Cut butter into pieces and mix into the flour leaving it in lumps, add water to bring to a firm dough. Wrap in cloth and set aside for 10 minutes in fridge, then roll on floured slab about 6" wide, 1" thick in long strip. Fold in three, turn round and bring the open edge towards you, roll out again this time rolling the paste to ½" thick. Fold in three and cool for 15 minutes. Repeat this process, i.e. two rollings, and one rest, twice more. Then the paste should be uniform in colour and show no signs of streakiness. Chill again before using. Be careful when rolling to use firm light strokes. Do not push for then the butter is pushed out of place: also you do not want to push so heavily that the butter comes through and sticks, which would mean using more flour, and in this recipe you don't want to do that.

Chocolate Crinkles

3½ tablespoons oil
2 oz cooking chocolate, melted
1 level teaspoon cocoa
6½ oz caster sugar
2 eggs
vanilla essence
5 oz flour
1 level teaspoon baking powder
½ teaspoon salt
icing sugar

Mix the oil with the chocolate, cocoa and sugar. Beat in the eggs one at a time and add a few drops of vanilla essence. Sift together the flour, baking powder and salt and fold into the chocolate mixture. Cover and chill overnight then roll into little balls and toss in sifted icing sugar. Place 2″ apart on a baking sheet lined with greaseproof paper. Bake in a moderate oven, 355°F (Reg 4) for about 10 minutes and allow to cool slightly before removing from tray.

Lemon Shaped Biscuits

4 oz margarine
4 oz caster sugar
8 oz plain flour
1 small egg
1 lemon

Beat the sugar and margarine together until pale and fluffy. Add the beaten egg and add the flour and grated lemon peel and juice. Mix well together and with your hands form a dough. Put this into the fridge for ¼ hour.

Now roll out the dough on a floured board and use different shaped biscuit cutters. Place the biscuits on a flat buttered baking tin and bake in the oven for 10 mins, 375°F (Reg 5).

You can have a few sesame seeds or caraway seeds on top if you like.

Florentines

8 oz plain chocolate
2 oz margarine
4 oz soft brown sugar
1 egg
5 heaped tablespoons desiccated coconut
3 heaped tablespoons chopped nuts
2 heaped tablespoons glacé cherries
2 heaped tablespoons mixed peel
2 heaped tablespoons sultanas

Melt the chocolate and spread over the bottom of a greased swiss roll tin and leave to set. Beat together the margarine and sugar, add the egg and the other ingredients. Spread mixture over the chocolate and bake in a slow oven, 325°F (Reg 3) for 30-40 minutes or until set and golden. Leave to cool, then cut into slices.

Scotch Sultana Cake

¼ lb softened butter
¼ lb caster sugar
2 large eggs, beaten
½ lb self-raising flour
pinch of salt
½ lb sultanas
juice and grated rind of an orange
juice and grated rind of a lemon
pinch of nutmeg and cinnamon

Mix the butter and sugar together until they are creamy, then gradually beat in the eggs until the whole mixture is light and fluffy.

Mix the flour, salt and spices together and fold this into the creamed mixture. Add the sultanas, the rind and juice of the orange and lemon and stir well.

Turn the mixture into a 6″ cake tin which is well greased and floured and bake at 350°F (Reg 4) for 1½-1¾ hours, or until it has risen well and is cooked through.

IX   RAINY DAYS AND CONVALESCENCE

Rain on the green grass
And rain on the tree
Rain on the house-top
But not on me.

* * * * * *

It's raining, it's pouring,
The old man's snoring;
He got into bed
And bumped his head
And couldn't get up in the morning.

* * * * * *

Rainy, rainy rattlestones,
Dinna rain on me,
Rain on John o' Groat's house
Far across the sea.

* * * * * *

I hear thunder,
I hear thunder,
Hark can you?
Hark can you?
Patter patter raindrops,
I'm wet through,
So are you.

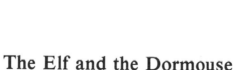

The Elf and the Dormouse

Under a toadstool crept a wee Elf
Out of the rain to shelter himself.

Under the Toadstool sound asleep,
Sat a big Dormouse all in a heap.

Trembled the wee Elf, frightened and yet
Fearing to fly away lest he got wet.

To the next shelter – maybe a mile!
Suddenly the wee Elf smiled a wee smile.

Tugged 'til the Toadstool toppled in two
Holding it over him gaily he flew.

Soon he was safe home dry as could be
Soon woke the Dormouse – good gracious me!

"Where is my toadstool?" loud he lamented
And that's how umbrellas first were invented.

Oliver Herford

179

Rainbows and Flowers

Great King Sun, who lights the world, has many messengers and servants to carry out his wishes upon the earth. Among these is the Wind, who can encircle the seven seas as well as all the lands with his breath. Then there are the Sun Fairies whose spears bring the Sun's light down to earth and the Rain Fairies who gather drops of mist from the clouds and turn them into raindrops that water the earth.

To these tiny Sun Fairies and Rain Fairies the great King Sun gave the special task of caring for the Plant-Children on earth. Because of this the Sun and Rain Fairies loved all the little Plant-Children and tried to win their favour! But once ......

Once there was a wee, shining, golden Sun Fairy who was **very** young and so thought that he knew a **very** great deal. When he was flying about, one day, he bumped into a Rain Fairy who was blue and cold, having fallen out of a cloud.

"How blue and cross you look, you poor, miserable, little rain-bringer!" the Sun Fairy teased.

"Miserable indeed!" responded the Rain Fairy. "You're not as bright as you think you are. Why without us, who would bring rain to the earth? Without us the little Plant-Children could not grow."

"As if the Plant-Children needed you!" said the Sun Fairy scornfully. "We Sun Fairies with our spears of light are the ones who help the Plant-Children grow."

"No, no!" cried the Rain Fairy. "We are the ones who help them."

"You are not!" shouted the Sun Fairy. "We are."

"No, we are!" the Rain Fairy began to swell with rage and look like a blue bubble.

"We are!" the Sun Fairy turned red with anger and his spear began to look like a red-hot flame.

They made such a hullabaloo that all the other fairies came rushing to the spot to see what was going on. Thousands and millions of light-bearing Sun Fairies swarmed toward thousands and millions of Rain Fairies who poured down from some drifting clouds.

The young Sun Fairy shouted to his bright brothers, "Come gather and listen. The Rain Fairies think they are the ones who help the Plant-Children grow!" And all the Sun Fairies flashed their golden spears with rage, and the spears glowed red like many flames of fire.

"Oo!" cried the blue Rain Fairy to his dark brothers, "the Sun Fairies say they are the ones who help the Plant-Children grow."

Now when great King Sun heard their quarrelling, he laughed, for he knew better; and he sighed, for he feared they would not believe him if he told them the truth.

Summoning the Wind, he commanded, "Go and blow the Rain Fairies away so the Sun Fairies learn a good lesson."

Then a great wind storm arose in the sky as the Wind blew the clouds away, and for many days thereafter not a cloud appeared in the clear blue sky.

Day after day the Sun Fairies flew among the Plant-Children showering them with sunshine. The days grew warmer and warmer and the Plant-Children began to get thirsty.

"We are so thirsty," they cried. "We want a drink of water."

The Sun Fairies pretended not to hear.

Then the ground became hotter and hotter, and the Plant-Children cried, "We are burning up!" And their little green coats began to scorch and turn brown.

Still the Sun Fairies paid no attention to their cries.

Then all the brooks and rivers dried up and there was no water anywhere. The Plant-Children turned black and curled up and died, all except the great Trees who were stronger than the rest. When they saw what had happened, they complained to their friend, the Wind.

"Oh, Wind," sighed the Trees, "the Rain Fairies have not visited us for so long that our little ones have died of thirst. Blow north, south, east and west, oh Wind, until you find where the Rain Fairies are hiding, and tell them to bring us rain."

So the Wind hurried away and found the Rain Fairies all hiding in a black cloud above a high mountain, and he told them to hurry down with rain to help the Plant-Children come to life again.

Then the Wind blew the great rain cloud down over the earth. The Rain Fairies leaped from the cloud splashing great showers of rain over the earth, and shouting at the Sun Fairies, who fled at their coming, "You have killed the Plant-Children with your red and yellow spears. We are the ones who really give them life."

High in the sky, above the clouds, great King Sun watched what was happening. He smiled to himself and sighed and decided that the Rain Fairies should have their turn and learn their lesson.

Day after day it rained. The rain made the earth wet again, and baby plants started to grow. Soon all the old black and brown and dead Plant-Children were hidden by new, green baby plants which grew well for a time. The Rain Fairies were very busy, making sure that it didn't stop raining. After a while the ground became too wet and turned into mud.

The newly grown Plant-Children cried, "We are too cold and wet!". Now the Rain Fairies pretended not to hear them.

Then the soil got so watery that it began to slide away in little streams of muddy water, leaving the Plant-Children with no covering for their roots.

Again the Plant Children cried, "Our feet are slipping. We will drown in all this water!"

Even then the Rain Fairies paid no attention.

Then the brooks and rivers filled up with so much rain water they overflowed their banks and the water spread out in all directions, flooding the land and drowning all the baby plants.

Again the big Trees saw what was happening and complained to their friend, the Wind, "Oh Wind, the Rain Fairies bring too much rain. They have flooded the land and our babies have drowned. Blow the Rain Fairies away and call the Sun Fairies back to dry up the water."

So the Wind blew and blew and, as the clouds scattered, the Rain Fairies saw that they had drowned all the little Plant-Children, and they were very much ashamed.

Now, as the Rain Fairies were flying away, they met the Sun Fairies coming back. This time they all knew better than to boast and fight. And so they stopped to greet each other in the sky singing, "The Plant-Children need us both. Not too much sunshine and not too much of rain. But both rain and sunshine will make them grow again."

When great King Sun heard this, he smiled again, and this time he did not sigh, for he knew that all was well.

Indeed, the Sun Fairies and the Rain Fairies decided to make peace with each other and each do their share to help the Plant-Children grow. To celebrate their new friendship they danced together in a great arch in the sky. And then something wonderful happened.

As the red Sun Fairies danced with the blue Rain Fairies, the arch shone with a violet light just the colour of the violets that bloom among the plants on earth. And as the yellow Sun Fairies danced with the blue Rain Fairies, a lovely green light shone in the arch, just the green that the plants wear in their stems and leaves. And soon there shone in the arch all the colours of the plant family. – violet, blue, green, yellow, orange and red – the colours of flowers and fruits and grasses.

So it is that the plants on earth flourish when the Sun Fairies and Rain Fairies share the work of caring for them. And when we see a rainbow in the sky, we know the Sun and Rain Fairies are having a good time together.

Dorothy Harrer

Waiting at the Window

These are my two drops of rain
Waiting on the window-pane.

I am waiting here to see
Which the winning one will be.

Both of them have different names.
One is John and one is James.

All the best and all the worst
Comes from which of them is first.

James had just begun to ooze.
He's the one I want to lose.

John is waiting to begin.
He's the one I want to win.

James is going slowly on.
Something sort of sticks to John.

John is moving off at last.
James is going pretty fast.

John is rushing down the pane.
James is going slow again.

James has met a sort of smear.
John is getting very near.

Is he going fast enough?
(James has found a piece of fluff).

John has hurried quickly by.
(James was talking to a fly.)

John is there, and John has won!
Look! I told you! Here's the sun!

A.A.Milne

Rain

The rain is raining all around,
It falls on field and tree,
It rains on the umbrellas here,
And on the ships at sea.

The Land of Counterpane

When I was sick and lay a-bed,
I had two pillows at my head,
And all my toys beside me lay
To keep me happy all the day.

And sometimes for an hour or so
I watched my leaden soldiers go,
With different uniforms and drills
Among the bed-clothes, through the hills;

And sometimes sent my ships in fleets
All up and down among the sheets;
Or brought my trees and houses out,
And planted cities all about.

I was the giant, great and still,
That sits upon the pillow-hill,
And sees before him, dale and plain,
The pleasant land of counterpane.

Two poems by R. L. Stevenson

No Pipe Dreams for Father

Though by no means a particularly sunny-natured child, my persistent grizzling one evening attracted Father's notice before he went off to the night shift. He picked me up on his lap, felt my burning forehead, and noticed my heavy eyes and quickened breathing with some concern. "Mark my words this young un be a'sickening fir zummat. The best place for 'er is bed an' a bit o'quiet."

He put a brick to warm in the oven, helped Mam to make a bed for me in their room, and lit a fire in its tiny grate. When the fire had warmed the bedroom and the hot brick my bed, Mam gave me a washdown mustard bath, covered me with extra blankets borrowed from a kindly neighbour, and my worried father went out in the darkness to walk to the pit.

When he came home in the early hours of the morning I was worse.

Father's only culinary achievement was invalid's soup and he proceeded to make me some. He poured some boiling water on a piece of bread in a basin, beat it to a cream, adding sugar, a little knob of butter and a drop of milk. When my normally greedy little stomach refused to touch the delicacy, alarm set in.

Mam made some invalid drink – boiling water poured on a piece of toast and allowed to get cold. My siblings went to bed with hushed voices and tip-toe manner.

"I be goin' for the doctor" said Father.

For the doctor's and pride's sake two shillings off the arrears we owed him had to be multiple-

182

borrowed from our impoverished neighbours, and Father ran through the woods to the doctor's house before going on his night shift.

Old Auntie, who had given up the struggle of getting upstairs to sleep, made a tortured ascent to sit with me whilst Mam did her evening chores and attended to the baby.

The doctor came, shook his head on my account, advised that the crisis would come shortly and my chance of surviving it was nil. His visit did not register on me; a black coma kept sucking me down. When I opened my eyes it was to unrecognisable surroundings. I could hear far away voices, and someone crying softly - "I be afeared we be gwine to lose the little wench, Maggie, fir I never knowed anybody as bad as 'er is to get over it - and to think that only a couple 'o' days ago 'er was threadin' me needle for me as right as rain." I could see no one, only weird terrible shadows on the wall and a pair of fiery tiger's eyes gleaming in the corner ready to pounce on me and eat me up. I must have screamed. Old Auntie pounded the floor with her walking stick, Mam rushed upstairs carrying the oil lamp. Some of the shadows disappeared, the tiger's eyes became the fire's reflection of the toe caps of a pair of treasured boy's boots someone had given Mam for my little brother to grow into. Mam had kept them shined and polished on the bamboo what-not in the corner of the bedroom.

"Dad, Dad I want our Dad" I begged from this little oasis of lucidity, Dad would make the witches' shadows go, and the tigers, and save me from the black pit that kept sucking me down. Several times I struggled to consciousness to see Dad's face - but he was still down in his own black pit hacking on his knees for the coal that nearly kept our bodies and souls together.

"Dad, Dad oh I want our Dad" - and he was there - allowed straight up to the invalid's clean bedroom in his pit dirt. That dear kind face with the crinkles at the corner of his eyes, held my hands in his pit calloused ones. I was safe now. Dad was home.

"There, there, my little wench, Faythers wum, an' I'll stop 'ere till thee bist better – now mind thees't got to make up thee mind to get better – for who's goin' to putt the taters in the dib 'oles for 'er old Dad, an' who's goin' to play wi' the babby whilst Mam do get on wi' the washin – now thee take a sip o' thee Mam's drink and goo to a nice nap and I'll stop 'ere by thee bed."

I took some spoonfuls from him whilst Mam fetched him up a cup of tea.

In the morning the doctor was amazed to find me still in the land of the living.

I had survived, but only just. I could make no headway with appetite or strength despite all the love and attention lavished upon me. My ten year old sister filled jars of flowers to put by my bed, Mam got little luxuries she couldn't afford to tempt my palate, but best of all I loved it when Dad come up to sit with me, to tell me stories or just to sit and read himself from one of the books a pit butty of his used to lend him.

One Friday, Dad came up with a cup and spoon in his hand and an expression of great pleading in his eyes. Beastly little daughter I must have been, for this was an ominous sign. Dad was a great believer in herbal medicines and often brewed his own from the herbs he gathered. I thought they tasted terrible and my pig-headed nature made me the most unco-operative of swallowers, but I noticed what I thought was a book wrapped in brown paper in Dad's pocket. Perhaps Dad was going to sit with me for a long time.

With the patience of Job, and his own incredible gifts of love and encouragement, he got me to take eight spoonfuls of his little brew; then to bolster the undeserved praise he lavished upon me, he drank the dregs from the cup himself.

Then from his pocket he took the brown paper parcel, but it wasn't a book! He unwrapped it and put it on my bed. I could hardly believe my eyes. It was the box of doll's furniture out of the post office window.

"There then, that's fir bein' a good little wench. Now thee try and start yuttin' a bit better and then theel't be able to get up and goo out on the tump to play to thee 'earts content wi' all the tother young uns. Now afore I do go out to do a bit 'o' gyardening I'll 'a' me a little nap." It was a little nap. As soon as he woke up it was always Father's habit to feel round for his beloved old pipe. He did so now, put it in his mouth, then took his baccy tin out of his pocket. There was nothing in it. He put it and his pipe back in his pocket, then sat sadly staring through the window.

I remembered – today was Friday, pocket money day! Sevenpence for doll's furniture – twopence for marzipan toffee, a penny for liquorice allsorts – there was only twopence left!

Winifred Foley

Indoor Activities

If convalescence and rainy days have a common element, it is the need for indoor activity which is less strenuous than outdoor play. If your child is recovering from a very serious illness, you will need professional advice as to guidelines. In the case of the more common childhood illnesses, there is usually a period when young children are well enough to be occupied but not well enough to go out. We hope some of the ideas in this section will be useful for such times.

First, it can be said that the bedridden child will benefit from any extra attention to 'little things' that you can manage. A houseplant or flowers brought specially to his or her window sill, or bedside, a pretty card or shell on the dinner tray, **small** portions of food presented to look nice rather than daunting large servings – these will be appreciated. Our Mother had trained in nursing, and true to her profession, always left a bell by the bed for ringing in 'emergency'. We had a sense of importance and safety, knowing we could summon her if we were in dire straits during mumps or chicken pox, or missing handkerchief or juice when heavy with cold.

Most households have the basic elements for indoor play: old scarves, tea-towels or a bag of 'jumble' for dressing up; clothes horse and blanket for making a 'house'; chairs to line up to be a train, newspaper to fold into hats or cut into paper chains, flour and water to mix paste for stick-on pictures, jars to fill with varying levels of water for sounding musical notes, a cardboard box to make into a castle or doll's house, scrap fabric to turn into puppets or dolly clothes, a brown paper bag to cut up into masks, a broom to be a hobby horse (put a wellington boot on the top end and it will look like a horse!); the list goes on, depending on your imagination and a readiness to forsake immaculate standards in the interest of an enjoyable, probably very constructive time!

Some of the craft activities in the following pages are geared to older children, but younger ones can join in with help.

One final note: in many families with small children one special privilege is reserved for when one is ill in bed – not to be enjoyed on normal days, but **only** when 'under the weather'. It might be looking through the very old family album, or having a special story, or looking in a bulging button box. When we were little, and sick, we were allowed to look through Mother's jewelry box, which we did with great care, handling her modest pieces as if they were the Crown Jewels. The tradition has carried over into the next generation, and now it is her daughter's box which is pored over by little hands at special times.

It may be that the limited use of some things warrants them more 'special'. If so, think about compiling your own 'box of tricks' for bringing out during rainy days or convalescence.

Basic Box of Tricks Ideas

Scrapbook(s)
Glue
Old Christmas cards, post cards or magazine for cutting up.
Scraps of interesting fabrics – lace, fur, prints, velvet, corduroy.
Needles and cotton.
Scissors.
Pieces of felt: the ideal for young children to sew as it does not fray.
Scrap pieces of hessian.
Old discarded rolls of wallpaper (the blank side is perfect for murals).
Elastic.
Odd buttons.
Odd balls of wool.
Feathers.
Small bells.
Books of puzzles or riddles for older children.

Empty matchboxes.   Clothes pegs for peg dollies.
Beads, if possible, for stringing.
Used matchsticks for tiny house-building.
Smooth pebbles for painting.
Basic paints.
Stiff card for paper dolls or knight's shield.
Pipe cleaners.
Pine cones or shells from past excursions.
Old wool bits, tights or other 'stuffing' for soft toys or puppet heads.
Soap for carving.
Empty cotton reels.
Bits of wood, sandpaper.

Picture Game

In **On the Banks of Plum Creek** Laura Ingalls Wilder recorded the following picture game, used for indoor fun during long stormy days a hundred years ago. Laura's mother used a simple slate to tell the story:

Far in the woods there was a pond like this:

The pond was full of fishes like this:

Down below the pond there lived two homesteaders, each in a little tent, because they had not built their houses yet:

They went often to the pond to fish, and they made crooked paths:

A little way from the pond lived an old man and an old woman in a house with a window:

One day the old woman went out to the pond to get a pail of water:

And she saw the fishes all flying out of the pond, like this:

The old woman ran back as fast as she could go, to tell the old man, "All the fishes are flying out of the pond!" The old man stuck his long nose out of the house to have a good look:

And he said, "Pshaw'. It's nothing but tadpoles!"

185

For the Bedridden Child

Susan Harvey, supervisor of Save the Children Fund hospital play groups, strongly encourages as much normal activity as possible in bed for the young child, if and when the child feels up to it. She suggests pushing bed or cot to the window if possible, putting breadcrumbs on the window sill to attract birds. One child had a box of snails to watch; another grew seeds and bean sprouts, watching their daily growth. Mrs. Harvey stresses that play is more than amusement, and particularly during illness it is reassuring to a child to be occupied and to feel life is as normal as possible. The family goldfish or bird could be brought to the room, and some odd jobs such as preparing vegetables or mending, can be done at the bedside. If it is a festival or holiday time the bed itself can be decorated.

With supervision and an old sheet or even a plastic table-cloth to cover the bed, it is possible to use water, dough and paint. Here are some of Mrs. Harvey's suggestions:

If there is no bed-table in the house a very simple one can be made from a strong cardboard box roughly 16″ x 18″ x 10″ according to the size of the child. Curves or rectangles can be cut out of the box to fit over the child's legs. It can be covered with stick-on plastic to make it attractive and waterproof. It is useful to have a ledge round the outside to prevent things falling off. If the box has a lid this can be stuck upside down to provide the ledge. In the same way the bookrest can be made from firm material, such as cardboard, pegboard or beaver-board. Two identical pieces, which will fit on the bed-table, can be hinged together. The drawing paper can be clipped on with bulldog clips, or two pieces of elastic or tape attached to the bookrest to keep the paper in place. Crayons, felt pens and collage pictures – make by pasting scraps of material, etc., on to paper or card (the sides of large cereal packets are a useful source of cardboard) – can, with a variety of other handwork activities make a variation from painting.

Water play, bathing dolls, washing up games or blowing bubbles can also take place in bed. These will probably need supervision. A polythene washing-up bowl is easy to provide. If parents feel enterprising and if their child is enthusiastic to use sand or clay, this can be made possible with the same equipment and precautions. Damp sand is usually more manageable than dry. Messy play is one of the best outlets for the tension which may build up in illness and it is worth making the effort to provide for it if the child is in bed for any length of time.

From *Mother's Help*

'I know an Animal'

This game is a 'time-passer', useful when you are needing to pass time. This might be during a long wait at the 'bus stop or in the doctor's surgery, when a bedridden child needs company, or even during tedious, lengthy car journeys. It's fairly appropriate from age four upward, but could be adapted to other age groups with "I know a city" or "country" or "book" etc. Small children particularly like it and never seem to run out of animals.

One person thinks of an animal and then gives hints so that others must guess. "I know an animal that's little, and has a long nose, and likes milk and has prickles. What is it?"   (Hedgehog).

Modelling

Don't panic if you can't get out to buy modelling material. The following is as good as anything, and you can make it in quantities as wished. Keep it covered when not in use, and if it seems to dry out after a while simply wrap in a damp cloth until softened.

Playdough

1 cup plain flour
½ cup salt
1 tablespoon oil
1 teaspoon cream of tartar
¾ cup water
food colouring

Mix all together.

Modelling for Older Children

The dough method of modelling at home enables older children to create figures which will last for a long time. This recipe may be used plain, but instructions are given for the use of colour as another option. Tools to use with the dough might include a rolling pin, garlic press for 'hair', knife, and a baking tray. For finishing figures you will need plain varnish and perhaps glue, (if pieces need assembling, as in a house or little furniture).

Ingredients for the dough:
6 cups plain flour
1½ cups salt
tins of red, blue and yellow cold water dye.
2¼ cups water to mix.

Mix the flour and salt thoroughly and divide into the following portions: 1 of 3¾ cups and 3 of 1¼ cups each. Add 18 tablespoons of water to the larger portion. To the second cup add 6 tablespoons of water with ½ small teaspoon of red dye dissolved in it, and to the third and fourth cups add the same amount of water with ½ small teaspoon yellow dye in one and ½ small teaspoon blue in the other. Knead each cupful for 5-10 minutes until a pliable consistency is reached.

For purple, orange and green dough combine small amounts of the primary coloured doughs. Experiment a little with the colours – to make a blonde hair shade add some plain dough to the yellow to make it paler and to make a deep brown add equal parts of red, yellow and blue. Make sure you mix the doughs well to get a consistent colour.

Try to see that figures or trees have a flat base so that they will stand. Bake them on the oiled baking tray, placed so that they are lying flat. Bake for about an hour at 325°F (Reg 3). When cool, paint each figure with three coats of varnish. If you wish a flat stand for figure or tree, sea for a boat etc., it is best to make this separately, place **baked** pieces on it and bake again before varnishing as above.

Items for the Doll's House

Here are a few very simple ideas for the doll's house.

Use a half walnut shell for a little baby's crib and fill with a little wool or a little material. You can make the baby out of some moulded wax or from some felt. Children who enjoy the story of Thumbelina will take to these little cribs!

Little chests of drawers can be made with, say, four matchboxes glued together and covered in material, with a little bead stuck on the front for each drawer.

A little mop can be made with a small piece of dowling and little bits of white yarn stuck to one end and a 'bissum broom' can be made with little pieces of twig or the pine needles from a fir tree fixed to one end of a piece of dowling with a little cotton.

Empty cotton reels make good bases for lamps, tables or little stools if covered.

Paper or Card Boxes

Made on a smaller scale these make delightful containers or you could do them in bright colours in several sizes so that each fit inside another in 'box of boxes' fashion.

Made on a larger scale of stronger card they can become houses, barns, or castles.

A. is the basic pattern to adapt to your scale. The dotted lines indicate folding for paper, and scoring for heavier card.

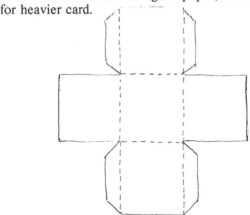

B. shows the simple folding up to make your box. Glue flaps to sides.

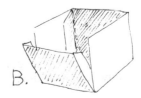

Cartons and packing cases are a good source of supply for corrugated cardboard which is excellent for rooftops, parapet or turrets.

Take the assembled box and cut out door and windows (or drawbridge?) as required.

Simple Tie-Dyeing

This is satisfactory and much easier than you might think.

You will need:
White cotton, fabric such as butter muslin, about 1 metre which can be cut into strips or squares to make scarves.
Cold water dye.
Thread for binding such as button thread, yarn or string.
Dye fix or soda, and salt.
4 bowls, plastic, enamel or stainless steel.
A measuring utensil, according to dye instructions.
Scissors, rubber gloves, washing powder and a large spoon.

Ideally your fabric should be washed in hot water and soap to remove the finish and make the cloth receptive to dye. Dry flat or iron. Now pleat the cloth in accordion fashion, with pleats of about 1 inch deep. When folded the cloth is ready for binding. The purpose of binding is to prevent dye from reaching parts of the cloth, thus creating a pattern. Wrap string tightly around the folded cloth, making bands of varying thickness, criss-crossing at intervals if you like. Any bits of cotton showing through will receive the dye. Fasten off the thread with a slip knot. (Loop thread loosely once around the cloth, slip thread through loop and pull taut). When you have bound your cloth, soak it in cold water while you prepare the dye. This is called "wetting out".

Allow the fabric one hour in the dye, stirring occasionally. Then remove and rinse in cold water until the water is clear. Now remove the bindings, wash the fabric in hot soapy water and rinse until water is clear. Dry and iron.

If you wish to apply a second colour, you could now repeat the entire process. Hem scarf or fringe the ends. Enjoy your pattern!

Tie-Dollies or Puppets

A pretty silk scarf, handkerchief, or plain cotton square can become a doll or puppet for a day's imagination. Or, if you have fabric to spare, this simple toy is a good addition to any play corner. All you need is a ball of wool or other stuffing for the head and thread or string for tying. Place your ball of stuffing in the middle of the cloth and tie for the head. Then knot the two drawn-up corners for hands.

On its own you have a pleasing dolly. For a puppet, tie string to hands and sew another string to top back of head. Join strings and use them to 'walk' the puppet, lift hands, nod head, etc. You could make several such puppets with a child, adding hair, crowns or simple capes as you wish. And this could lead into the child's own puppet show or play.

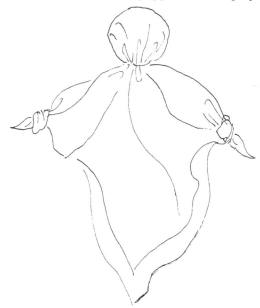

Handkerchiefs and Sock Puppets

Draw a face on a handkerchief or cloth square and tie it on your hand so as to make it move.

You can do wonders with old single socks. Sew on buttons for eyes, perhaps a red felt tongue and bit of wool for 'hair' and you create an instant snake or dragon with character; the length of the sock going up the arm. Children can also stuff the 'toe' end firmly and tie this off to be a doll puppet head, adding facial features or hair as they wish.

Wool Dolls

For wool dolls you need only wool, card and scissors. They take very little time to make and are versatile for play.

Take the card and cut a piece the width you want the arms and body to be. Wind the wool around about a dozen times, then slide off and tie (**A**). Now cut a card for height, wind the wool around it 25 times and slide off. Tie off head (with 'topknot' if wished). Then slip arms through body and tie again. (**B**) For a girl leave as it is for a skirt effect. For a boy, divide for legs and tie off feet.

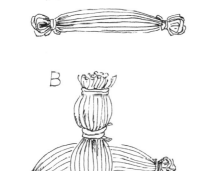

Tied to a string or length of wool, these little dolls can be made to 'walk' or 'jump' in puppet fashion if wished.

Windmills

You will need:

piece of card or stiff paper
paints or crayons
pencil, ruler
a strong pin or small tack
length of thin wood, bamboo or even an unsharpened pencil
cork

A. Draw a square 8″ x 8″ and make lines in from each corner of 4″. Cut along these.

B. Colour in the four divisions. Now fold every other corner to centre and secure with the pin.

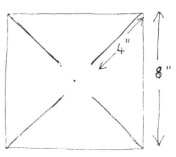

C. Fasten pin firmly to stick or pencil, putting a small cork on it first to allow space for movement this way the windmill should spin easily.

Print Making

You can use water colours, powder paint, or poster-paints. Cover the table with newspaper and have a rag or two on hand for wiping spills. Potatoes, turnips and swedes provide the sort of solid surface for cutting an image to print. Cut them in half, remember you need enough to hold onto, and use a sharp knife, peeler, or even a small pastry cutter to cut a simple design or letter. Either dip this into paint or use a brush to apply colour to your pattern. Then press down on paper.

Many items will print, after being dipped in paint, without any cutting. These are ideal for younger children to experiment with themselves, and include: vegetables (cut in half)

carrots	turnips
celery	cucumbers
green peppers	beets

nature items:

sticks	stones
flowers	weeds
nuts	bark
seeds	cones, feathers

toys:

old cars – dip wheels in paint and make tracks
blocks – of any size or shape; plastic or old wooden ones (paint may remain on wood)
sponges – cut into any shape
pipe-cleaners – bent in any fashion
paper doilies.

Dressing-up Hats

For Indian bands or crowns, take a rough measurement of the child's head using a piece of string or wool. This gives you the length of paper or ribbon to cut. For a crown use tissue paper, newspaper, or even card covered with silver foil. Zig-zag the edge as you cut.

The Indian band may be cut plain but could be decorated with bright spirals or any design. If you haven't a tall feather to glue on the back, simply cut one out of paper, fringing the edge.

For a sailor's hat, have a sheet of newspaper about 12″ by 18″. Place this flat on tabletop or floor, and fold in half to 12″ by 9″. Working from the fold, turn the two upper corners to the centre so that they meet exactly, and press down.

A.   Now on both sides of the hat turn up the remaining paper beneath the fold.
B.   Fasten as needed with sellotape.

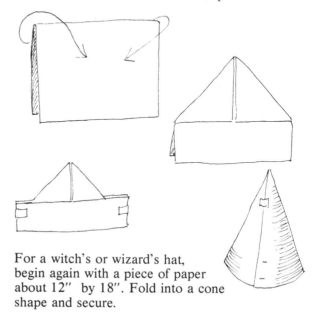

For a witch's or wizard's hat, begin again with a piece of paper about 12″ by 18″. Fold into a cone shape and secure.

Pom-pom Animals

For chicks or ducks use yellow wool if possible; try white for a rabbit, or white and brown.

Cut out 2 circles of cardboard, 3″ across with a small circle inside about 1″ across. Wind wool around both cardboard rings until the hole in the middle becomes too small to continue. If you can thread it a few more times with a darning needle. When the centre is too tiny for this, cut the wool around the edges – between the outer rings. Now tie a piece of string or strong thread between rings and tightly knot this. Remove the cardboard and fluff out the ball shape.

Using the same method, make a smaller ball for the head, and sew together. Cut out a beak or long ears of felt and sew these on.

190

Papier Mâché

1. Tear lots of newspaper into small pieces and place in an old saucepan with enough water to cover the paper. Bring gently to boil, and stir. Then let the mush soak for a while.
2. When lukewarm, put in a bucket and stir in 1 tablespoon cellulose wallpaper adhesive – leave for 15 minutes.
3. The papier mâché is now ready to use. You can make anything you like. If it feels too mushy squeeze out some of the liquid.
4. Put your model in a warm place, like an airing cupboard, to dry.

Collage

If you have a good glue and cloth, paper or hessian backing, you can do collage pictures with almost anything at hand. Bits of fabric, wool, buttons, egg shell and ingredients from the store cupboard are ideal. Think of orange lentils, dried peas, red kidney beans, sunflower seeds, cloves, rice, and pasta. Only small amounts of these items are required. Younger children will simply enjoy spreading glue and using the different textures and colours. Older children may wish to plan out a picture, using a real twig or cut cloth for a tree, felt for birds, silver paper or tin foil for crowns or wheels; whatever they may come up with. As they handle materials, ideas will come. Tweezers are a help for gluing on fiddley things like grains of barley or tiny beads.

Throughout the year you can gather a rich variety of collage materials from the park, the garden, seashore or countryside. Bring home the dry seed heads of poppies, cow parsley, teasel and grasses. The 'keys' of ash and maple, different bits of bark, shells, bits of driftwood, and attractive pebbles are all ideal.

Traditional Paper Dolls

You need a strip of paper about 10″ x 4″, newspaper or half a piece of typing paper. Fold this in half (to 5″ x 4″), then in half again. Fold in half once more. Now place the paper as shown with fold edge to your right.

Draw in half a person on the folded edge. The arm is the connecting link and must reach the opposite edge. Cut out through all the layers of paper and unfold.

Star Box (based on traditional Jewish holiday box)

You will neeed plain paper for a pattern, paper for the box, scissors, pencil, ruler and glue.

First make your pattern for a six-pointed star from paper at least 9″ square. Make a hexagon pre-fold (A) and cut once as shown in (B). Unfold paper.

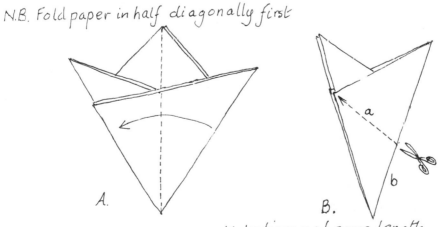

N.B. Fold paper in half diagonally first

A.

B.

a

b

Make lines a & b same length

191

Place your pattern star on paper and draw around it, as shown by dotted lines in (C) then use the ruler to add tabs all around. Cut out along tabs.

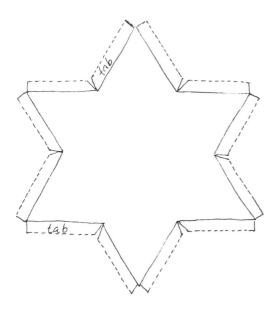

For the sides of the box, cut strips of paper 3″ wide and glue together until you have a strip 1 yd. long. Fold up tabs, have them upright and glue your long piece against the tabs, all around the star. Make creases to conform to points.

You may make a lid by making your basic star again with a strip 1″ wide to glue to tabs.

Paper Basket

You will need a rectangular piece of paper or card for this basket, the size of the paper depending on the size basket you wish. Try a model first with plain paper about 4″ x 5″. Fold about a quarter down from the top and the same up from bottom of the paper. Then fold in from each side to the middle so that your folds look similar to A. when the paper is opened flat.

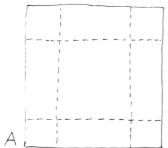

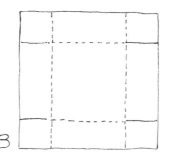

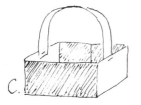

Now cut as on solid lines in B.

Bring sides and ends up along folds, bend end flaps in and glue. Add a simple handle of paper (either glue or staple it on) C.

These may be made deeper by allowing wider folds on your paper.

192

X   EXTRA TOUCHES

Life is often busy, even hectic, in most homes. There may not be enough time to organise a children's party; perhaps members of the household have to work on festival days. Perhaps, then, it is possible to live into the situation as it is, but adding a few 'extra touches' to daily life if wished.

For example, the table we eat at is an important place; sometimes the only place which finds us gathered together to share the day's events. We introduced a simple grace at mealtimes not only because of a religious need but also because it provides a minute's space after the hassle of preparing and serving a meal, making sure everyone has what they need, we sit and hold hands and say:

A blessing on the meal and peace on the earth.

What you say can vary but the point is that we are sharing something together, food that has been prepared with thought. Perhaps we owe thanks to the earth, the sun and rain for providing us with good things to eat. Children so often launch into their food without a moment's hesitation and it is good to make them aware of others around them and a moment's pause helps them consider whether everyone has what they need!

If there is space in the middle of the table or a little nook nearby you can use this to bring the treasures of the season or something simple made. For example:

Spring a little egg-cup with spring flowers in – primroses, crocus, grape hyacinth, any little ornament with baby animals, little beeswax or plasticine models of nests and suchlike; empty egg shells with cress growing in them.

Summer a bowl of summer flowers and perhaps some well-loved shells collected from a holiday.

Autumn a little dish of rosehips or berries, things made out of conkers or acorns or a little garden with moss and precious stones – everything is returning to the earth at this time for the winter. Food is being stored by the animals now and we do the same when we use the summer's harvest to bottle, preserve, and pickle. Sometimes we put a miniature pot for each of the children of a favourite jam we have made in the centre of the table and they love to have their very own at teatimes. A decoration of apples and berries can look very beautiful.

Winter perhaps a few hyacinths or crocus bulbs in a bowl to remind us of things to come. A few crystals or stones on a bed of moss. At Christmas time a candle arrangement with some yew or evergreen and pine cones will look very effective.

THE PEACE OF GOD

GRACE

Earth who gives to us our food
Sun who makes it ripe and good
Dearest Earth and Dearest Sun
Joy and love for all you have done.

The Peace of God,
The Peace of Christ,
Be upon each thing my eye takes in,
Upon each thing my mouth takes in,
Upon my body that is of earth
And upon my soul that came from on high.

Celtic Prayer

193

APPLESEED GRACE

The Lord is good to me
And so I thank the Lord
For giving me
The things I need
The rain, the sun
And the Apple seed
The Lord is good to me.

The verse to the left is based on the American legend of Johnny Appleseed, who is said to have walked barefoot from coast to coast carrying his Bible and a sack of appleseeds, which he planted as he travelled.

Johnny Appleseed

The Lord is good to me and so I thank the Lord, for giving me the thing I need, the sun, the rain and the apple seed, the Lord is good to me.

The Robin's Song

God bless the field and bless the furrow,
Stream and branch and rabbit burrow,
Hill and stone and flower and tree,
From Bristol town to Wetherby –
Bless the sun, and bless the sleet,
Bless the land and bless the street,
Bless the night and bless the day
From Somerset and all the way
To the meadows of Cathay;
Bless the minnow; bless the whale,
Bless the rainbow and the hail,
Bless the nest and bless the leaf,
Bless the righteous and the thief,
Bless the wing and bless the fin,
Bless the air I travel in,
Bless the mill and bless the mouse,
Bless the miller's bricken house,
Bless the earth and bless the sea,
God bless you and God bless me!

Old English

Prayer of St. Francis

Praised be God for brother Sun,
Who shines with splendid glow,
He brings the golden day to us,
Thy glory does he show!

Praised be God for sister Moon
And every twinkling star;
They shine in heaven most bright and clear,
All glorious they are.

Praised be God for brother Wind
That storms across the skies,
And then grows still, and silent moves,
And sweetly sings and sighs.

Praised be God for Water pure,
Her usefulness we tell,
So humble, precious, clear and good,
She works for us so well.

Praised be God for brother Fire
Friendly and wild and tame,
Tender and warm, mighty and strong,
A flashing, flaring flame.

Praised be God for mother Earth,
Who keeps us safe and well,
Whose mother heart all warm with love,
Dark in her depths doth dwell.

Transcribed by Lawrence Edwards

In the Dark

I've had my supper,
And had my supper,
And HAD my supper and all;
I've heard the story of Cinderella,
And how she went to the ball;
I've cleaned my teeth,
And I've said my prayers,
And I've cleaned and said them right;
And they've all of them been
And kissed me lots,
They've all of them said "Good-night."

So – here I am in the dark alone,
There's nobody here to see;
I think to myself,
I play to myself,
And nobody knows what I say to myself;
Here I am in the dark alone,

What is it going to be?
I can think whatever I like to think,
I can play whatever I like to play,
I can laugh whatever I like to laugh,
There's nobody here but me.

I'm talking to a rabbit .....
I'm talking to the sun .....
I think I am a hundred –
I'm one.
I'm lying in a forest .....
I'm lying in a cave .....
I'm talking to a dragon .....
I'm BRAVE.
I'm lying on my left side .....
I'm lying on my right side .....
I'll play a lot tomorrow .....
I'll think a lot tomorrow .....
I'll laugh .....
   a lot ....
      tomorrow ....
       (Heigh-ho!)
        Good-night.

A.A. Milne

Lullaby

I gave my love a cherry that had no stone
I gave my love a chicken that had no bone
I gave my love a ring that had no end
I gave my love a baby with no crying.

How can there be a cherry that has no stone
How can there be a chicken that has no bone
How can there be a ring that has no end
How can there be a baby with no crying.

And so to bed ...

A cherry when it's blooming has no stone
A chicken in the egg has no bone
A ring when it's rolling has no end
A baby when it's sleeping has no crying.

I gave my love a cherry

I gave my love a cherry that had no stone, I gave my love a chicken that had no bone, I gave my love a ring that had no end, I gave my love a baby with no crying.

Mockingbird

Hush little baby don't say a word,
Papa's going to buy you a mocking bird.

If that mocking bird don't sing
Papa's going to buy you a diamond ring.

If that diamond ring is brass
Papa's going to buy you a looking-glass.

If that looking-glass gets broke
Papa's going to buy you a billy-goat.

If that billy-goat don't pull
Papa's going to buy you a cart and bull.

If that cart and bull fall over
Papa's going to buy you a dog called Rover.

If that dog called Rover don't bark
Papa's going to buy you a horse and cart.
(slower)
If that horse and cart fall down
You'll still be the sweetest baby in town.

Golden slumbers kiss your eyes
Smiles awake you when you rise
Sleep pretty darling do not cry
And I will sing a lullaby.

Care you know not therefore sleep
While I over you watch to keep.
Sleep pretty darling do not cry
And I will sing a lullaby.

Go to bed first,
A golden purse;
Go to bed second,
A golden pheasant;
Go to bed third,
A golden bird.

A Cradle Song

Sleep, baby, sleep!
Thy father watches the sheep,
Thy mother is shaking the dreamland tree,
And softly a little dream falls on thee!
Sleep, baby, sleep!

Sleep, baby, sleep!
The large stars are the sheep,
The little stars are the lambs, I guess,
The fair moon is the shepherdess;
Sleep, baby, sleep!

Sleep, baby, sleep!
I'll buy for thee a sheep,
With a golden bell so fine to see,
And it shall frisk and play with thee;
Sleep, baby, sleep!

Sleep, baby, sleep!
Thy father watches the sheep,
The wind is blowing fierce and wild,
It must not wake my little child;
Sleep, baby, sleep!

Evening Song

Who has the nicest white sheep?
The silver moon on high
Who lives behind the treetops
Up yonder in the sky.

She comes late in the evening
When everyone's asleep,
So slow and calm she wanders
Across the heavens deep.

All night she guards her white flocks
In meadows blue and deep
For all the little twinkling stars,
Are only her white sheep.

Evening Song

Who has the nicest white sheep, the silver moon on high, who lives behind the tree tops up

yonder in the sky.

Chinese Cradle Song

Dear little baby,
Don't you cry;
Your father's bringing water
From the brook near by.

A red-tasseled hat
He wears on his head,
Your mother's in the kitchen
Baking you some bread.

See, from mother's shoe tips
Peep three pretty toes!
Now baby's laughing
There he goes!

Willow leaves murmur, hua-la-la.
Sleep precious baby, close to mama.
Hua-la-la, baby, smile in your sleep;
You'll have only sweet dreams
While my watch I keep.

Hindu Cradle Song

From groves of spice,
O'er fields of rice,
Athwart the lotus-stream,
I bring for you,
Aglint with dew,
A little lovely dream.

Sweet, shut your eyes,
The wild fireflies
Dance through the fairy neem,
From the poppy bole
For you I stole
A little lovely dream.

Bye, baby bunting,
Father's gone a-hunting,
Mother's gone a-milking,
Sister's gone a-silking,
Brother's gone to buy a skin
To wrap the baby bunting in.

Wynken, Blynken and Nod

Wynken, Blynken, and Nod one night
Sailed off in a wooden shoe –
Sailed on a river of crystal light,
Into a sea of dew.
"Where are you going and what do you wish?"
The old moon asked the three.
"We have come to fish for the herring-fish
That live in this beautiful sea;
Nets of silver and gold have we,"
Said Wynken, Blynken, and Nod.

All night long their nets they threw
To the stars in the twinkling foam –
Then down from the skies came the wooden shoe,
Bringing the fishermen home;
'Twas all so pretty a sail, it seemed
As if it could not be,
And some folks thought 'twas a dream they'd
dreamed
Of sailing that beautiful sea –
But I shall name you the fishermen three:
Wynken, Blynken, and Nod.

The old moon laughed and sang a song,
As they rocked in the wooden shoe,
And the wind that sped them all night long
Ruffled the waves of dew.
The little stars were the herring-fish
That lived in the beautiful sea –
"Now cast your nets wherever you wish –
But never afeared are we";
So cried the stars to the fishermen three:
Wynken, Blynken, and Nod.

Wynken and Blynken are two little eyes,
And Nod is a little head,
And the wooden shoe that sailed the skies
Is a wee one's trundle-bed.

Eugene Field

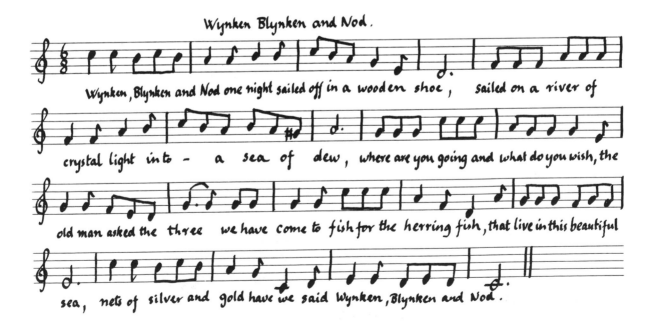

198

Good Night

No more work and no more play,
Every toy is put away,
Ended is the lovely day,
Then – good night!

Drink the milk all white and creamy,
Have your bath all warm and steamy
Close your eyes all tired and dreamy,
Then – good night!

Through the window stars are peeping,
From their holes the mice are creeping,
Your white bed is soft for sleeping,
Then – good night!

Ruth Ainsworth

Prayer for a Young Child

Spring put a sprig in his mind,
Prosper his enterprises.
May the hand that gropes in the roosting-box
Lift out an egg.

His hope blow like a rose in the morning,
And may the grunt of thunder
And the rush of rain
Relieve the pressure of the summer sun.

May his foot find a way
Among the fallen leaves,
As the sun blazes over the Severn
And the night falls cold.

The nip of winter house his sword
And exercise his centre;
The stars of the dark flare in his eye,
The frost preserve his resolutions.

Unleasher of seasons,
Keep in the nooks a wink
For the murky-hearted,
A rush-light for the lonely.

Light him at last
To sleep in his scallop,
The sea singing renewal
And the life to come.

Lanny Kennish

Prayer for the young

God be in my head
And in my understanding.

God be in mine eyes
And in my looking.

God be in my mouth
And in my speaking.

God be in my heart
And in my thinking.

God be at my end
And at my departing.

199

Children are the reward of life

Congolese proverb

Let your love be like the misty rain, coming softly, but flooding the river.

Madagascar

A little rain each day will fill the rivers to overflowing

Liberia

The moon moves slowly, but it crosses the town

Ashanti

Sunrise

Look to this day!
For it is life, the very life of life.
In its brief course
Lie all the verities and realities of your existence:
    The bliss of growth
    The glory of action
    The splendour of achievement,
For yesterday is but a dream
And tomorrow is only a vision,
But today well lived makes every yesterday
    a dream of happiness
And tomorrow a vision of hope.
Look well, therefore, to this day!
Such is the salutation to the dawn.

From the Sanskrit

XI   BIRTHDAY CALENDAR

JANUARY

1.
2.
3.
4.
5.
6.
7.
8.
9.
10.
11.
12.
13.
14.
15.
16.
17.
18.
19.
20.
21.
22.
23.
24.
25.
26.
27.
28.
29.
30.
31.

FEBRUARY

1.
2.
3.
4.
5.
6.
7.
8.
9.
10.
11.
12.
13.
14.
15.
16.
17.
18.
19.
20.
21.
22.
23.
24.
25.
26.
27.
28.
29.

MARCH

1.
2.
3.
4.
5.
6.
7.
8.
9.
10.
11.
12.
13.
14.
15.
16.
17.
18.
19.
20.
21.
22.
23.
24.
25.
26.
27.
28.
29.
30.
31.

APRIL

1.
2.
3.
4.
5.
6.
7.
8.
9.
10.
11.
12.
13.
14.
15.
16.
17.
18.
19.
20.
21.
22.
23.
24.
25.
26.
27.
28.
29.
30.

MAY

1.
2.
3.
4.
5.
6.
7.
8.
9.
10.
11.
12.
13.
14.
15.
16.
17.
18.
19.
20.
21.
22.
23.
24.
25.
26.
27.
28.
29.
30.
31.

JUNE

1.
2.
3.
4.
5.
6.
7.
8.
9.
10.
11.
12.
13.
14.
15.
16.
17.
18.
19.
20.
21.
22.
23.
24.
25.
26.
27.
28.
29.
30.

JULY

1.
2.
3.
4.
5.
6.
7.
8.
9.
10.
11.
12.
13.
14.
15.
16.
17.
18.
19.
20.
21.
22.
23.
24.
25.
26.
27.
28.
29.
30.
31.

AUGUST

1.
2.
3.
4.
5.
6.
7.
8.
9.
10.
11.
12.
13.
14.
15.
16.
17.
18.
19.
20.
21.
22.
23.
24.
25.
26.
27.
28.
29.
30.
31.

SEPTEMBER

1.
2.
3.
4.
5.
6.
7.
8.
9.
10.
11.
12.
13.
14.
15.
16.
17.
18.
19.
20.
21.
22.
23.
24.
25.
26.
27.
28.
29.
30.

OCTOBER

1.
2.
3.
4.
5.
6.
7.
8.
9.
10.
11.
12.
13.
14.
15.
16.
17.
18.
19.
20.
21.
22.
23.
24.
25.
26.
27.
28.
29.
30.
31.

NOVEMBER

1.
2.
3.
4.
5.
6.
7.
8.
9.
10.
11.
12.
13.
14.
15.
16.
17.
18.
19.
20.
21.
22.
23.
24.
25.
26.
27.
28.
29.
30.

DECEMBER

1.
2.
3.
4.
5.
6.
7.
8.
9.
10.
11.
12.
13.
14.
15.
16.
17.
18.
19.
20.
21.
22.
23.
24.
25.
26.
27.
28.
29.
30.
31.

XII YOUR OWN IDEAS : NOTES

INDEX

Advent, 121
    biscuits, 122, 126
    calendar, 122
    wreath, 121

All Souls Day, 91

Almond paste, 13, 70

Angels,
    mobiles, 135
    of sheepswool, 133

Animals
    at Christmas, 136
    at Midsummer, 52
    bread horse, 166
    hedgehog to make, 114
    pom-pom chicks, etc., 190
    satsuma animals, 166
    song, 100

Apples
    apfelstrudel, 110
    apple butter, 75
    appleseed grace, 194
    cakes and tarts, 110, 111
    Christmas, 141, 149
    cutting, 109
    decoration – "apple pig", 100
    games, 85
    song, 109
    toffee, 100
    twelfth night tradition, 154

Baskets
    custom, May, 25
    Easter, 18
    heart-shaped, paper, 135
    paper, 192
    sculptured, dough, 30

Bay leaves, for open fire, 115

Beach, 54

Birds
    feeding, 119
    goose round, 101
    lark's song, 28
    robin's song, 194
    white dove's songs, 49
    Whitsun bird, 50

Birthdays, 159
    cake ideas, 163-4
    family ritual, 160
    party food, 163-166
    party games, 160-163
    pinata, 163
    verse, 159

Biscuits
    aniseed, 124
    butter, 125, 175
    carob fingers, 174
    chocolate orange, 176
    chocolate shortbread, 176
    Christmas tree, for hanging, 136
    crinkles, 178
    Easter, 23
    flapjacks, 97
    florentines, 178
    gingerbread man, 98
    Granny's, 177
    hazelnut, 123
    lemon, 178
    lizzies, 125
    macaroons, 48
    New Zealand, 176
    oat ginger, 174
    oatmeal, 125
    parkin, 93
    peanut butter, 176
    pinwheels, 124
    pumpkin, 90
    ragged robins, 175
    roll, 126
    sand tarts, 126
    shortbread, 175
    shrewsbury, 176
    speculaas, 129
    speculatius, 124

Black Peter, 126

Box of tricks, 184

Bread
    croutons, 94
    garlic, 94
    herb soda, 39
    malt, 172
    nut, 95
    pita, 173
    plaited harvest, 69
    pumpkin, 90
    spiced apple, 111
    stollen, 129
    wheat sheaf, 70

Cakes
    apple, 110-111
    brownie, 177
    caraway angel, 14
    carrot, 96
    cheesecake, 62, 63
    chestnut, 148
    chocolate log, 148
    Christmas, 130
    Columba di Pasqua, 22
    date and walnut, 96
    Easter, 24
    Epiphany, 154
    German honey, 128

gingerbread, 97, 98
gooseberry, 62
Halloween, 87
harvest fruit, 69
madeira, 23
paskha, 22
Scotch sultana, 178
simnel, 13
soul cakes, 91
Victoria sponge, 26
Welsh cakes, 172

Candlemas, 7

Candles,
   decorating, 8, 134
   floating, 151, 164
   making, 7-8

Cheese
   cake, 62, 63
   flan, 56
   herb cream cheese, 38
   straws, 99

Cherry stones, counting, 54, 55

Christmas Eve, 137
   meal ideas, 137
   songs, 138-40

Christmas, 140
   breakfast, 141
   crackers, 147
   decorations, 131-136
   pudding, 130
   songs, 138-40, 152, 153
   stories, 141-147
   stories, 141-147

Chicken pieces, 57

Chutney
   beetroot, 76
   country, 73
   gooseberry, 72
   green tomato, 74
   marrow, 74
   plum, 75

Colcannon, 87

Collage, 191

Conkers
   conker men, 112
   furniture for dolls house, 114
   necklace, 112

Convalescence, 184, 186

Corn-cob pipes, 68

Corn dollies, 66, 67-68

Cornish pasties, 57

Crackers, 147

Crullers, 26

Crumpets, 172

Decorations
   Advent, 121
   birthday, 163-166
   Christmas, 131-136
   Easter, 16
   gingerbread house, 98
   Halloween, 86
   May Day, 25
   seasonal, table, 193

Dips, 58

Dolls,
   corn dollies, 66, 67
   dolls house furniture, 114, 187
   maize dollies, 68
   tie-dollies, 188
   wool dollies, 189

Doughnuts, 12

Drinks
   bishops wine, 129
   blackberry cordial, 75
   blackberry syrup, 76
   elderberry syrup, 72
   elderflower fizz, 65
   elderflower syrup, 72
   ginger beer, 65
   herb teas, 39
   lambs wool, 155
   lemon and grapefruit barley water, 65
   lemonade, 64
   milk shakes, 65
   orange and lemon, 65
   spiced tea, 120

Easter, 16
   basket, 18
   cakes, 22-24
   Easter pole, 16
   Easter tree, 16
   eggs, 17
   egg hunt, 20
   egg rolling, 21
   hare, 16, 18, 19
   'nests' for eating, 21
   stories, 18-20

Eccles cakes, 175

Epiphany, or Twelfth Night, 154
   cake, 154
   legend from Russia, 155
   tree, 157

Fairies
   child's imagination, 138
   decorations, 113, 114
   Midsummer, 51
   story, 180

Father Christmas
    as tradition, 138
    decoration, 134

Flans
    cheese, general, 56
    cranberry and apple, 149
    pizza, 56
    sage and onion, 38
    spinach tart, 57
    wheaten lattice, 165

Flowers
    drying, 80
    kitchen use, 37
    May Day, 25
    marzipan, 169
    poem, 44
    pot pourri, 39, 40
    press, 31
    seasonal, for table, 193
    seeds, easy growing, 15
    sugared rose petals, 164

Fruit
    ambrosia, 149
    frosted fruits, 164
    fruit and nut sticks, 169

Games (See also Ring Games)
    apple bobbing, 85
    beans are hot, 160
    Chinese laundry, 160
    cobbler cobbler mend my shoe, 161
    fly away sparrow, 161
    hunt the pairs, 160
    I know an animal, 186
    matchbox game, 160
    muffin man, 162
    nut on the mound, 86
    oranges and lemons, 162
    picture, 185
    treasure hunt, 161
    twirling the plate, 160
    up jenkins, 149

Gnomes
    child's imagination, 138
    sheepswool, 113
    table decorations, 112

Good Friday, 15
    hot cross buns, 15

Guy Fawkes, 93
    bonfire songs, 100-105

Halloween, 83, 87
    games, 85-86
    games, 85-86
    jack-o-lantern, 83
    trick or treat, 85

Hats, to make for dressing up, 190

Harvest, 66
    breads and cakes, 69-70
    corn mother, 66
    corn dollies, 67-68
    preserving, 70-76

Herb vinegar, 72

Herbs, 33-40
    bouquet garni, 40
    drying, 37
    growing and uses, 35-36
    pot-pourri, 39-40
    recipes, 37-39
    sachets, 40
    teas, 39

Hot cross buns, 15

Ice creams, 63-64

Icing
    butter cream, 26
    cream cheese frosting, 97
    glace, 14
    royal, 26

Jams
    apple and blackberry, 76
    chestnut, 76
    hodgkin, 72
    lemon curd, 71
    plum, orange and walnut, 75
    raspberry, 72

Jelly
    boats, 165
    gooseberry and elderflower, 76
    hedgerow, 75
    quince and apple, 76

Kites
    making one, 82
    story of, 81

Lanterns
    jack o lantern, 83
    Martinmas, 106
    paper decoration, 133
    songs, 107

Leaves
    chocolate, 164
    dried, for pictures, 112, 115
    preserving, 79
    song, 79

Lemon curd, 71

Lentils
    roasts, 96
    salad, 60
    soup, 94

Lullabies, 197

Maids of Honour, 177

Maize dollies, 68

Marmalades, 71

Martinmas, 106
    lanterns, 106
    songs, 107

May Day, 25
    baskets, 25, 30
    cake, 25-26
    pole, 25, 27, 28

Meat loaf, 57

Michaelmas, 80

Midsummer, 51
    bonfire, 51
    elves and fairies, 51, 53

Mincemeat for mince pies, 130

Mint sauce, 73

Mobiles
    beechnut, 113
    Christmas, 135
    feather, 113
    pinecone, 114
    walnut, 134

Mothering Sunday, 13
    cakes, 13-14

Muffins, 173

Nettles, 32

New Year's Eve, 151
    fortune telling, 151
    traditions, 152

Nuts
    almond rice roast, 96
    bread, 95
    Halloween tradition, 85
    nut balls for soup, 95
    poem, 112
    proverb, 141
    rissoles, 95
    roasts, 95
    walnuts (see separate heading)

Pancakes
    plain, 11
    scotch pancakes, 172
    sour milk, 12

Paper dolls, 191

Papier mache, 191

Pastry, 177

Peel, candied, 131

Persephone, 2

Pickles
    bean, 75
    dill, cucumber, 74
    onions, 74
    piccalilli, 73
    pickled cucumber, 73

Picnics, 55
    food ideas, 56-59

Pies
    apple, 110
    pumpkin, 90

Pip-counting, 55

Play dough, 186, 187

Poems, by title
    Apple Harvest, 111
    Among the Nuts, 112
    A'Reaping, 66
    Bed in Summer, 42
    Child's Song in Spring, 4
    Colour, 78
    Daddy fell into the Pond, 44
    Elf and the Dormouse, 179
    Elfin skates, 118
    Flowers, 44
    Good Night, 199
    Harvest, 78
    Haytime, 52
    Here's to the old Apple Tree, 154
    In the Dark, 195
    It was Long Ago, 43
    Land of Counterpane, 182
    Logs, 115
    Midsummer Night, 51
    Mother Earth, 66
    Prayer for a Young Child, 199
    Pudding Charms, 115
    Rain, 182
    Red in Autumn, 78
    Slumber in Spring, 3
    Spring goeth all in White, 48
    Summer Sun, 42
    The Calendar, VII
    The Hag, 83
    The Lavender Bush, 44
    The Months, VI
    The Old Cricketer, 4
    Twelfth Night, 154
    Waiting at the Window, 181
    Winter Morning, 118
    Witch, 84
    Witch's spell, 84
    Wynken, Blynken and Nod, 198
    You are going out to Tea today, 171

Potatoes
    baked, fillings for, 94
    casserole, 95

hot-pot, 37
shaped, 95

Pretzels, chocolate, 122

Printing, 189

Pudding
charms, 115
plum, 130
pumpkin, 88
summer, 63

Pumpkin
biscuits and bread, 90
jack-o-lantern, 87
recipes, 88-90
song, 89

Puppets, simple to make, 188

Rainy Days, 179-182
indoor play, 184
things to make, 186-192

Ring Games
cuckoo and the donkey, 29
farmer in the dell, 162
here we come gathering nuts in May, 30
here we go round the May pole high, 28
here we go round the Mulberry Bush, 119
Lady Spring, 6
Oats and Beans, 6
old Roger is dead, 108
oranges and lemons, 108
poor Jenny is a-weeping, 45
sent a letter to my love, 9
water, water wallflower, 5

Salads
bean, 62
beansprout, 61, 62
carrot, 60
celeriac, 60
cottage cheese, 62
cucumber, 61
leek, 60
lentil, 60
pasta, 60
picnic, 55
potato, 61
ratatouille, 62
rice, 62
tomato and lentil, 61
winter, 137

Sandwich fillings, 58

Scones
savoury, 175
wholewheat, 172

Shrovetide, 11
Lent, 11
pancakes, 11-12

Snowflakes
paper, cut-out, 132
song, 119

Songs, by title
Animals, 100
Bells at Midnight, 139-140
Cradle Song, 196
Dame get up, 139
Evening Song, 197
Father Sky, 107
From Heaven's Arch so High, 123
Glimmer, Lantern, Glimmer, 107
Gloucestershire Wassail, 152
Goose Round, 101
Herb Song, 34
Here we come A-Wassailing, 153
I gave my Love a Cherry, 195
John Barleycorn, 105
Johnny Appleseed, 194
Kookaburra, 104
Lark in the Morn, 28
Leaves be Green 79
Little White Doves, 49
London's Burning, 104
Mockingbird, 196
My Nice Red Rosy Apple, 109
Old John Braddlelum, 101
Old Roger is Dead, 108
Pedlar's Caravan, 46
Pumpkin Pie, 89
Scarborough Fair, 33
Snow Song, 119
Soul Cake, 91
Spring is Coming, 3
Summertime, 47
Sunlight Fast is Dying, 107
There was an Old Woman, 102
We wish You a Merry Christmas, 138
When I first came to this Land, 103
White Dove Song, 49
Wynken, Blynken and Nod, 198

Sorrel, 32

Soups
cold cucumber, 59
cottage pea, 60
iced tomato and courgette, 59
lentil, 94
nettle, 32
pumpkin, 88
sorrel, 32
vegetable, 93
vichyssoise, 59

Spiral, paper hanging, 134

Stars
box, 192
card, 132
paper, 133
straw, 131

St. Francis, prayer of, 194

St George, legend, 80

St John, 51

St Martin, legend, 106

St Nicholas, 126-129

St Swithin's day, 42

St Valentine, 9

Stories
  Baboushka, 155
  Christmas Rose, 143
  Easter Hare, 18, 19
  Epiphany tree, 157
  Gingerbread man, 97
  Persephone, 2
  Rainbows and Flowers, 180
  Robin Redbreast, 143
  Star Mother's Youngest Child, 141
  St George, 80
  St Nicholas, 128
  The Kite, 81

Sweets
  apricot crunches, 169
  brandy snaps, 148
  butterscotch, 168
  chocolate brazils, 168
  coconut ice, 167
  fruit and nut sticks, 169
  fudge, 168

honeycomb, 167
honey toffee, 169
Italian torrone, 148
marron glace, 169
marzipan, 14, 169
noisette chocolates, 168
peppermint creams, 168
sesame chews, 169
turkish delight, 167

Tie-dyeing, 188

Twelfth Night, see Epiphany

Valentine's Day, 9
  biscuits, 10
  cards, 9

Walnuts
  boats, 151
  decorations, 134
  for tiny gifts, 134
  furniture for dolls house, 187

Weaving, autumn mat, 114

Whitsun, 48
  songs, 49
  Whitsun bird, 50

Windmills, 189

Witches
  decorations, 86
  poems, 83, 84

XIV   References and Acknowledgements

We are grateful for the kind permission by these authors to use their work: Lanny Kennish, for **Prayer for a Young Child;** Margret Meyerkort - for kind permission to use several stories and for using material collected by the Steiner Kindergarten teachers; Ruth Ainsworth for **Good Night,** Norman Hunter for **Pancake Day at Great Pagwell** from **The Incredible Adventures of Professor Branestawm,** which is reprinted by permission of the author and The Bodley Head; Erdmute Lloyd of Rudolf Steiner Press for **St. George** and **Praised be to God for Brother Sun** from **The Key of the Kingdom;** Eileen Hutchins for **Mother Earth;** Robin Crofts Lawrence for **Rainbows & Flowers** by Dorothy Harrar from **Nature Ways,** New York Rudolf Steiner School; Winifred Foley for excerpts from **No Pipe Dreams for Father;** Pumpkin Pie Folksingers of Stroud for **Pumpkin Pie;** Laurie Lee for **The Three Winds** from **The Sun My Monument** and two extracts from **Cider with Rosie;** Methuen & Co. Ltd. (London) for excerpts from Astrid Lingren's, **Midsummer in Bullerby** and **The Six Bullerby Children.**

We also acknowledge the following authors, and publishers, and literary agents for permission to reproduce their work: Louise Moeri for **The Star Mother's Youngest Child** published by Houghton Mifflin Co. Ltd., Boston and Macdonald and Jane's Publishing Group, London; David Higham Associates Ltd. for excerpts from Dylan Thomas' **Quite Early One Morning** and **A Child's Christmas in Wales,** published by J. M. Dent; Methuen Childrens Books Ltd. for A.A. Milne's **Waiting at the Window, In the Dark** and **Cherry Stones** from **Now We are Six;** William Blackwood Publishers for **Daddy Fell into the Pond** by A. Noyes; Oxford University Press for excerpts from Flora Thompson's **Lark Rise to Candleford;** J. M. Dent & Sons Ltd. for Percy Ilott's **The Witch** from **Songs of Childhood;** Evans Brothers Ltd. for **The Apple Harvest** by H. Leuty, **Colour** by A. White, **Pudding Charms** by Charlotte Druitt Cole, **Haytime Poem** by I. Pawsey - taken from **The Book of a Thousand Poems;** Miss A. Fleming for Elizabeth Fleming's **The Lavender Bush;** Curtis Brown Group Ltd. for Ogden Nash's **Winter Morning** from **Silver Sand & Snow** published by Michael Joseph; D. Higham Associates Ltd. for Eleanor Farjeon's **It Was Long, Long Ago;** Lutterworth Press for extracts from Laura Ingalls Wilder's **Farmer Boy;** D. Higham & Associates Ltd. for excerpts from Eileen Bell's **Tales from the End Cottage;** Floris Books for **The Christmas Rose** by Selma Lagerloff from **Christ Legends And Other Stories;** A.M. Heath & Co. Ltd. for B. Euphan Todd's **The Calendar** from editor Kaye Webb's **I Like This Poem** (Puffin).

Whilst every effort has been made to trace the owners of copyrights, in a few cases this has proved impossible, and we take this opportunity of tendering our apologies to any owners whose rights may have been unwittingly infringed.

Other acknowledgements: for ring games see **Therapeutic Games,** compiled by E. & M. Le Fevre, Glencraig Curative School, Craigavad, Holywood, Co. Down, N. Ireland; M. Meyerkort editor of Book of Seasons e.g. **Spring, Summer, Autumn, Winter,** printed and published by Wynstones School - for kind permission to use several stories such as **The Easter Hare, The Story of a Kite,** the Martinmas songs; **Robin Redbreast, St. Nicholas, An Epiphany Story of The Tree, The Night before the Birthday,** and **Evening Song;** for Celtic prayers see **The Sun Dances** editor Alexander Carmichael, Christian Community Press 1960; Susan Harvey, **The Child in Bed** excerpt from editor Susan Dickinson, **Mother's Help,** Collins 1972.

The publication of this book has been generously supported by the Mercury Provident Society Ltd., George & Gelda Perry, Frances Woolls, Honor Mackenzie and others.

THE AUTHORS AND EDITORS

Diana Carey is from London and trained as a social worker. She now works as a counsellor in the Cotswolds. She is married, with four children.

Judy Large is American and has lived in England for eleven years. She is a Course Tutor for the Open University in modern history and is married with three children.

They both participated for three years in the Gloucestershire Ariadne Women's Group, and feel that many of the themes of this book arose from Ariadne discussions.

THE CHILDREN'S YEAR
Stephanie Cooper, Christine Fynes-Clinton
and Marye Rowling.
Full colour cover; 10½″ × 8½″ (267mm × 216mm);
192pp; several hundred illustrations.
ISBN 1 869 890 00 0

Here is a book which hopes to give the possibility to adults and children alike to rediscover the joy and satisfaction of making something that they know looks and feels good and which can also be played with imaginatively. It takes us through Spring, Summer, Autumn and Winter with appropriate gifts and toys to create, including full, clear instructions and illustrations. There is children's clothing as well, particularly meant to be made of natural fabrics to let the child's body breathe while growing. There are soft items for play and beauty, and there are firm solid wooden ones; moving toys such as balancing birds or climbing gnomes; horses which move when you add children to them! From woolly hats to play houses, mobiles or dolls, here are 112 potential treasures to make in seasonal groupings.

You needn't be an experienced crafts person to create something lovely, and the illustrations make it a joy to browse through while choosing what to make first. *The Children's Year* offers handwork for all ages and individualities, it reminds us of the process of creating as opposed to merely consuming, and all this in the context of nature's rhythm through the year.

The authors are parents who have tried and tested the things to make included in *The Children's Year*, with their own families.

WHO'S BRINGING THEM UP?
How to break the T.V. habit:
Television and child development — Martin Large

Television is the context for many families. "We would not be a family without our television," said one child. Some children watch television more than they are in school. Half the children in a recent survey had a set in their bedrooms. People joke about being hooked on the 'plug in drug'. These observations prompt the questions:-

How does the T.V. 'Pied Piper' exert it's magic?
How does T.V. affect children's behaviour?
What activites are displaced by T.V.?
What effects does T.V. have on attention spans, reading and health?
What effects does viewing — regardless of programme content, have on children's developing language, imagination, senses, thought and play?

This book explores the relation between television and child development. The examples given by parents, doctors and teachers are used to back up research on the effects of viewing.

How can the T.V. habit be broken?

Parents frequently ask how they can break the T.V. habit, so their families can lead a fuller life. Both gradual and drastic ways of cutting down on viewing are explored using family examples. Practical guidelines are given that will enable you to control T.V. — instead of being controlled by it.

Martin Large is being brought up by four children. He works in business and management development.

"An interesting and provocative read" The Guardian.
"Thought provoking" John Rae, Times Educational Supplement.
"A clear and accessible book for the concerned parent" New Internationalist.

192pp; £5.95 or US $9.95; paperback; publication date March 1990.
ISBN 1 869 890 24 8; Lifeways Series

THE INCARNATING CHILD
Joan Salter.
Full colour cover; 8¼″ × 5¼″ (210 × 135mm);
220pp approx.; illustrations and photos.
ISBN 1 869 890 04 3

Even in today's modern technological world, the mystery and miracle of conception, pregnancy and birth stir within many people a sense of wonder. *The Incarnating Child* picks up Wordsworth's theme "our Birth is but a sleep and a forgetting ..." and follows the Soul life of tiny babies well into childhood. It is full of practical advice for mothers, fathers, relations or anyone concerned with childcare. Joan Salter examines pregnancy, birth, early infancy, babyhood, childhood, on up to adolescence. She addresses physical and spiritual development, the formation of healthy personalities, nutrition, clothing, environment, toys and learning, immunization and health, and the acquisition of skills and thinking ability. She writes with an astounding attention to detail, and the voice of years of experience in her field.

Joan Salter is a specialist in maternal and childcare, and has a nursing background which included work with migrants from many countries. She is the founder and director of the Gabriel Baby Centre, since 1976 a centre for maternal and child welfare in Melbourne, and is essentially concerned with the upbringing of the child in the home.

ORDERS: FESTIVALS, FAMILY AND FOOD

Copies may be obtained from Hawthorn Press is not readily available locally. Please send payment with orders. Sterling cheque/P.O. payable to **Hawthorn Press** £7.95 plus £1.00 p&p UK, Europe and Australia. US $14.95 post free. Two copies to same address post free.

Bankfield House, 13 Wallbridge, Stroud, Gloucestershire. GL5 3JA
Telephone Stroud (0453) 757040
Fax (0453) 753295

Printed and bound in Great Britain
by Billing & Sons Limited, Worcester.